How To Restore & Modify
PORSCHE
914 & 914/6

Patrick C. Paternie

Technical photography by Wayne Demsey

MBI Publishing Company

First published in 1999 by MBI Publishing Company, 729 Prospect Avenue, PO Box 1, Osceola, WI 54020-0001 USA

Special photography by Wayne Dempsey, courtesy of Pelican Parts, www.pelicanparts.com

The information in this book is true and complete to the best of our knowledge. All recommendations are made without any guarantee on the part of the author or Publisher, who also disclaim any liability incurred in connection with the use of this data or specific details.

We recognize that some words, model names and designations, for example, mentioned herein are the property of the trademark holder. We use them for identification purposes only. This is not an official publication.

MBI Publishing Company books are also available at discounts in bulk quantity for industrial or sales-promotional use. For details write to Special Sales Manager at Motorbooks International Wholesalers & Distributors, 729 Prospect Avenue, PO Box 1, Osceola, WI 54020-0001 USA.

Library of Congress Cataloging-in-Publication Data
Paternie, Patrick C.
    How to restore & modify your Porsche 914 & 914-6/Patrick C. Paternie.
      p. cm.
    Includes index.
    ISBN 0-7603-0584-6 (pbk.: alk. paper)
    1. Porsche 914 automobile—Conservation and restoration.
2. Porsche 914 automobile—Customizing. I. Title.
TL215.P75P38   1999
629.28'722—dc21   99-26203

On the front cover: Porsche introduced a completely different car design in 1970 to replace the short-lived 912. The company's original intent was to release the 914 as an entry-level car that would embody the trend for mid-engine sports cars. Porsche aimed the 914 directly at young people who wanted a Porsche but could not afford a 911. Between 1970 and 1976, Porsche sold more than 118,000 914s and 914/6s. The yellow 914 on the cover is a 1973 2.0-liter owned by Bill Anders and the black car is a 1974 with a 2.7-liter, six-cylinder conversion owned by Don Bierce.

On the back cover: Top: Porsche 914s readily lend themselves to updates, modifications, and performance upgrades. Renegade Hybrids of Redlands, California, recently finished updating the first 914 ever converted to a V-8. C-2 wheels, slight flare to rear quarters, and discrete dual exhaust outlet only hint that a sleeper V-8 lies under the skin.
Inset: Many Porsche 914 owners use their cars for autocrossing or roadracing. 914s readily accept several components designed for its more powerful sibling, the Porsche 911, such as these huge 12-inch cross-drilled rotors that now help stop a 1.7-liter 914 at California motoring events.

Printed in the United States of America

Contents

Acknowledgments

If you think maintaining and restoring a 914 can be tedious, annoying, never-ending, aggravating work, you ain't seen nothing until you try writing a book about doing it. But just like driving the 914 on a nice sunny day with the top off when everything is functioning properly, there is a fun and rewarding side to the experience.

And while automobiles can provide their own mechanical brand of joy and companionship, it's the people you meet hanging around them that provide life's real pleasures. I owe some of those people a big thank you for helping me write this book.

At the top of the list is my wife, Linda, who not only has the "real job" in the family but has continuously provided me with the encouragement, advice, and editorial critiques that a writer needs to successfully ply his trade. She also puts up with my weird work hours and methods. A smart woman, but she still loves me.

Matt Stone, quintessential car maven and auto writer, has done so much for me and opened so many doors as a role model, mentor, data source, and damn good car buddy that I could fill a book about it, but I'll just say, "Thanks, Matt."

My gratitude goes out to Zack Miller at MBI Publishing Company for giving me the chance to write this book and John Adams-Graf for putting up with all the whining, wheedling, excuses, and headaches I have given him during our journey through 914 land.

Thanks to all the 914 fanatics who have provided their time, knowledge, and energies to this project. I am especially grateful for the support of Wayne Dempsey and Tom Gould of Pelican Parts, who let me share their knowledge and photography of many of the procedures in this book. Brian Kumamoto went above the call of duty in supplying 914 tips and even free legal advice. Old friends Lars and Bev Frohm generously pitched in when I called. Bill Bartee, Ron Mistak, and Andy Leaney also made special contributions. Mitch Rossi was generous with his time and talent.

Klaus Parr and Jens Torner of Porsche were also very kind and helpful in providing information and materials.

Last, but not least, wherever he may be, a special thanks to Larry B., the Mad Hatter who started me on the path that let me follow my dreams.

Introduction

This is a 914 user's manual. Unlike most books about Porsches, this one can go out to the garage and get its pages dirty. It's not a glossy tribute to the 914, to be jauntily displayed just so on your coffee table when company comes over. If you do leave it out when your 914 buddies come over, it won't even hurt my feelings if they occasionally use it as a beer coaster.

Nor is it the definitive illustrated guide to every part, nut, and bolt the factory ever screwed together to make a 914. That's why they make shop manuals.

A user's manual is not to be confused with an owner's manual. The owner's manual is the little booklet in the glovebox buried under a bunch of fast food napkins and a flashlight with dead batteries that tells you pretty basic stuff like how to shift gears by first depressing the clutch or how to use the jack. For some reason, owner's manuals tend to get separated from their vehicles over the years. We'll assume you have a pretty good idea of how to drive and roll up the windows, turn on the lights and other basics. We'll also assume that you have a basic set of tools and a general understanding of automotive technology like how to change oil and what spark plugs do.

So what does a user's manual do? It's a practical guide to enjoying the 914. Advice on finding, buying, restoring, repairing, and/or modifying a car that will come closest to meeting your expectations of 914 ownership. Remember that word *practical*. This is not the ultimate restoration guide to prepare a national concours winner. It's also not intended to provide all the details on building a car that will let you blow off Hans Stuck. I have no interest in the former and the latter would be impossible.

This is a book about reality. Maybe it's the reality that sets in when you go looking to buy a Porsche and find out that the only Porsche you can afford to buy and maintain is the 914. Or the reality that sets in after you buy a 914 when you discover that not a whole lot of current material is readily available to help you keep this car running the way you imagined a Porsche sports car should run. I know, because that's the situation I was in a few years ago and came to that same conclusion. So you might say I wrote this book in self-defense. People I met and tricks I learned from my own initiation into 914 ownership.

I have owned a 911 for many years, but still wasn't prepared for the unique experience of owning a 914. After all, you're not going to find too many cars with two large trunks, an air-cooled motor in the middle, a removable top, and the ability to out-handle almost anything else on the road. OK, maybe the Boxster, but in the short time the Boxster has been around there has probably been more written about that car than you can find about the 914. You can also buy 10 exceptionally nice 914s for the price of one Boxster.

The 914 is a rare combination of a real sports car that offers reasonable degrees of practicality and economy. And even though some people panned its styling when it was introduced, the 914's looks have successfully stood the test of time.

But there's a dark side to owning a 914 that Charles Dickens could have appreciated. Conceived in the freewheelin' 1960s, the 914 hit the market just as emissions laws and safety laws were being forced down the throats of the auto makers. The little roadster bore the brunt of compliance at the expense of performance and driveability. If that weren't enough, it suffered an international identity crisis that orphaned it from its Porsche and Volkswagen parents. James Dean's infamous 550 Spyder may have been named the "Little Bastard" but the 914 lived that life.

What I have tried to do here is pull together everything you need to be a knowledgeable owner and user of the Porsche 914. You'll find notes on the car's history along with maintenance and performance tips. I've also included information on the 914/6. Even 911 owners will be able to relate to some of the mechanical aspects regarding those cars.

Of course, every man has his dreams. And for some strange reason, the 914 triggers some of the best, and worst, of them. I've tried to concentrate on the former. You'll see that there are some pretty devoted and creative people still actively experimenting to attain the perfect 914. Many of these are race cars, but I've included V-8 powered street cars as well for all the 1.7 and 1.8 914 owners who've decided that they're mad as hell and not going to be pushed around at traffic lights anymore.

Speaking of fast driving and racing, the 914 is the car of choice for many Porsche enthusiasts who like to autocross, time trial, or club race. For many Porsche fans, the 914 has served as a great introduction to racing. That's why, in addition to discussing modifications and set-up for speed events, I thought it would be helpful to provide a few basics on how to get started driving your 914 in competitive events.

Whether you race it or just cruise the highways in it, the true joy in owning a 914, like any sports car, is to use it. Hopefully this user's manual will help you wring all the joy you want out of your 914.

What Is a 914?

There's one question regarding 914s that always pops up sooner or later, so let's get it out of the way first:

Is the 914 really a Porsche? Or is it a VW?

In the United States, we say it's a Porsche and we've got the Porsche Club of America to back us up on this. That's the quick and dirty answer you'll want to give on most occasions when telling people what kind of car you drive. The exception being, of course, your insurance agent, to whom you will swear it's really a VW that they just call a Porsche. The full-length answer comes down as the automotive equivalent of explaining the chicken-and-road conundrum by saying "to get to the other side." For the 914, the "other side" was crossing the Atlantic Ocean to America.

The public's dilemma regarding the true identity of the 914 began when it was introduced at the Frankfurt auto show in September 1969. As 914s became available to buyers in Europe shortly thereafter, the cars were badged as VW-Porsches with VW emblems on the hubcaps and the Wolfsburg crest embossed on the steering wheel hub. They were sold through VW-Porsche dealers. When the cars showed up in the United States in early 1970, they also were devoid of any

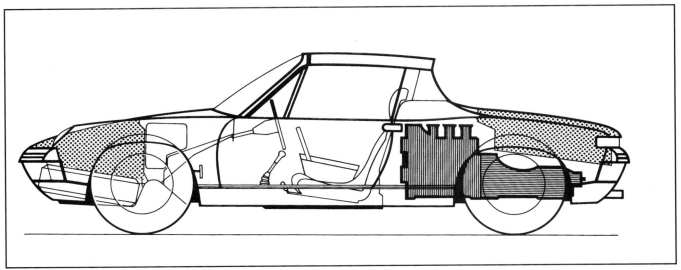

Porsche's original plan for the 914 was as an entry level car that would embody the current trend at the time for midengine sports cars. With two trunks and six cylinders, the 914/6 could have been a very successful car, if the selling price could have been lower. Porsche AG

Porsche emblems, although this was the only country in which they were sold through Porsche dealers. The word "P-O-R-S-C-H-E" was carried on the engine lid grille and a subtle Porsche crest replaced the VW coat of arms on the steering wheel.

Here's an interesting bit of trivia while we're on the subject of emblems and signage. No 914 ever came with a Porsche crest on the front trunk lid, although they are certainly a popular aftermarket add-on. The same applies to any right-hand drive 914 you may see, as the factory only produced left-hand drive versions.

The VW masquerading as a Porsche issue was further confused by the Porsche Club of America. The PCA has a strict set of rules as to what constitutes a "Porsche" to determine if an owner is eligible for membership. You must own a Porsche to be a member. There was no question as to the pedigree of the Porsche factory-assembled 914/6 with its 911 engine, but a strong debate raged about the VW roots of the engine in the four-cylinder cars. Conveniently forgotten by those opposing the 914 was the origin of much of the componentry in the early 356s. All 914s were eventually deemed acceptable for PCA membership.

As 75 percent of the 914s produced came to call the United States home, the car's acceptance by PCA makes it safe

The 2.0-liter from the 1969 911T was the power plant for the 914/6. Porsche AG

The 914 four put the engine in front of the transmission for better weight distribution and balance than a 911. Front suspension was similar to 911, while coil springs replaced torsion bars in rear. Porsche AG

to call it a Porsche. But the technically proper, and historically correct, answer is that it's a VW-Porsche. The cars were conceived through a joint agreement between Porsche and Volkswagen, the bodies were built by Karmann, a supplier to both firms, and the suspension and transmission were Porsche parts while the four-cylinder cars had Volkswagen engines.

Why and how all this came about is important for an understanding of why the 914 was built the way it was, and why, ultimately, it had such a short lifespan. I also think that, as in most mechanical projects, there will be times as you travel the path to restoration or modification of your own 914 when you may hit a bumpy stretch prompting you to loudly and profanely question your car's genealogy. I feel a little historical knowledge may be useful in soothing one's temper at those times. Rather than resorting to base vulgarities, please remember the free-love attitude of the Swingin' Sixties and think of the 914 as a Porsche-VW "love child."

Speaking of the 1960s, by the middle of the decade, you didn't need Bob Dylan to tell you that the times were a changin' in the world of automobile racing as well as other institutions. A look at the race results, and the starting grids, showed that placing the engine behind the driver and ahead of the rear wheels was the way to go. The Cooper-Climax grand prix cars led the way in Formula One and by 1961, all F1 cars had followed suit. Ferrari won Le Mans in 1963 with a midengine racer, while Jim Clark's 1965 win at Indy in the Lotus-Ford sounded the death knell for the ponderous front-engine roadsters.

Midengine cars offered better weight distribution, taking weight off the front wheels and putting it closer to the rear. This improved traction for the rear driving wheels. It also meant a lower polar moment of inertia, centering most of the mass of the car, which improved handling and steering response. Without staring over, or around, the engine, the driver had a better view of the road.

Naturally, what works in race cars soon becomes the latest vogue in sports and GT cars. By 1967, when Ferry Porsche began discussions with his good friend Heinz Nordhoff, the head of Volkswagen, about producing a modern, reasonably priced sports car, the world's enthusiasts were already drooling over midengine wonders like the Lamborghini Miura, Ferrari Dino 206GT, the DeTomaso Mangusta, and the Lotus Europa.

Porsche, of course, had been building "rear-engined" sports cars, with the motor hung out behind the rear wheels. All of its race cars, however, from the early 550 and RSK Spyders on up to the 904, were midengine cars. Building a midengine sports car seemed logical and feasible.

On the subject of Porsche history, while my purpose is to give you a basic understanding of the 914's development and

The final deal with VW worked out over distribution of cars changed the face of Porsche marketing in the United States, creating Porsche+Audi. In Europe, the cars were sold as VW-Porsches. Porsche AG

evolution, a more comprehensive study is presented in the book *Porsche, Excellence was Expected* by Karl Ludvigsen. It expansively embraces the complete history of the company and its cars. It's not something you need to work on your 914, but it is a valuable reference tool for anyone who is a Porsche enthusiast.

Back to 1967, here's what Ferry Porsche and Heinz Nordhoff each needed that they felt could be best achieved by working together. Porsche was doing well meeting the

The 914 was aimed directly at young people who wanted a Porsche but couldn't afford a 911. Porsche AG

While an entry level Porsche, the 914 still boasted innovations like dual trunks and a stowable targa top that couldn't be found in the competition. Porsche AG

world's demand for 911s and 912s, but the prices of these cars had risen to a point where the company felt that it needed a less expensive, so-called "entry level" Porsche, to keep its dealer network alive and well. Making this car a midengine model would also help Porsche's overall marketing image, providing a connection to the technology it used in its successful racing program and showing that Porsche was in

step with Ferrari, Lotus, and company by turning out its own midengine car. From a manufacturing standpoint, aligning itself with Volkswagen, a company with which it already had a long-standing relationship, gave Porsche the economic benefits of mass production without having to invest in the expansion of its own facilities.

Volkswagen, on the other hand, was undergoing a sales slump and desperate to expand its product line. It was going up market with a new car, the 411, for which it had designed a new four-cylinder engine. Its European competitors all had sporty models to offer customers, while VW struggled to sell the Type 2 version of the Karmann-Ghia. By putting the 411 engine in a new sports car produced by Karmann, VW could solve a number of problems with one move. Karmann had been producing bodies for Porsche since 1961, so the transition from the Karmann-Ghia to a Porsche designed midengine sports car was not thought to be that much of a stretch.

Nordhoff and Porsche shook hands on a deal that would have Porsche design and develop a midengine sports car around the 411 engine. This car was to be Volkswagen's new sports car. Porsche would also be able to take bodies produced by Karmann, at cost, and add its own engines to sell the resulting cars as Porsches. A fairly straightforward arrangement between two long-term business partners.

Or so it seemed. In the two ensuing years before the 914 was ready to go to market, significant changes would

Everywhere but the United States, cars carried VW's "Wolfsburg crest" on the steering wheel. Porsche AG

In the United States, both the four- and six-cylinder cars carried Porsche emblems. Porsche AG

In true 1960s fashion, the 914 came into the world as the love child of two German auto makers. **Porsche AG**

Even the 911-powered 914/6 suffered an identity crisis outside the United States. **Porsche AG**

occur that not only affected this new midengine sports car but significantly altered the way both Volkswagen and Porsche conducted business. The first came when Heinz Nordhoff, shortly after his meeting with Porsche, took seriously ill, eventually passing away in April 1968. His successor was Karl Lotz. Lotz knew nothing of the handshake deal between Ferry Porsche and Nordhoff. All he had to go by was a contract stating that Porsche was designing a sports car for Volkswagen's exclusive use. If Porsche wanted bodies for its own purposes, they would have to buy them from Volkswagen at a cost higher than what Nordhoff and Porsche discussed. This would severely impact Porsche's

plan for using the 914 as a lower price entry level Porsche. As things turned out, because of VW's cost accounting methods, the 914/6 bodies turned out by Karmann cost Porsche more money per unit than the 911 bodies being made in the same facility.

After much gnarling and gnashing of teeth, the agreement that was finally hammered out created a new entity, VW-Porsche Vertriebsgesellschaft GmbH, shortened to VG, to sell sports cars for both companies. In the United States, a new division of VW was created, called Porsche+Audi Division, to sell Porsches and Audis from new showrooms that were separate from VW dealers. Lotz needed to bring the Audi to the U.S market, and he felt that selling it through VW dealers would cheapen its image. Naturally, this created an upheaval amongst the existing independent Porsche dealership network, despite the fact that 75 percent were affiliated

Porsche developed the 914/6GT, with its distinctive fender flares, to carry wide racing tires and wheels. **Porsche AG**

On the inside, the 914/6GT, despite racing seats and safety harness, remained in stock trim. Porsche AG

with VW dealers. The car model positioned on the point for this new marketing network was the 914.

In addition to its distribution, the new marketing plan also impacted the 914's appearance. To meet Volkswagen's sales goals, the new car couldn't look like a rehash of an old Porsche design. It had to be distinctively different. Therefore an outside firm was considered to be a better source to handle the car's styling.

Gugelot Design GmbH was one of Germany's top industrial design firms. Its client base included Braun and Kodak among many other major companies. The company's only automotive work was for the German plastics manufacturer Bayer. Gugelot had designed a car to showcase Bayer's work with an experimental manufacturing process that molded a fiberglass frame and body together to save weight by eliminating the use of steel or other metals. The process turned out to be economically unfeasible, but the automotive design study caught the eye of

Three 914s were entered in the August 1970 Marathon de la Route. Cars 1 and 3 were Group 6 cars because of their 8-inch rear wheels. Car 2 was a Group 4 entry. Porsche AG

The Marathon de la Route in 1970 was an 86-hour enduro held at the Nurburgring, in which Porsche entered the 914/6, as it had done to show off the Sportomatic transmission in 1967 and the 911E in 1968. Porsche AG

Larousse/Haldi/Marko (1) covered 6,293 miles in 86 hours of racing to win the event. Car 3 was second and Car 2 was third. The 914s had no problems, other than a flat tire, two blown fuses, a burned out taillight, and two loose window cranks. Porsche AG

Butzi Porsche, the designer of both the 911 and the 904, who suggested its use as the starting point for the 914.

Although it was originally conceived as a front-engine vehicle, the clean, functional lines of the Gugelot car were easily adaptable to a midengine configuration encompassing ample front and rear trunk space. The most distinctive feature of the design was the location of the front turn signal/running lights, perched along the forward edge of the fenders. These lights were carried over to the 914 and became one of its major styling features. Not that the resulting flat and angular appearance of the 914 would be judged guilty of having major styling features when it was unveiled to the public. One prominent automotive magazine described it as a "potato cart." Time has proved to be much kinder to the looks of the 914, its minimalist styling faring better

A routine pit stop in the Marathon for the car driven by Claude Ballot-Lena and Guy Chasseuil, the same teammates who drove a 914/6GT to sixth overall at the 1970 Le Mans race. Porsche AG

This 1971 photo shows Christian Jurgensen in a 914/6GT with radical fender flares and cornering attitude. **Porsche AG**

than some of its contemporaries, whose looks will eternally be stuck in the 1970s.

While not a styling sensation, the 914's strength was in function following form. Its wide, flat body allowed the two trunks to have a combined capacity of 15.9 cubic feet. There was also a generous-sized fuel tank sitting below the front trunk to carry 16.4 gallons. Capable of better than 25 miles per gallon, the four-cylinder version not only was able to move two people and a lot of their luggage, but it could carry them over 400 miles without refueling.

An interesting comparison of the 914 to the 911 reveals that although it was shorter in overall length by 7 inches (156.8 versus 163.9 inches), its wheelbase was longer by the same amount (96.5 versus 89.3). It was also wider than a contemporary 911 by 1.5 inches (65.0 versus 63.4). Its overall height was 48 inches, making it 4 inches shorter than the 911. The 914/4 weighed 268 pounds less than a 911 (1,982 pounds versus 2,250 pounds), while the 914/6 tipped the scales at 2,070 pounds. In addition to being lighter, the 914 also carried its weight more evenly distributed than the 911. The average 911 of that time had about 58 percent of its weight biased toward the rear while the 914 was a bit closer to even with a front to rear ratio of 46/54.

Despite these statistical differences, the 914 did share a number of things with the 911. Front suspension, consisting of struts and longitudinal torsion bars, was carried over, as was a modified version of the 911 rack and pinion steering. The 914/6, besides the obvious 2.0-liter (1,991-cc) six-cylinder engine that was used in the 1969 911T, also had Porsche five-lug hubs and wheels with ventilated 11.12-inch front disc brakes and 11.25-inch solid discs in the rear. The basic 914 relied on the hubs, wheels, and solid 11.05-inch front discs of the VW 411. At the rear, in a concession to its sporting personality, 11.10-inch disc brakes were added in place of the VW's drum units. The rear suspension for both 914s avoided the 911's torsion bar setup and used boxed steel trailing arms, with coil-over shocks to locate the rear wheels. The 911 five-speed transaxle was used in both models, although turned around and modified for the midengine location.

The four-cylinder version of the 914 was powered by a 1.7-liter (1,679-cc) motor developed by Volkswagen for its new 411 sedan. While the six had sporty overtones like overhead cams and a pair of Weber triple-throat carbs, the VW powerplant was a bit more mundane with its pushrods and a modern but less aurally inspiring electronic fuel injection.

The first four-cylinder 914s, labeled as 1970 models, began to trickle into the United States in January 1970. The price was $3,595 on the East Coast while West Coast buyers had to ante up an extra 100 bucks. The 914/6 showed up in March and was priced at $5,999 in the East and $6,099 for Left Coasters. Unfortunately, these prices were not considered to be bargains by the automotive press or potential customers. The base price of the Datsun 240Z, which also debuted as a 1970 model, was $3,526, although greedy dealers did bump that up by $1,000 or more. Even Porsche enthusiasts had to wonder about the wisdom of buying the austere 914/6, when a 911T offered similar performance and a bit more comfort and prestige for less than $500 more.

Now before the 914 diehards start reaching for poison pens, or even worse, poison darts, and the rest of you start thinking about trading in this book for the *MGB Buyer's Bible* and *Illustrated History of Warm Beer*, let me make it perfectly clear that the 914 package possessed unique capabilities to offer sports car enthusiasts. We'll get into them and the comparisons in performance and handling of the 914 against its competitors in chapter 2, when we explore the who, what, why, where, and how much issues of acquiring a 914 to restore or modify in today's world. But from a historical standpoint, and ultimately a potential restorer's perspective, like it or not, we need to point out that the 914's high initial selling price plagued the car throughout its short existence. It cost Porsche too much to produce and to continue developing, unlike the 356 and 911. The sensitive issue of the 914's comparative price in the marketplace was compounded by the escalating strength of the German mark versus the U.S. dollar throughout the 914's life.

The 914/6 bore the brunt of the price/value problem. Porsche made only 3,360 914/6 cars in a little over two years, before the model was dropped. For the model years 1970–1976, factory records indicate that 115,596 four-cylinder cars were produced. What follows is a year-by-year analysis of what was offered to 914 buyers, as Porsche tried to tailor the car to the demands of the marketplace while battling increasing government regulations regarding safety and emissions. The trim and equipment contained in this listing does not reflect special options for countries other than the United States.

A limited run of 11 916s were also produced in 1971 and 1972. These cars featured the fender flares and wider wheels of the 914/6GT but were true street GTs with leather interiors, fixed roof panels, and the mechanicals and running gear of a 1972 911S.

Sales of the 914/6 were so dismal after its first year on the market that very few, 443 to be exact, were produced during 1971. It was still part of the catalog in 1972 but none were officially sold in the United States, although 240 cars were made. Some of those last cars may have had the new 2.4-liter 911 engine, since Porsche had obtained EPA certification for

914/4

1970–1971

Standard Equipment:

- 1.7-liter, 80-DIN horsepower @ 4,900 rpm, four-cylinder engine
- 4.5x15-inch four-bolt painted steel VW 411 wheels with hubcaps
- 155SRx15 radial tires
- Bumpers painted body color
- No antiroll bars
- Fixed passenger seat with tethered movable footrest for "adjustments"
- Column-mounted ignition switch
- Dash-mounted two-speed wipers with manual washer button
- 7,000-rpm tachometer, 120-mile-per-hour speedometer, fuel gauge, brake/fuel warning lights
- Hard rubber steering wheel

Options:

- Appearance Group with items that were standard on the 914/6, including vinyl-covered targa bar sides, dual horns, chrome bumpers, fog lights, 5.5x15-inch steel wheels with hubcaps, 165HRx15 tires, leather-covered steering wheel, top headliner, and pile carpet
- Upholstered "third seat" pad for tray between seats
- 5.5x15-inch Pedrini cast alloy wheel with eight cooling slots
- Choice of basket-weave vinyl, corduroy, or cloth seat insert trim
- Air conditioning
- Various radios

1972

Changes to Standard Equipment:

- Adjustable passenger seat
- Shorter rear valance panel
- Basket-weave pattern door panels replaced previous smooth surface covering at midyear
- Retractable seatbelts at midyear
- Washer/wiper switch moved to steering column; washer still powered by spare tire air pressure
- Adjustable air vents added to either side of dashboard

Rear trunk received full-length padding as insulation from muffler heat

Options:

Same as 1970–71

1973

Changes to Standard Equipment:

- Improved shift linkage
- California emissions reduces 1.7-liter to 72 horsepower @ 5,000 rpm (compression ratio lowered from 8.2:1 to 7.3:1)
- Wheel hubs machined with circular lip for improved wheel mounting
- Black bumpers instead of painted bumpers
- Front rubber bumper guards
- Black metal "914" and "1.7" logos on rear panel
- "PORSCHE" in silver letters instead of gold on engine lid
- Black window cranks, inner door handles, and threshold covers
- Conventional handbrake replaced collapsible unit
- Doors reinforced by steel side beams to meet U.S. safety laws (added 110 pounds.)

Options:

- 2.0-liter, 95-DIN horsepower @ 4,900 rpm four-cylinder
- Appearance Group fitted to 2.0-liter models
- Center console with hinged lid to fit between seats
- Center console with three VDO gauges—clock, oil temp, voltmeter
- Intermittent wipers
- Fuchs "2.0-liter" 5.5x15-inch forged alloys part of Appearance Group for 2.0-liter cars and optional on others
- Pedrini alloy updated for revised hubs
- Mahle 5.5x15-inch cast alloys introduced
- Heated rear window
- Sway bars, 15-millimeter in front and 16-millimeter in rear, fitted to 2.0-liter and optional on others

1974

Changes to Standard Equipment:

- Displacement increase from 1.7 liters to 1.8 liters (1,795 cc) producing 76 DIN horsepower @

4,800 rpm for all states; switch from Bosch D-Jetronic to L-Jetronic fuel injection
Rubber bumper guards added to rear
Standard wheel now 5.5x15-inch steel "sport" wheel
Black plastic windshield washer jets replace silver-colored jets
Vinyl-covered targa bar side panels on all models
Black headlight surrounds and retaining ring
Plastic exterior lettering and numbers
Seatbelt warning light

Options:

Pedrini alloys no longer available
Leatherette replaces leather on optional steering wheel
Limited Edition—consisting of 2.0-liter engine, special front spoiler extending below bumper, delete vinyl trim on targa panels, Mahle wheels, sway bars, center console, leatherette steering wheel, and choice of three color schemes. Choice of black with yellow valances, rocker panels, bumpers, spoiler, wheel centers, and "PORSCHE" side stripe; or white with either green or orange in place of the yellow trim on the black model

1975–1976

Changes to Standard Equipment:

Catalytic converter on California cars
Emissions controls reduce power of 2.0-liter to 88 DIN horsepower @ 4,900 rpm
Fuel pump relocated to front of car to reduce vapor lock tendencies
Black "shock absorber" 5-mile-per-hour safety bumpers added
New rear license plate light arrangement
Revised ignition switch
VW Rabbit window cranks installed
Wider basket-weave pattern on interior panels
California cars had additional bumperettes

Options:

Plaid cloth seat inserts
Rectangular fog lights
Performance Group—front spoiler, sway bars, alloy wheels

914/6

1970–1972

Standard Equipment:

2.0-liter 110 DIN horsepower @ 5,800 rpm six-cylinder engine (same as 1969 911T)
Steel 5.5x15-inch five-lug 911 wheels with hubcaps
165HRx15 radial tires
Chrome bumpers
Vinyl-covered targa bar side panels
"914-6" emblem on rear panel
Fog lights
Dual horns
Dash-mounted 911 ignition switch
Hard rubber steering wheel
Hand throttle
Fixed passenger seat with tethered movable footrest for "adjustments"
Column-mounted wiper/wash with three-speed wipers/electric-powered washer
8,000 rpm tachometer, 150-mile-per-hour speedometer, combination fuel/oil temperature gauge

Options:

Leather seats
5.5x15-inch cast magnesium Mahle wheels
5.5x14-inch forged alloy Fuchs wheel with 185HRx14 radial tires
Air conditioning
Various radios
M471 Package (March 1971 to 1972)—steel fender flares, matching steel front valance, no rear valance, flared fiberglass rocker panels, 6x15-inch forged alloy Fuchs wheels, 185/70VRx15 tires, 21-millimeter wheel spacers, extended wheel studs.

the 1972 914/6 so equipped. The 914/6 died a quiet death. For 1973, Porsche introduced the 2.0-liter four-cylinder, which offered only slightly less bang for a lot less bucks. It also was a more profitable car for Porsche to produce. Originally,

the U.S. Porsche+Audi marketeers dubbed it the 914S but Porsche quickly squashed that title, not wanting to chance the possibility of eroding all the good will that the 911S had built up over the years.

An "all-star" exhibition race at Ontario Speedway, California, in August 1970 had 914/6s driven by celebrity teams like Dick Smothers and Bobby Unser (3) and Astronaut Pete Conrad with Mario Andretti (7). **Porsche AG**

The 914 could not cure Volkswagen's financial woes. Kurt Lotz resigned in late 1971 and was replaced by Rudolf Leiding. Leiding made a decision in 1972 that all future VW products would be front-wheel drive and water-cooled. Obviously the 914 didn't fit in his plans. Work was begun on a successor, which evolved into the 924.

In 1974, Porsche bought out Volkswagen's share of the VG marketing operation. Part of the deal was that the 914 would remain a VW-Porsche everywhere with the exception of the United States. Porsche would have sole marketing responsibility for the 914. It's ironic that even though the 1973 and 1974 2.0-liter cars were the best of the 914s produced, the car would soon fade from the marketplace with production slowly phasing out during the 1976 model year. By then the price of a 2.0-liter had reached $7,250. Plans were already in progress to replace it with the 924. With sales of 118,976 units in a little over five years, it could hardly be called a failure for Porsche. And the car has certainly withstood the test of time among enthusiasts. Striking parallels

can also be drawn to Porsche's most recent success story, the Boxster. That car also shares suspension components with the latest 911 in addition to having two trunks and a midengine configuration.

If there is a villain in the 914 story, then it must be Volkswagen's inability to get the most out of Porsche's design work. Selling 75 percent of its production in the only market where it carried the Porsche nameplate is pretty strong evidence. So to end this long discussion of whether to call the 914 a Porsche or a VW, let's concentrate on the positive side and call it a Porsche.

Short, but Sweet—The 914 Competition History

Porsche has always believed in the old racing axiom of "What wins on Sunday sells on Monday." Racing is a major part of the company's marketing program. So what better way to pump up the sales of the slow-moving (off the showroom floor) 914/6 than to demonstrate how fast-moving it was on a race track.

A 914 racing in the Targa Florio in 1971. Porsche AG

At this point in time, the Porsche competition department was still headed up by Ferdinand Piech. Piech was the driving force behind Porsche's rapid rise to becoming one of the world's most feared factory race teams. His evolutionary development of prototype racers, starting with the 906, had culminated in the ultimate endurance weapon, the 917. But his engineers were kept busy on a number of other projects.

An example of one of these projects was the building of two special 914s before the car was introduced to the public in 1969. Other than slight fender flares, the cars looked to be 914/6s but carefully tucked away amidships was the 3.0-liter, flat eight-cylinder racing engine from the 908. One of these cars, slightly detuned to produce 260 horsepower equipped with a complete street exhaust system, was a present to Ferry Porsche in honor of his 60th birthday. He drove

the car for a number of years before it was retired to the Porsche museum.

The other car was used by Piech primarily at the Weissach test facilities, although it did see limited road use. With the full race engine setup installed plus a muffler system, the car still managed 300 horsepower. Those who drove it compared its performance to that of the 930 Turbo when it appeared in 1977.

These two cars proved the capability of the 914 chassis to handle the extra horsepower required in a successful GT racing program. In the United States, Porsche+Audi aimed their sights at the SCCA Production Class. Eventually, as sports car racing so often requires political power as much as horsepower, the 914 successfully ended up racing in IMSA. On the international scene, the factory set out to follow the 911's success in rallying and endurance racing.

A 911S duels with a pair of 914s at Le Mans in 1971. Porsche AG

The FIA is the governing body for international auto rac-ing, and to qualify to race under the Group 4 rules for production cars at that time, it was necessary to prove that 500 cars were produced in the configuration that was being raced. Cars meeting these requirements were said to be homologated, or approved, to compete. Porsche determined that what was needed for the 914/6 to be competitive under the rules was to take advantage of the extra 2 inches allowed and widen the fenders of the 914 to fit bigger wheels and tires. To meet the homologation requirement Porsche made available to anyone interested the wider steel fender flares, wheel spacers, and wider alloy wheels that made up what came to be called the 914/6GT. This kit was later sold as the M471 Option. Details aren't clear as to how many kits ended up in the hands of privateers, or even how many 914/6GT racers were actually built. While the total was originally thought to be 11 cars, later studies of factory records indicate

that as many as 47 cars may have been produced by Piech's busy crew.

Other changes made to the 914/6GT include fiberglass bumpers, front valance, rocker panels, and deck lids. The top was strengthened by a steel cross brace that was bolted in place. Brakes were from the 911s with 908 calipers added up front. The chassis was also stiffened in key spots. Various engines were run, but the "standard" powerplant was a twin-plug 2.0-liter with Weber carburetors.

The most famous 914/6GT is the one prepared for Sonauto, the French Porsche distributor, for the 1970 Le Mans race. With a modified 2.0-liter engine putting out between 210 and 220 horsepower, the white No. 40 was driven by Guy Chasseuil and Claude Ballot-Lena. Thanks to a very wet and stormy 24-hour period that caused all but seven cars to be classified as finishers, the 914 motored on, averaging 99.27 miles per hour, to finish sixth overall. It not only averaged over

13 miles per gallon, it never had to change tires or brake pads. It won the overall GT category and the 2.0-liter class.

Later that year, in the 86-hour Marathon de la Route run over the north and south loops of the Nurburgring, Porsche entered three 914/6 racers. One was fitted to the Group 4 9146GT specs, while the other two, running 8-inch rear wheels, were classified as Group 6 prototypes. The cars finished 1-2-3 in the event, easily outdistancing their competitors. The winning Group 6 car completed 6,293 miles during the event.

The 914 did not fare as well as a rally car. The factory rally drivers preferred to stake their chances with the winning reputation of the 911. But the factory forced them to use 914s in the 1971 Monte Carlo Rally. The Rally's ensuing snowy conditions, ideally suited to the rear-weight bias of the 911, rendered the 914s totally uncompetitive and the 914 rally program was forgotten.

Meanwhile, back in the United States, Josef Hoppen was in charge of competition for Volkswagen of America, which included the racing plans of Porsche+Audi. He devised a plan that would place the 914/6 in the hands of experienced racers across the country to boost the car's image nationwide. The six-cylinder cars would go up against the 240Z and Triumph TR-6 running in SCCA's C Production. Factory support from the main players made this the most competitive of the SCCA "amateur" racing programs. Hoppen chose longtime Porsche racer Richie Ginther to run cars on the West Coast, Bob Hindson and Art Bunker in the Midwest, and a promising racer named Peter Gregg in the Southeast. By competing in a number of regions across the country, Hoppen not only gained nationwide exposure for his efforts, but he also guaranteed himself that a number of Porsches would qualify on a regional basis to run at the national championships at Road Atlanta. The most distinctive features of these cars were the cut-down windscreens.

Alan Johnson and Elliott Forbes-Robinson drove the Ginther-prepped cars to seven regional wins to qualify both for the finals. Nine 914/6 drivers made the national championship race, only to lose to the more powerful Z cars. Forbes-Robinson finished fourth with teammate Johnson behind in fifth. Factory support went away the next year, but one of the new privateers who qualified a 914/6 for the finals was to go on to great success driving other Porsches, Al Holbert.

Hoppen's political battles with the SCCA over classification of the new 914/6GT in 1971 led to the start of another important chapter in Porsche racing history. One that would ultimately involve Holbert, but in the beginning established Peter Gregg and Hurley Haywood as leading Porsche racers. Hoppen switched Porsche's racing efforts to support the newly organized IMSA series. Gregg and Haywood won every race they entered that year, sweeping the GTU (under two-liter class), and they were the overall winners in three events. The 914 went on to many more wins in IMSA over the years in the hands of private entrants.

Today the 914 still enjoys popular status as a PCA club racer and in many vintage races.

2

Buying a 914

Walk up to a 914 owner and ask him why he bought it and the answer you'll hear the most often is because it's a true entry level Porsche. It may not be the fastest, best looking, or most reliable Porsche there is but it is the least expensive way to become a Porsche owner. It drives like a Porsche and it gets you in the Porsche Club. Getting in the Porsche Club means you can compete in autocrosses, time trials, and club racing events. And that's where you'll discover another important reason for owning a 914—they regularly outhandle all other types of Porsches at these events.

Don't let the misbegotten history of the 914 lead you to think that the car was a failure as a Porsche. The 914 outsold the revered 356, another Porsche with a DNA pattern very similar to that of a VW, by almost 40,000 units. And it did so in a production span that was half as long.

Remember, too, that with the exception of the Carrera models, the 356 wasn't the fastest car in the world from 0 to 60, but it did introduce the world to a unique driving experience. The "Porsche experience"—an inimitable combination of sounds and sensations that puts both car and driver in synch with themselves and with the

Advertising for the 914 stressed the youthful image and entry level, for a Porsche, price tag. Porsche AG

Despite the presence of a 911-based six-cylinder in the engine room, the 914/6 was a dismal seller. Porsche AG

Nimble handling and excellent balance are the 914's strong suits. Porsche AG

Painted bumpers and hubcaps kept the price down on the base 914. Porsche AG

Early four-cylinder cars had the wiper switch on the dash. Porsche AG

Base 914/6 lacked pizzazz when shod with base hubcaps. Porsche AG

Interior of the 914/6 was spacious but stark. Note tray for center console between seats. Porsche AG

twists and turns of the road. Anyone who has driven a Porsche, especially an air-cooled model, will recognize this sensation immediately upon driving another Porsche. Porsches are highly responsive to driver input, whether it's good or bad. They are cars that respond and reward good drivers. Because they are so responsive, they also inspire people to become better drivers.

The Porsche experience does not appeal to everyone, but it's something that anyone who is looking for a sports car should sample. It can be intimidating as well as exhilarating. It's also seductive and expensive. And that brings us back to owning a 914. All things considered, the 914 is still the least expensive way to enjoy the Porsche experience.

So much for the metaphysics of owning a 914. What if you're not looking for a rolling religious experience but just want a low-buck vintage sports car to fix up and enjoy on

Advent of the 1973 2.0-liter models also saw the debut of Fuchs forged alloys, which came to be known as 2.0-liter alloys. Porsche AG

sunny weekends? The choice is pretty much the same one that you would have had back when the 914 was new. The leading contenders are the MGB, Triumph TR-6, and Fiat 124. While browsing through the used car ads for sports cars, you may also be tempted by cars like MG Midgets, Triumph Spitfires, Datsun Z-cars, and the occasional Alfa Romeo Spider.

As we have seen from our study of the 914's history, the 1970s was a rough time to be an automobile manufacturer because of the ever-increasing smog and safety legislation. These were especially tough times for building sports cars. As a general rule, sports cars are quick and nimble performers

1973 saw Porsche jazz up both looks and performance of the 914 by coming out with 2.0-liter four-cylinder and a center console gauge package. Porsche AG

Not all the midlife additions to 914s were positive. Seatbelt interlock systems came on board in 1974. Porsche AG

In 1974 a "Limited Edition" run of 2.0-liter 914s came equipped with Mahle alloy wheels and a special front spoiler. Unfortunately, they also came with garish paint jobs that haven't done much for value to collectors.
Porsche AG

because they get the most from efficient, highly tuned small-displacement engines mounted in lightweight chassis. Meeting emissions and safety standards served up a double whammy to sports cars. It meant adding more weight and detuning engines. Further compounding problems for cars designed for handling agility was the fact that because of the "five miles per hour" bumper laws, not only was weight being added, a good portion of it was going in exactly the worst spot, the extreme ends of the car.

This was especially true for cars like the MGs and Triumphs that were originally designed in the early to mid-1960s without anticipating the legal complexities that would surround them a decade later. The MGB had a dual carb 1.8-liter (1,798-cc) engine that put out 98 horsepower at 5,400 rpm in its early years, before steadily losing power, along with one of its carburetors, through the years. It declined from 92 horsepower in 1970 to an anemic 62.5 horsepower before it was put out of its misery in 1980. It also gained over 400 pounds in weight as it got older.

In its best years, the MGB could probably accelerate as quickly as a 1.7-liter 914 but would be no match for a 2.0-liter version. Once the road deviated from a straight line, the 914 would easily leave the MGB behind. The MGB also was limited to a four-speed transmission (electric overdrive was available and you know about English electrics), lever action 1930's vintage shock absorbers, and a tiny trunk. For a number of years, lowering the top involved unsnapping the top from its frame, then disassembling the frame. Quite a contrast to the five-speed, fuel-injected, four-wheel disc, twin trunk, easy-on/easy-off roof setup of the 914 that still would qualify as fully equipped today.

The MGB does have its merits. It's still cheaper to acquire, restore, and maintain. It also has its own top-down, exhaust muttering, wind in the face appeal that can't be denied. What it lacks is the practicality of the 914 and, by a wide margin, the overall performance.

The Triumph TR-6 did come with a 2.5-liter (2,498-cc) six-cylinder, but despite the extra cylinders, it only made around

Rubber bumpers and standard steel wheels with "mag look" were featured on 1975 and 1976 914s. Porsche AG

Mahle alloys were optional on late 914s. Porsche AG

106 horsepower, putting its 0–60 performance in the same league as the MGB and the less powerful 914 motors. The TR-6 came out a year before the 914, in 1969, but was allowed to fade away much like the Porsche during the 1976 model year. Both the 914 and the TR-6 were terminated in favor of cars thought to be light years ahead of the sports car market. Triumph's TR-7 was billed as "the shape of things to come." It was a shape that came and went even quicker than the noisy, underpowered 924 that succeeded the 914. Thanks to the engineering efforts of Bob Tullius' Group 44, the TR-6 duked it out with the 914/6 for SCCA's C Production Class honors. Some serious rules politicking by British-Leyland helped as well. Unless you get Tullius to help, the 914 in either four- or six-cylinder flavors is the high performance choice these days.

Spitfires and Midgets suffer from the same faults as the MGB, in addition to coming in much smaller and slower packages.

The Fiat X1/9 shares many of the design qualities of the 914 but its small size and matching performance make it come up short, literally and figuratively, when compared to the 914. Parts availability and a history of reliability woes also work against the X1/9. The Fiat 124/2000 Spider suffers in the performance and parts categories as well.

As for the Alfa Romeo Spider, the 914's biggest edge would be in "bang for the buck" over the long haul. It comes down to the Porsche experience versus the Alfa mystique. It might be a fun touring car, but the 914, including the 914/6, would have the racer's edge over the Alfa.

There is one other car that might be raised as a natural competitor to the 914, having been introduced in the same year and at about the same price as the four cylinder. That car is the Datsun 240Z and its later iterations as the 260 and 280 models. I do not consider it a direct competitor in the used sports car market primarily because it is a GT and not an open-top sports car. While its price was more or less equal to the base 914, its performance, thanks to a larger six-cylinder engine making 150 horsepower, was better than the 914/6 with a 0 to 60 time of around 7.5 to 8 seconds. That made it about a second quicker than the 914/6 in acceleration. But a sports car is about handling and that's where the 914, four or six, easily outpaces the Datsun. Z cars are cheap to buy and can be made into fast, decent-handling, fun cars. Like the 914, many of them have also led hard lives and been consumed by rust. The biggest difference, apart from the closed cockpit, is they lack the 914's Porsche heritage.

As a combination of a practical tourer and/or a potential racer, the 914 must get the nod over the ranks of its competitors in the lower price range of the used sports car market. It's by no means perfect, as we shall discuss a little later in this chapter, but it does have significant advantages, as pointed out above. Most importantly, as we said in the beginning, it's a Porsche. If you haven't driven many Porsches, now's the time to go out and sample a few. See if you can feel what everyone means when they talk about the Porsche experience. Hey, the first few rides are free—just remember my warning about it being addictive.

Decide How You Will Use Your 914 Before You Look at What's for Sale

No matter how much money you have to spend on your 914, there are two important rules to follow as you shop. The first is to decide how you want to use your car. Are you looking for a reliable daily driver that will put a little more fun in your commute? A car that can provide a little fun in the sun on weekends, too. Or do you want a weekend warrior to run time trials or maybe even do a little wheel-to-wheel racing? Maybe you're one of those fussy individuals who is on a personal crusade to have a perfect 914, one that's cleaner and better assembled than the ones that rolled off the assembly lines. A real concours queen. Odds are your needs lie somewhere in between a couple of these extremes. It's up to you to decide what you want and then follow the second shopping rule—to buy the best car that you can afford that meets your needs.

This sounds like pretty basic advice, and it is, but there are a few things that can complicate matters and cloud your judgment when it comes to choosing the best that you can afford. The first is the nature of the 914 market. While prices tend to fluctuate according to used car prices in general, rising in good times and falling a bit during recessions, for the better part of the last decade you could expect to pay around $1,500 to $2,000 for a running four-cylinder in poor condition, about $4,000 to $5,000 for a decent example, and roughly $6,500 to $8,500 for a perfect example. The market for a clean 914/6 hovered around $12,500 for a long time but has lately been creeping up with pristine low mileage cars demanding up to $20,000.

Because of the 914's relatively low price, many of the people you'll find selling them are not dedicated Porsche enthusiasts. They bought their cars because they were cheap, only to discover that while the price of admission may be lower than for most Porsches, the cost of parts and repairs, other than routine maintenance like tune-ups and oil changes, is comparable to other Porsche models. Once they find out that "parts is parts" when it comes to pricing Porsche

Mack McFadgen's 914/6 with its 1970-style Porsche side stripe is about as original a car as you could find today.

McFadgen can tell stories of his days as the Bosch rep assigned to Can Am races, and working with Bruce McLaren and the Penske team. The 914 was driven on high speed runs to Nevada as weekend fun trips with famous racers.

items, they try to sell the car for about what they paid for it. This tends to keep prices fairly steady, but it also means that the cars are not receiving the proper care they require.

That's why I caution you to buy the best car for your intended purpose that you can afford. If you're looking for a concours quality car or a dependable daily driver, you will generally be better off in the long run spending a bit more up front for a well-maintained, well-equipped car. Better to pay an extra $2,000 or so than to end up putting $20,000 into the restoration of a car that might at best be worth half that much. It's not a bad idea to send away for a catalog from one or two of the parts suppliers listed in the appendix to familiarize yourself with the availability and cost of various parts before you start 914 shopping in earnest. Another good source would be the ads in magazines specializing in Porsches, most notably *Excellence*. You'll be amazed at the price variations for the same or similar parts. Just remember that when it comes down to choosing a supplier to order parts, make sure that in getting the best price you'll also be dealing with a firm that offers qual-

ity merchandise and can deliver it promptly and reliably. Having someone who can offer advice as to installation or what's best for your particular needs is also worth something. Check with other Porsche owners to see what experience they have had with various vendors.

Chances are that whatever car you end up buying will need something, so you better leave room in your budget for any necessary repair items. Maybe we should alter our shopping rule to getting the best car that you can afford, including any necessary parts.

If you plan on building a track car or aren't a stickler for making your car a 100 percent original, you can afford to look at some of the lower priced "fixer-uppers." As long as the car is solid and has the essentials to meet your needs, you can save yourself a nice chunk of change. Just remember to factor in the cost of adding whatever pieces may be missing or in need of replacement. Fortunately, there is a decent market of used parts available. Most dedicated 914 owners tend to be hands-on when it comes to doing their own repairs and maintenance.

Mack's 40 years with Bosch as a fuel injection expert earned him the nickname "Dr. Diesel." The irony is that he has only the carburetted version of the 914. Bought new in Portland, Oregon, and driven home to northern California, the car has only 57,000 miles.

Interior has padded center console cushion and "adjustable" passenger footrest.

Since Mack is usually the car's only occupant, the footrest is almost brand new.

Some even fall in the tinkerer class. After all, Porsche repair shops aren't cheap and many of them are better skilled at working on newer 911s and 944s than a 914. Your wallet, and probably your 914, will benefit from whatever work you can perform on your own. That's why you bought this book, right?

What to Look For and When to Run Away

Speaking of owners who tinker and "improve" their cars, what modifications increase or decrease the value of a 914? Again, it depends on how you intend to use the car. The concours fanatic will want a car that's 100 percent stock and original. The racer will probably appreciate any suspension upgrades or chassis stiffening improvements. Obviously a big factor is how the work was performed and if the seller can provide necessary receipts to back up his claims. This is especially important regarding any claims as to engine or transmission rebuilds.

Items that I would consider to be acceptable improvements to a 914 would be:

- Installation of improved shift linkage, e.g., a side-shifter, to a pre-1973 car
- Installation of a 911 front suspension
- Conversion to five-bolt wheels
- Installation of larger brake master cylinder (A common upgrade at one time, but one that is being questioned lately. See chapter 7.)
- Larger brakes
- Conversion to six-cylinder if done properly including suspension, braking, and wheel/tire upgrades
- Fender flares, depends on quality of workmanship/ materials
- Electronic ignition

I would avoid cars that have radical bodywork or V-8 engines, although a company called Renegade Hybrids has

been doing reliable conversions for years. "Big bore" four-cylinders of over 2.0-liters could also be potential disasters. The same goes for anything with wild cams and high compression ratios. Engines like these may be exciting while they last, but they tend to lead shorter lives than the less stressed stock displacement motors. If you are planning to use your car as a daily driver, a stock displacement motor with the fuel injection intact would be the most reliable and efficient choice. Stock cars also tend to maintain their resale value more than modified cars.

All 914s were equipped with electronic fuel injection. These systems can be quirky at times, but if properly adjusted and maintained they are superior to carburetors. You will run across cars for sale that have been converted to Weber carbs. This usually indicates that somewhere along the line the owner had a problem with the fuel injection and opted for the carbs as a quick fix. This could be indicative of a car whose owner scrimped on spending when it came to carefully maintaining the car, or used a mechanic who was either too lazy

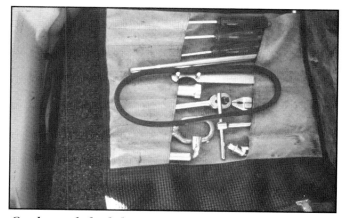

Car has only had three sets of tires in its life and still carries the original tool kit.

or poorly trained to solve the problem. Most of the time, the carbs proved more difficult to adjust than the fuel injection they replaced, running too rich at certain rpm and too lean at other parts of the rev range. Either symptom can affect the life expectancy of an engine.

An added consideration is that the carburetors will not pass smog requirements in many states. Before California adopted a law exempting cars over 25 years old from smog checks, the used car ads were filled with these "bargain" 914s. Even if you didn't mind the high expense involved in converting back to the fuel injection, many of the necessary parts of the original emissions controls have long since disappeared. California buyers should remember that it is still illegal to alter the emissions systems for any given year vehicle, pre-1973 or not. It's just that the exemption from smog checks decreases the chance of being caught.

When it comes to the 914/6, my personal opinion is that I would be hesitant to pay a high price for a car that has been materially altered by the addition of a larger six-cylinder engine. A rebuilt 2.0-liter that has had some performance improvements would be acceptable. As for four-cylinder cars that have been converted to sixes, as long as the complete package, including brakes and suspension, has been upgraded to handle the extra power, I have no objections. Many times they offer better performance and shifting than the original factory six-cylinder cars. This assumes the work was neatly and properly done. I would not, however, pay a price equivalent to that of an original 914/6 in similar condition. By the way, the 914/6 cars carry different serial numbers from the fours, so it's very easy to tell the real ones from the impostors.

If you are buying a car to go racing, be sure to check a copy of the rules as enforced by the appropriate sanctioning body. The Sports Car Club of America (SCCA), Porsche Club of America (PCA), Porsche Owners Club (POC), and various vintage racing associations all have their own sets of rules regarding the 914 and how it may be modified. Don't buy a car unless you know that you can legally race it in your club.

To further help you with your 914 shopping, I have compiled a listing by model year outlining the desirability and drawbacks for all the cars:

Only nonstock item is the rear trunk handle, added to keep the lid from becoming dented when opened or closed.

1970–71: Not the most desirable models. Very stark interior, fixed passenger seat, lack in-dash air vents, generally equipped with skinny tires and wheels; balky shift linkage (tail-shifter); 1.7-liter not very powerful, but cars are lightest in weight.

1972: Improved interior, including fresh air vents in dash, adjustable passenger seat, and windshield wiper switch on steering column. A better buy than a 1970–71 or 1975–76.

1973: 2.0-liter introduced. This is the most desirable of all 914s. Much improved performance. Shift linkage greatly improved. Chrome bumpers, fog lights, and other appearance items make it look as good as it performs. 5.5-inch Fuchs alloys. Better insulation. The 1.7-liter lost eight horsepower and gained over 100 pounds in weight to further cramp its meager performance. The 1.7 with its improved shifting could be a good bargain.

1974: 2.0-liter almost as desirable as 1973. Cars equipped with Sport (Fuchs alloy wheels, sway bars) and Appearance Group (center console, chrome bumpers, dual horns, leather steering wheel) options essentially the same as the 1973 2.0-liter on which this equipment came standard. Shorter seat tracks and rear bumper extensions are a minor difference from the previous year's model. One thousand Limited Edition 2.0-liter cars sent to United States. These cars had special paint along with spoilers, sway bars, and special alloy wheels. Somewhat rare, but selling price doesn't reflect this. 1.7-liter pumped up to 1.8-liter. Horsepower jumps from 72 to 76. This engine uses the L-Jetronic fuel injection which is less desirable than the D-Jetronic of the other 914s. Not a very desirable model.

1975–76: New bumpers and snazzy plaid interior don't make up for power loss in the 2.0-liter. Safety bumpers add more weight. California cars get catalytic converter and EGR system. Despite weak performance, some people prefer the appearance and the fact that these are the newest models. This works to keep prices just below the 1973–74 models.

Summary: Most 914 enthusiasts would recommend the 1973–74 2.0-liter cars to anyone looking for the best possible iteration of the 914. Surprisingly, more than a few will pick

The 916 is the rarest of 914s. This is what they looked like.

these cars over the stock 914/6. Certainly, the 2.0-liter six has the edge in suspension and braking systems plus the glorious sounds so unique to an air-cooled 911 motor, but the performance edge is not that much better. Factoring in the cost of purchase and maintenance, the four-cylinder 2.0-liter cars are definitely the better overall buy.

It may take a while to find a clean one in original condition, but if you have the patience to keep looking until you find one, the 1973–74 2.0-liter should be well worth the wait.

Now that you know the pros and cons of each year in the life span of the 914, let's look at problem areas to avoid for all 914s in general. Rust is the No. 1 problem facing the 914. You'll discover cars that look OK on the outside but are ready to break in two underneath. It's a sick feeling to insert a jack in the appropriate location under the rocker panel and, after furiously cranking away for a minute or two, look up to see the wheels still on the ground while the middle of the car is now several inches higher.

Not a pretty sight, but not the worst rust problem you can have in a 914. Open the engine lid and notice where the battery is located. It sits high on a shelf on the right side of the compartment. Over the years, battery acid, assisted by rain water dripping through the air grille, can seep down from the battery, corroding everything in its path to the ground. Unfortunately, a major item in this path is the right rear suspension. To save yourself a lot of time and to ensure a quick getaway from a car that is a rolling disaster site, this is the first place you want to inspect for rust. Over the years, cars may have been repaired and fitted with replacement battery trays. Check for signs of this type of repair. Make sure the work was done properly. While you're at the rear of the car, open the rear trunk and check around the rear shock towers for signs of corrosion that have spread through from the engine compartment. Also check for signs of water seepage around the taillights that can rust out the floor of the trunk. This is not a big structural problem but it pays to look.

The next big problem area is along the rocker panels. Check the jacking points. As I mentioned before, the exterior jacking point locating holes may look fine but the bracing behind them may have been eaten away. Dirt, grit, and leaves can build up in the rockers over the years, trapping moisture and causing the longitudinal supports of the car to fall prey to rust. Pull off the rocker covers to thoroughly give this area the twice over. Another good test is to remove the top and have a hefty friend sit in the passenger seat. The passenger door should open and close as easily as it did with the roof on. If not, you may not be getting all the 914 you deserve or at least think you're getting. If the door sticks and everything looks good underneath, check the rubber where the window meets the edge of the targa bar. Sometimes new

Space-saver tire was part of 916 equipment.

Rear view of the 916.

replacement rubber may cause a hang-up here. That's not a big problem.

Believe it or not, water does leak into a 914 after a heavy rain. For this reason, pull up the carpet behind the seats and check the floor for dampness and/or rust. A loose rear window (bad rubber seal) may also cause a leak in this area. Check for rust at the corners of the windshield and along the seal of the front compartment.

Look under the car for rust and any signs of major front end damage. If you see the latter, move on to the next, and hopefully straighter, 914.

A rust-free 914 is getting hard to find, even in California. Use your judgment regarding the overall appearance and maintenance of the car to determine if minor rust could grow into a big future problem. You'll still want to pass on cars with any damage in the areas affecting the car's basic structure. In chapter 3, we'll go back over this territory again in order to discuss ways to repair and/or avoid corrosion damage.

All 914s have awful shift linkages when compared to more conventional cars. Some are a lot worse than others. Remember that starting in 1973, the shift linkage and transmission was improved, so any later car you drive should shift better than an early one. Engaging first gear does feel awkward. Minor grinding can usually be cured by adjusting or replacing the clutch cable. I would be more wary of problems getting into second gear. Replacing synchros can get expensive, although judicious double-clutching can keep you going for years if the synchros are only slightly worn. Converting the linkage on an early car to the later side-shifter is an expensive procedure. An early car that has had this conversion might be a good deal if everything else checks out and the price is right. Replacing worn shifter bushings, fairly easy and inexpensive, can do wonders in improving the feel of shifting any year 914.

All the normal used car rules apply to checking the brakes, tires, shocks, and other parts on the car. Be especially observant regarding the condition of the fuel lines. Worn and leaking fuel lines have made 914s as prone to spontaneous combustion as drummers for the rock band in the pseudodocumentary film *Spinal Tap*. Inspecting and upgrading the fuel lines should be one of the first things you do after buying a car.

Another place where danger may be lurking is in the heater boxes that are part of the exhaust system. Rusted heater boxes may allow carbon monoxide to creep into the cockpit.

Also be wary of people who have had their cars for less than a year and are now selling them. A long string of short-term owners is not a good sign. The fewer owners and the more recorded maintenance history a car has, the better. Porsche club members, as a general rule, appreciate and take better care of their cars than the general public.

Keep your guard up for cars being advertised as "low mileage" specials. Almost all 914 four-cylinder cars have been driven on a daily basis for most of their lives. Their lower market value makes them driveables, not collectibles. Because the odometers, which are prone to failure, do not read beyond 100,000 miles, it's easy to claim that the 75,000 miles shown doesn't have a 2 or a 3 preceding it. Do the math. The newest car is 23 years old and the average person drives at least 10,000 to 12,000 miles a year. That's why maintenance records are important. You can also tell a lot by the condition of the seats and the pedals, and even the knobs on the dash and the armrests. It's not unusual for the ignition key to wear out over the years. Play detective and look for clues of wear and abuse. You may not solve any crimes like Colombo did, but you'll have a much nicer car than his.

Where to Look

Dedicated owners take the best care of their cars, so Porsche club members would be a good place to start. Contact information for the Porsche Club of America, Porsche Owners Club, the Porsche 914 Club, and the 914 Owners Association can all

be found in the appendix. They all publish a newsletter or magazine that will have a listing of cars for sale. PCA puts out a monthly magazine that alone is worth the $36 in annual dues. The magazine is called *Panorama* and averages 100-plus pages of articles, tech info, local and national events, and a huge section of classified ads for cars and parts. The only problem is that joining PCA is a bit of a Catch-22 situation. You need to already own a Porsche to be eligible for membership. Actually, you just need to own the serial number of a Porsche for application purposes, if you know what I mean. (Wink, wink, nudge, nudge.) The Porsche Owners Club tends to be very competition oriented, so it would be a good starting point if you're thinking about racing a 914.

The Internet also has web sites and listings of cars for sale. The 914 Club web site and Pelican Parts are two of the better places to find 914 devotees. Refer to the appendix for details.

We've already mentioned *Excellence,* which calls itself "The Magazine About Porsche." It's published eight times a year. It's another great source for technical info, classifieds, and pages of ads by suppliers of Porsche parts and equipment. *PML* is a monthly listing of Porsche ads from around the country. It features a different type of Porsche each month, listing technical details and current market prices. It's a great source to see how prices for any given model of Porsche are doing. Again, you'll find subscription information on these magazines in the appendix.

Of course you always have the local newspapers and weekly *Auto Trader* photo ads. Checking with any shops specializing in Porsche repair may lead to one of their customers who is interested in selling a 914. This gives the advantage of knowing a little of the car's history before you buy it. It also may lead you to a 914 that has led a better life than most of them.

Speaking of Porsche mechanics, unless you are very confident in your mechanical investigative skills, it would be a wise investment to pay a qualified Porsche mechanic to do a prebuy inspection of any 914 that you are seriously considering. It may cost you around $100, but it could save you much more in grief down the road. If a seller is reluctant to have this inspection done, you may save yourself both the inspection fee and the potential problems. If you do have an inspection done, you could use any findings or recommendations of the mechanic as bargaining chips to negotiate a lower price, in which case the inspection pays for itself.

Take your time and do your homework before settling on a car. You may want to read through the rest of the chapters in this book to familiarize yourself with the various subsystems and components of the 914 to help you in your search for a car. If you already have a car, feel free to roam around the book and key in on any areas that will help you enjoy your 914 as much as possible.

Body and Trim

While hot rodders and musclecar fans can cruise along humming the Beach Boys, the closest anyone has come to recording an anthem for 914 owners was Neil Young's "Rust Never Sleeps." As we've discussed, history and political wrangling conspired against the 914's basic engineering strengths to make it less than perfect. Over the years remedies and fixes for many of the 914's ailments and shortcomings have evolved, but corrosion, because it attacks the basic platform to which all the improvements are attached, continues to be the car's leading cause of death. And it's a silent killer, gnawing away until the suspension collapses or the middle of the unibody folds in two.

Sure, you can buy partial and complete floor pan replacements, along with other major structural parts, to raise a deteriorated 914 carcass from the ashes of red dust, but that's an expensive proposition requiring the precision and expertise of restoration experts. You have to weigh the cost of such repair work against the value of the finished product. With the possible exception of maintaining the "originality" of a 914/6, it's a lot cheaper to locate a solid, or at least less infested, replacement chassis.

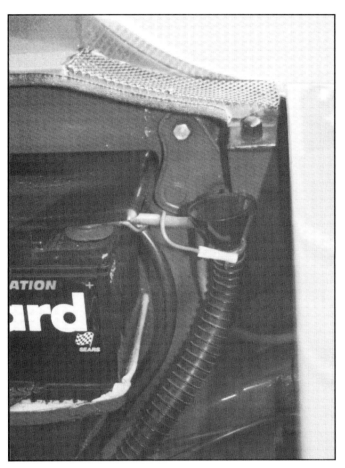

Making sure that the water drip tray is in place, and that its drain hoses work, is a good way to prevent rust in a 914.

This may sound like blasphemy to the hardcore 914 zealots who toil away in the flashing light of their MIG torches like mad monks clad in welding helmets and aprons. While their efforts may reward them spiritually, economically the 914 has not reached the investment level of the Porsche 356, a car with an investment value that warrants expensive rebuilding work.

For now, the main attraction of the 914 is that it remains a reasonably priced sports car with advanced features for its time that delivers performance potential higher than its cost of entry. And the best way to keep that cost of entry as low as possible is to start out with as rust-free a car as you can find. That's why I'll concentrate on how to avoid rust, as opposed to how to repair its damage. For anyone who still intends to plunge ahead with a "fixer upper," I offer the sincerest best of luck and a reminder that unless you can either perform or afford the highest quality work, you are only wasting your time, and maybe endangering your safety, by

Look below the carpets of trunks to spot rust damage in a 914. Not all cars will look this clean inside.

hanging an engine, suspension, and brakes on a foundation that is misaligned or flawed in some way.

Looking for Rust in All the Right Places

The previous chapter included information on where to look for rust when shopping for a 914. Let's expand that inspection process to include some thoughts on how to remedy whatever damage you find, or avoid any future problems.

Let's cut to the worst-case scenario right away. Approach a 914 from the right rear and check to see if the rear tire on that side is standing reasonably perpendicular to the ground. If it tilts in severely at the top, causing the right rear corner to sag, you may not want to get any closer to this car. This indicates that the right rear suspension console, the inner mounting point for the control arm on that side, has rusted out. It's a common problem primarily caused by the location of the battery at the top right of the engine compartment.

Rear trunk should look like this, without any rust. Note jack location and new top clips.

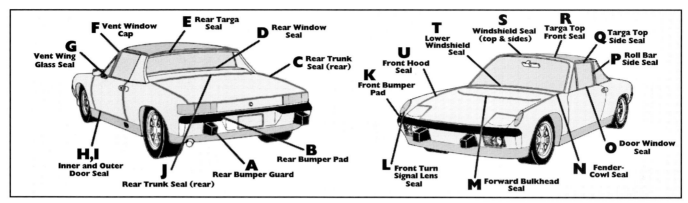

Replacing the weather stripping on a 914 can be expensive but worth it, as a part of the 914 owner's battle against rust and corrosion. New rubber also makes the cockpit a little quieter and a lot drier. www.pelicanparts.com

Perched on a shelf just below the engine lid, the battery is easily accessible not only to you or your mechanic, but also to any water that passes through the grille work of the engine lid. This water drains off the battery, mixing with battery acid, and drips down onto, and ultimately through, the engine compartment shelf. Its path then continues onto the suspension console directly below. During its rust-inducing journey, this moisture also weakens the tray holding the battery. This can cause the battery to break free and wreak all kinds of havoc in the engine compartment. Things can get real exciting back there when the resulting sparks hit any leaking or ruptured fuel lines.

As dire as these problems sound, parts are available to remedy them. The battery shelf and its support are fairly inexpensive

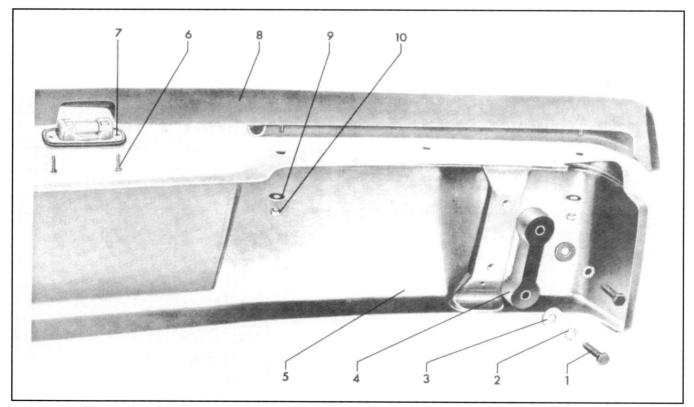

Early bumpers, like this rear unit, used dog bone–shaped insulators, No. 4, in mounting bumper to chassis. www.pelicanparts.com

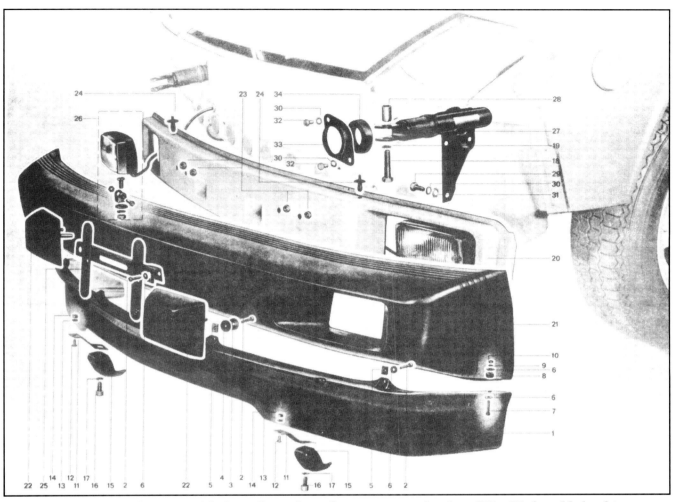

Later cars had rubber bumpers with five-mile-per-hour "impact energy absorbers," No. 27, for added safety.
www.pelicanparts.com

and easy to attach, but the parts for repairing the rear suspension console plus the labor to properly weld it in place so the suspension alignment is correct can get pricey. It's much cheaper to find a car that already has had this work properly done, or even better, never needed it in the first place.

While you're poking about in the engine compartment making sure that the battery is securely mounted, look down into the compartment's forward corners, where water can accumulate and do damage. Even if everything looks OK, you still want to crawl under the car and check out the condition of the trailing arm mounting points for rust. Wear protective gloves and carry a big screwdriver to prod around potential weak spots.

After checking out the rear suspension, direct your attention farther forward along the bottom of the car. Inspect the condition of the floor pan, especially the seat mounting points. Obviously, no part of the seats should be hanging down here.

Check the rocker panels and the jack post supports. Leaves, dirt, tire dust, various liquids, mud, and anything else that can get kicked up by the tires into the wheelwells can wedge its way into place between the external rocker panel covers and the pan. A row of screws along the bottom edge holds the lower part of the outer rocker panels in place. There is also a bolt to secure each end of the panel. These are located in each wheelwell. Loosen these screws and ease the panel out a bit to inspect for rust and debris. Pay particular attention to the jack post holes and supports.

Replacing the jack post holes and supports can be done cheaply and easily. Just be sure that whatever ate out these parts hasn't spread deeper into the floor pan. The outer rocker panels can also be easily replaced if they are damaged. OEM-type metal pieces are available as are slightly cheaper fiberglass replicas. The latter come finished in a black gel coat

Brian Kumamoto's 1974 2.0-liter is a near-perfect example of a stock 914.

Brian's homemade paint job looks better than many from professional shops.

The red car is a daily driver with over 200,000 miles, with new paint and engine work done by its owner.

which saves you the additional work of painting them. If you don't own a black car, these panels can provide a racey look in contrast to the overall body color. Another advantage of the plastic rockers is that they won't rust. Automotion also offers a set of ABS plastic rockers that have "Porsche" spelled out in raised letters for a further custom touch. Installing the new rockers is pretty much a bolt-on job. Besides the previously mentioned mounting screws along the bottom and in each fender well, pop rivets are used to secure the top of the rockers to the door sills.

Back to our rust inspection tour. Still under the car, keep moving forward. Check for rust below the front trunk, especially where the suspension mounts are located. Like other areas we have discussed, you have to gauge the severity of the problem in relation to the overall shape of the car. Or your capabilities as a welder. Remember, as at the rear, you must not only deal with the sheet metal repair but also with ensuring that the suspension will be mounted properly and safely to avoid misalignment and, even worse, the possibility of it coming adrift at speed, in a corner . . . you get the picture.

Now it's time to look topside. Inspect the floor of the front trunk, especially the seams. While you're in there look for any signs of collision damage in the panels behind the front bumper. Don't worry too much about replacing a damaged hood; that's a cheap and easy fix, but looking deeper at the walls of the trunk could provide evidence of more severe damage that has bent the chassis.

Deteriorated or missing rubber gaskets and seals can lead to rust-producing water leaks. New OEM rubber is not cheap. Reproduction pieces can reduce the cost by at least half to two-thirds, but quality varies, and pieces are not available for all applications. You may also have to do a little trimming to ensure the proper fit on your car. We'll talk about this a little later in this chapter.

The headlight buckets are another area to check for rust. Porsche engineered drain holes to keep water from collecting there. Unfortunately, over the years, just as with the rocker panels, this area becomes a receptacle for dirt and leaves that can clog up the drains. To inspect this area, raise the headlights and disconnect the battery. The plastic shroud surrounding the light is held in place by three Phillips head screws. Remove the shroud so you can look down in the well where the headlights retract when not in use.

Another place to look for rust is on the cowling near the corners of the windshield. Bent, loose-fitting, or missing windshield trim can cause water to collect here and cause damage. Also make sure that the little rubber seals are properly fitted where the front fender meets the cowl. It's another place where water can seep in and do damage over the course of time. New seals only cost a couple of bucks versus the cost of replacing and repainting rotted sheet metal.

Close-up of what your targa top rubber seals and front top latches should look like. Porsche AG

When you open the door to look for rust from the inside of a 914, it should open easily. It should also close as easily. Make sure that the windows are up when you do your test. If the rear edge of the window glass hangs up on the rubber seal attached to the targa bar, it could be a sign of rust damage causing the body to buckle below the doors. A good test is to put someone fairly heavy in the passenger seat and then try to open the door. The added weight will put enough stress to make the body sag if it is weak. If a car fails this test, you better crawl back underneath and do some more screwdriver prodding near the inner rockers and right rear. Before you panic and viciously attack a car that looked pretty solid at first

glance, make sure that tight-fitting new rubber window trim isn't the culprit.

While you have the doors open, check the sills and door jambs for rust. Then move inside and pull up the carpeting around the pedals. Check the floor around the seat mounts. Since most 914s tend to leak during heavy rainstorms, check the area behind the seats. Water accumulating here can rust out the floor and the firewall. Another problem in this area is caused by worn seals around the rear window. Look for more rust on the outside of the targa panel and around the rear window.

Finally, check inside the rear trunk for damage caused by water entering through the taillight assembly and rotting away the rear floor just before the bumper. Many cars will already have been repaired in this area, thanks to aftermarket floor panel parts. It's an easy fix. Since you have the rear trunk carpet lifted to check for rust, be sure to check for the insulation pad that should be separating it from the metal trunk floor. The muffler sits right under the rear portion of the trunk and things can get hot back there. At first, on the 1970–71 cars, an abbreviated pad that only covered the rearmost floor of the trunk was used, but later models had a full pad. Starting sometime in the middle of 1974, this pad received a plastic covering. It's pretty easy to retrofit this pad to an early car. You can even make your own pad out of insulated foam padding material.

Speaking of heat and mufflers, there is one other potential rust spot that is not a body part but should be checked because of its potential for danger. Like any rear-engined Porsche or VW, heat exchangers (heater boxes) are part of the exhaust system. They supply warm air for interior heating and defrosting. They also tend to rust, causing exhaust leaks that could result in carbon monoxide entering the passenger compartment.

New replacement heater boxes and mufflers for 914/4s can be expensive and double that for the 914/6. Fortunately, stainless steel aftermarket heater boxes are available that are a bit cheaper, although still not cheap, and will eliminate the

Close-up of rear targa top latch and rear window seals on a new 914. Yours should look this good. Porsche AG

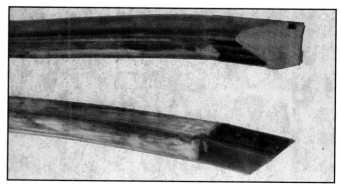

Brand new left and right targa top seals ready for installation. www.pelicanparts.com

New seals should slide into channels alongside top after applying silicone spray. www.pelicanparts.com

rust worry. If you don't need a heater, headers can also solve this problem for less money.

Rust Prevention

Inspecting a 914 for rust damage, or even worse, finding rust and repairing it, as illustrated in our preceding discussion, can involve a lot of work. It's much easier to keep your 914 from becoming infested with the metal-eating rust bug. Here are some preventive maintenance routines to follow.

1. Wash and wax your car on a regular basis. This includes a good hosing to the underside and wheelwells. See chapter 13 for the proper techniques and tricks.
2. Inspect and repair all weather stripping and rubber seals. Check the rear window for looseness indicating a bad seal. Check for top and windshield leaks.

3. Buy a battery cover.
4. Even better, buy a sealed battery and inspect it once a month for leaks and corrosion.
5. Don't remove the water drip pan from the engine cover grille. If your car is missing the drip pan, install one, and make sure the accompanying funnel and drainage tubes are clear and properly fitted. There are also drain tubes up front, inside the cowl vent between the windshield wipers. If they are cracked or worn, water can seep into the area around the fuel tank causing damage to the chassis and the tank itself. Fixing them requires removing the fuel tank, so it's a good job to do when replacing old fuel lines or adding a front sway bar. (See chapter 6.)
6. Inspect, replace, and repair leaky pedal assemblies. (See chapter 4.)
7. Inspect and clean the headlight buckets at least once a year.
8. Loosen outer rocker panels and flush out dirt at least once a year.
9. Inspect the exhaust system. Avoid short trips, especially in cold weather, that increase the chance for corrosion-causing condensation to form.
10. If the car is to sit idle for extended periods of time, see that it is properly stored and not exposed to the elements.

Smoothing Out the Way to a Fine Finish— A Primer on Painting Your Car

CAUTION: State, local, or other laws may limit or restrict your ability to legally paint your car in your garage or driveway. Additionally, many professional paint products are extremely

Be sure that slit on rubber seal fits over metal tab on channel for proper fit. www.pelicanparts.com

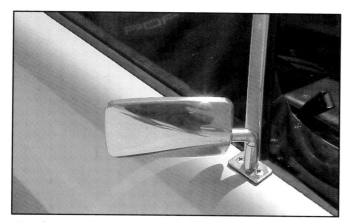

No, the negative is not reversed. Left and right side 914 mirrors are interchangeable. Here's a left-hand mirror turned over to become a right-hand mirror. www.pelicanparts.com

hazardous to your health. Proper ventilation, breathing equipment, gloves, and other safety precautions should always be observed when working with professional paint products. Additionally, the fumes of many paint products can be explosive. If you are painting in your garage, any flames (e.g., water heater pilot lights) or spark sources (e.g., electric motors) should be eliminated.

The above is the kind of stuff you expect to hear from an attorney when you ask him about do-it-yourself auto painting. In fact, I got the above warning from my attorney friend Brian Kumamoto when I brought up the subject of someone testing their artistic talents with a spray gun on a 914. Brian's

daily driver is a showroom-new looking 1974 2.0-liter that he painted himself, so I thought he'd be a good guy to share his experience with any of you considering a similar task. About the only thing he knew about painting when he started was that his friend had a compressor he could borrow.

Brian wanted a quality paint job but didn't want to bend the family budget to get it. The estimate he got from one of the discount chains was almost $900 without a guarantee that all the panels would be straightened completely. The upscale body shops began the bidding at $2,000 and went up. That's when he decided to try his own hand at painting.

The simplicity of the 914's design gave him the courage to take on this project. It has relatively straight lines with flat surfaces and panels that are relatively free of moldings and other adornments. This makes it one of the easier cars to paint. It is still a time-consuming and tedious task if you want good results, but not technically difficult.

Step one for Brian was going to the library and reading up on all the available material about painting and bodywork. The next step was meeting with an automotive paint supplier to learn more about the paint and supplies necessary for his specific project. These are both excellent ideas for anyone considering doing his own paint job.

As far as physical labor goes, if you're following in Brian's footsteps, the first task is stripping the car to the bare essentials. This includes the bumpers, door handles, lights, engine grille, antenna, mirror(s), trunk lock, emblems, chrome trim, windshield washer nozzles, and the wipers.

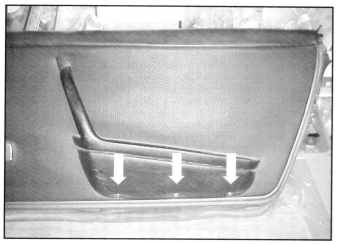

Arrows point to three screws that hold bottom of passenger armrest in place. Once screws are removed, this piece will slide out toward rear of car. www.pelicanparts.com

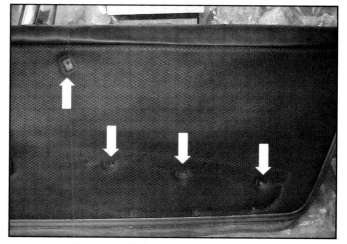

Passenger door handle has already been removed for clarity so arrows can show where the four bolts are located that attach handle to door. www.pelicanparts.com

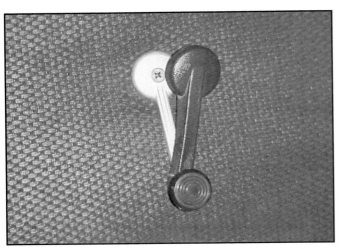

After prying the plastic cover off, mounting screw for window winder is revealed. www.pelicanparts.com

Door panel is held in place at the bottom and along the sides by plastic clips. Be careful not to break them when snapping the panel back on. www.pelicanparts.com

After that, you're ready for a very important step in getting a professional and long-lasting paint job. The car must be degreased and stripped of any old wax. The silicones in most modern wax products will affect the durability and adhesion of any paint sprayed over them. The car should be washed with detergent and then cleaned carefully with a commercial wax and silicone remover.

Now the car can be wet sanded using 220-grit wet/dry sandpaper on sanding blocks. Don't be afraid to use plenty of water. It's not necessary to go down to the bare metal except in areas where the car is in very bad shape or to remove loose or shrunken body filler. Your main objective is to get a nice, even working surface.

Retaining screw that holds plastic backing plate for door release. www.pelicanparts.com

Here's when the hardest work comes in. After sanding, you should now be able to detect the "high" spots from the "low" spots of the car's surface. The high spots are where you sanded down to the bare metal. The low spots were barely grazed by the sandpaper. The objective is to get the entire surface level and smooth. Take a small hammer and pound out any of the larger dings and dents. Use a catalyzed polyester body filler—call it a high tech "Bondo" if you want—to fill in the smaller imperfections. These new fillers will not shrink over time like the traditional body fillers. Follow the directions on the can.

Once you have applied the filler and it is dry, take a spray can of primer and spray a "guide coat" of primer over the repaired areas. All you need is a light coat of primer in a color easily distinguishable from the car's original paint. Once the primer is dry, do more sanding to reveal the remaining high and low spots. Use 220-grit paper and a long board about 16 inches long and 2 inches wide. The board should be slightly flexible to conform to the body contours. Keep repeating the guide coat process, using more filler if necessary, until all parts of the car are smooth and level.

In the next step, you get your first action with the spray gun. What you will be applying is a primer/sealer. There are many such products available. Brian was highly pleased with a product called SEM Prime, a catalyzed polyester primer surfacer. This is what you use to fill in tiny imperfections so your finished painted surface will come out smooth as glass.

By the way, before you start spraying, make sure the area that you are working in has adequate ventilation and you have on a properly rated aspirator. You can pick these up at

Use a punch from the bottom to make a starting mark for the drill bit. Gradually increase size of bit until holes are large enough for mounting screws. www.pelicanparts.com

any professional paint store. A simple dust mask won't do. You shouldn't need an attorney to point this out, because it's just common sense. And no, let's not get into a debate about common sense, the law, and the kind of attorneys who don't work on their own cars.

When the primer/surfacer is dry, it's time to lay on another guide coat of primer and lightly sand with 240-grit sandpaper to find more uneven spots. As the surface smoothes out, keep on applying the guide coat but move on to a finer 400-grit sandpaper.

Make sure you prime and paint bare metal around mounting holes to fight rust. Use a rubber mirror gasket for best fit and further rust prevention. www.pelican-parts.com

Once you are satisfied that the car is as smooth as it can be, remove all the old masking paper and remask the car in preparation for a sealer and then the paint. This will protect against any sanding dust or residue sticking to the finish.

Before he applied the paint, Brian sprayed the entire car with Velva Seal Sealer, a product that increases the adherence and color uniformity of the paint. He called a number of body shops to find out what type of paints they used. The discount shops use synthetic enamel, which is the least expensive, but slow drying and not the most durable. Many shops recommended lacquer because it dries quickly. The rapid drying reduces the likelihood of dust and other foreign substances sticking to it, and lacquer can be easily sanded and resprayed in case of mistakes. Lacquer, however, can crack over time. It also requires an application of 8 to 10 coats.

Brian decided on acrylic enamel with a catalyzed hardener. It dries fairly quickly, does not have to be buffed to make it glossy, and only requires three coats for coverage. It is also reasonably priced. The hardener increases its durability.

Before painting his car, Brian did one more thing. He visited a high quality paint shop to watch an expert at work, hoping to pick up some last-minute pointers. He discovered that common amateur mistakes include standing too far away when spraying and moving too slowly. This wastes paint because the material goes on too dry and doesn't cover properly. He advises standing about 8 inches from the surface, which seems unnatural but works best.

Brian sums up his painting experience by saying that it took longer than expected. He spent about 130 hours after work and on weekends. It was also messier than expected, primarily because of all the dust from sanding. Even though

This is what your door handle should look like on its inner side. www.pelicanparts.com

If your door handle doesn't open or close properly, chances are it looks like one of these on the inner side. (top) part of broken flapper arm is missing; (middle) mounting tab is broken; (bottom) plastic door latch cam broken. www.pelicanparts.com

he turned his garage into a "spray booth" with long plastic sheets before he began, he was continuously cleaning up sanding dust that had drifted over the washer and the dryer, and to other locations. It cost him about $450 in materials and supplies. The compressor isn't included in that total, but it does include a high quality spray gun. He feels the result was well worth the effort. You can judge for yourself from the pictures of Brian's car.

Another option you can have is to do all the prep work and then turn over the final painting to a professional or a friend who has the experience and talent.

Getting Tight—Resealing Rear Windows

Resealing the rear window eliminates one of the major causes of rust in 914s by stopping water from leaking down into the floor behind the seats during a hard rainstorm or when you wash the car, and it insulates the passenger compartment from road and engine noise. Once you've renewed the rear window seal, you'll notice the overall "feel" of the car is improved. It seems solider, and definitely quieter.

The rear window is primarily held in place by a sticky bead of black windshield seal. Over time, this seal dries out and shrinks, causing the window to work loose. Replacing it is fairly simple and inexpensive, but it does take time. It also helps to have a willing assistant during part of the procedure. Finding one may be the hardest part of the job, but don't dismay if your pleas for help fall on deaf ears (it could be that noisy passenger compartment) because it's not impossible to do it all by yourself if you're careful.

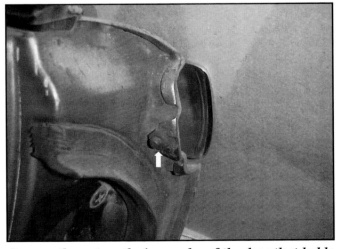

Remove the nut on the inner edge of the door that holds one end of the door handle in place. www.pelicanparts.com

This is a door stay in good shape. www.pelicanparts.com

All you need to do this job is a new roll of windshield seal, a screwdriver or two, a thick pair of gloves, and a warm sunny driveway or well-heated work area. The windshield seal can be found at most auto supply stores. It looks like a long, thick roll of black licorice wound around wax paper to prevent it from sticking to itself. The instructions on the package may say that a heat gun is needed to make it adhere to the glass, but for the 914's rear window application, as long as you're working in warm conditions you should get a tight bond without it. Some people use a hair dryer as a substitute for the heat gun.

OK, let's get to work. Remove the targa top. Slide the driver's seat forward all the way, then reach underneath to push up on the spring that releases it from the seat rail tracks. Pull the seat a bit more forward, up and out. Do the same for the passenger seat.

With the seats out of the way, it's time to remove the backpad. It's attached by a few upholstery screws and slide-in tabs along the top. Locate and remove these screws, so you can lift the backpad out of the car. You may also have to unscrew the engine lid release knob as part of this process.

Now you're ready to remove the roll bar padding. It's held in place by screws that are recessed into the roll bar trim. Start at the sides and remove these screws, then do the top. You need to be real careful at this point, because this trim may be the only thing holding your rear window in place. This is the part where an assistant is nice to make sure the window stays put while you take out the trim.

Once you've completed the removal of the trim, it's time to carefully remove the window. Don't worry if a few small plastic spacers come out with the window. These were used by the factory to ensure a tight fit between the glass and the window frame. Your new seal should be thick enough to ensure a nice, tight fit without these spacers in case they are missing or lost.

The old seal, if it is original, should just peel off the glass. You will need to remove as much of the old seal as possible before reinstalling the window. This is also a good time to give the entire rear window glass a good cleaning.

Unroll the new seal and place it in the channel from which you removed the old seal. Reinstall the rear window. Put on a thick pair of gloves and start pressing the window against the seal. Push firmly along the edges to get a tight seal. Don't push in the middle of the window or you'll crack it! Keep pressing until you're satisfied with the bond. This is where a heat gun or hair dryer could be used to make sure the seal strip is warm and sticky.

Reinstall the roll bar trim, backpad, and seats, as they say, in the reverse order of removal. It's not a bad idea to go through and thoroughly clean your interior while everything is out of the car. While you're digging around, you may even find enough loose change to buy a cold drink when you're done.

Once all the interior bits are back in place, take some rolled up towels and wedge them firmly behind the headrests to keep pressure on the rear window. For best results, let the car sit like this for a day or so. If you do need to drive it, wait at least a few hours before doing so.

Backdating Bumpers

It is tempting to take a quick path to improving the performance and handling, and some would say looks, of your 1975 or 1976 914 by retrofitting a set of early bumpers. While shedding at least 50 pounds of weight hanging off the ends of the

If this looks familiar, watch out for those swinging doors. www.pelicanparts.com

car may produce slight gains in acceleration and cornering, it also reduces the safety margin for body parts, vehicular and human.

If you decide it's worth the risk, removing the newer bumpers is a straightforward case of unbolting them from the energy absorbing shocks and then unbolting the shocks themselves. Remember to disconnect the fog lamps up front and the rear license plate light before removing the bumpers. Once you have the bumpers off, you will be able to see how the energy absorbing shocks are mounted.

The fenders on cars equipped with the newer bumpers have mounting tabs on which the ends of the rubber bumpers are fitted. Before bolting on the older style bumper, these must be ground off, primed, and painted for rust protection and appearance purposes. The holes through which the energy absorbing shocks protruded should also be filled in and painted as well.

When bolting on the older style bumpers be sure to use the factory mounting holes and the rubber "dogbone" insulator gasket for proper fit and alignment. Make sure all mounting brackets and bolts are secure before you consider the task completed.

Squeaks and Leaks—Targa Top Repair and Maintenance

The cheapest, easiest, and most enjoyable way to eliminate all of the squeaks and rattles from the 914's top is to drive around without it. As for leaks, follow the advice given in the preceding sentence, but drive faster.

Now let's talk about a less enticing, but more practical, alternative. Naturally, this involves spending money and a bit more work.

One of the first things you can do to eliminate the creaks and groans emanating from the top is getting out the silicon spray lubricant and applying liberal doses to all the rubber seals. This may do the trick if all of your rubber is in very good shape.

Another quick fix would be adjusting the front top latches. The latches are mounted to the roof by two nuts. Loosening these nuts allows you to slide the latch back and forth until you find a position that snugs the top down nice and tight.

The next step, and most expensive and time-consuming, is replacing all the rubber seals. In July 1973, Porsche made a change to the 914 top (commencing with serial number 4732926222 to be exact) that improved its weather resistance. The front and rear seals were changed, and side seals were improved with an extra lip where they met the side windows. These seals can be retrofitted to early cars. There is also a seal that fits over the top and down the sides of the windshield. If it looks as if your car has a three-piece instead of a

Mounting bolts for a door stay. www.pelicanparts.com

Close-up of front retaining clip for storing targa top in rear trunk.

one-piece seal around the windshield, it's clearly time for replacement. The best way to install the new piece is, after thoroughly removing the old rubber and cleaning out the mounting tracks, to slide down the driver's side almost all the way then work on the passenger side. Once both sides are even and almost fully in place, press the top portion of the seal in place. Work the corners down as you finish sliding down the sides. Slick down the rubber with silicone spray lubricant (high tech approach) or dishwashing liquid (low tech, but your hands smell nice) to make easy work of sliding it in place.

If your top is looking a bit tattered, shopping the swap meets or used parts purveyors should get you a replacement for reasonable money. No one seems to have perfected a way to duplicate the "grain" of the original. Spraying the top with Wurth Matte Black paint comes very close to the stock color.

Some people simply sand the top smooth and paint it to match the body color. A simple solution, but getting the roof perfectly smooth is almost as difficult as replicating the grainy finish.

Installing a Right Side Mirror

Dual outside mirrors are standard equipment on almost every new car and truck these days. Unfortunately, the 914 came to market just before a passenger side mirror became an essential piece of safety equipment, thanks to crowded highways and the resulting high frequency of lane-hopping. It also comes in handy at the race track, assuming you intend to pass people.

Coming across a 914 that was originally equipped with a passenger side mirror is quite rare, although the option did exist. While specific right side units with convex mirror glass did exist, common practice is to mount a left side mirror with the head swiveled in the appropriate direction. Fortunately, Porsche did foresee a need for mirrors on the passenger's side and welded two mounting nuts on the inside of the right-hand door skin. All that's needed to mount the mirror is to remove the inner door panel in order to access these nuts and drill out the holes. Besides the mirror, the only parts you'll need are the two mounting screws and a mirror base gasket. New mirrors are expensive, so prowl the swap meets and wrecking yards for good used ones.

Step one is to remove the inner door panel. Remove the lower part of the armrest by unscrewing its three attachment screws and then sliding it rearward to disengage it from the door handle. Four bolts, usually Allen head bolts, hold the handle in place.

Now it's time to remove the window crank. Working on the round end of the window crank, pry off the plastic cover to reveal the attachment screw. Take out this screw and remove the crank. By the way, should you ever need to replace a window crank, the cheapest and easiest replacements are the ones for Volkswagen Bugs.

A single screw is all that holds the plastic surround for the door handle. Once that piece is out of the way, carefully tug at the lower and side edges of the door panel to unsnap it from the door. A screwdriver can be used to pry the panel loose, but be gentle so as not to bend the panel or pull it loose from the plastic snaps that attach it to the door. The top of the panel is held in with metal clips. To avoid damage, don't try to pry it loose from the top. After you have unsnapped it at the bottom and sides, simply swing it up from the bottom and away from the door.

You may find a clear plastic sheet attached to the door after removing the panel. This plastic is intended to protect the inner door panel from water that may enter through the window. Try not to damage this plastic sheet if you can.

With the window rolled up, locate the two mounting nuts welded inside the door. Using a nail or punch, gently tap through the nuts from the inside to make an impression on the outer door skin. These will be your guide marks for drilling the mounting holes. From the outside, use a center punch on these marks to make a starting point for your drill bit. Starting with very small drill bits and working up to larger sizes, drill out the holes. Keep test fitting the mounting screws each time you change bits, so you don't drill too large a hole. Be careful not to go too deep and damage the threads on the mounting nuts. They are not mounted flush with the door skin, so exercising a little care should eliminate the probability of drilling out the threads.

Once you have holes large enough to fit the bolts through, it's simply a matter of putting the gasket and mirror in place and bolting them down. Don't forget the gasket. It ensures a tight fit and protects against rust. Touching up the metal around the new holes with rust-resistant paint is also a good idea. The mirror base will cover up any little mistakes you may have made while drilling out the mounting holes.

All that's left is to remount the inner door panel, window crank, door handle surround, and door handle/armrest. In just about an hour's time, you have added a safety feature to your 914 that could someday save your neck, or at least cut down the strain of swiveling it around in traffic.

Targa top retaining clip at rear edge of trunk. Replacing broken clips avoids top damage as well as trunk rattles.

Popular option is rear "PORSCHE" reflector panel, actually a 911 piece cut to fit the space between 914 taillights.

Holes are drilled in the rear panel for the reflector mounting screws. An electric trunk release must also be installed to operate rear trunk lid. The stock lock button can be maintained, but the hole for it must be meticulously drilled out in the reflector panel. This hole will deface the "S" in Porsche.

Replacing Outside Door Handles and Door Locks

Aesthetically and aerodynamically, the outside door handles of the 914 were ahead of their time. Unfortunately, the bright thinking that went into their design did not carry over to the choice of material used to make them. A cheap pot-metal guarantees fatigue from daily use. Sooner or later your 914 will need either replacement or repair of its door handles.

Damage occurs in a number of ways. The flapper arm that moves the handle can crack and fall off. Or the mounting tab that attaches to the door will break off. A third problem is the failure of the plastic door latch cam, which can break after years of use. Replacement or repair is fairly simple, but new handles are expensive. Your best bet is finding a good used one. They do come in left and right applications, but can be swapped if you don't mind a minor appearance transgression from stock and aren't a fanatical concours competitor.

To repair or replace a door handle, first remove the inner door panel as described in the section for mounting a passenger side mirror. After the inner panel is removed, you will see how the handle mounts to the door in two locations. A hex nut bolt holds the middle of the door handle to the door frame. Remove this bolt using a long 4.5-millimeter hex key. Be careful when removing the bolt that it doesn't fall into the bottom of the door.

Now look for the nut that mounts the forward edge of the door handle to the door. Remove this nut and pull out the door handle. Don't lose the washers that fit over each mounting bolt. You can either try to repair the broken handle or just install a working handle in its place.

While you have the handle out, it is a good time to rekey the lock on the door handle so that one key will work both

doors. Put the key in the lock cylinder, remove the single mounting screw and pull the lock cylinder out of the door handle using the key. Note how the lock cylinder return spring and eccentric are mounted before removing the lock cylinder from the door handle. If you have the patience, you can take needle-nosed pliers and fiddle with a set of tumbler pins until you match up to the key that fits both door locks. Or you can have a locksmith do it for you.

Replacement is the reversal of removal.

Teach Your Door to Stay

We already talked about Neil Young crooning about the 914, so why not bring up Bob Dylan while we're on the subject of 914 doors. "Blowing in the Wind" is what many doors start doing sooner or later. This is the result of a failure by the door stay. The door stay consists of an arm, or strap, that works in conjunction with spring loaded rollers to hold the door either completely or partially open. What happens is that either the strap breaks or the rollers wear out causing the springs to fall off. When this happens, your door will flop wide open, possibly bending the edge of the front fender as it completes its unrestricted arc.

The solution requires removing the inner door panel to get to the two mounting bolts that hold the door stay in place. You already know how to remove the inner door panel on the passenger side from our lesson on installing a right side outside mirror. The driver's side has a map pocket that requires a little different procedure than the passenger's armrest. After that everything is the same.

To remove the map pocket, you need to remove two screws on either side of it. Depending on the condition of your car, these screws may be hidden behind plastic plugs.

Remove the plastic plugs, then remove the screws. You will need a set of metric hex keys to remove these screws. The bottom of the map pocket is held in place by three more screws. Once you remove these, you can pull off the map pocket and get on with the business of removing the inner door handle shroud, window winder, and, finally, the door panel itself.

Before you remove the bolts holding the door stay, use needle-nosed pliers to remove the cotter pin from the clevis pin that attaches the door stay to the car. You should be able to reuse the cotter and clevis pins. Now unbolt the door stay and remove it. Put in the replacement (left and right door stays are interchangeable), bolt it on, and put in the clevis pin.

Replace the door panel and map pocket. Make sure the bottom screws for the map pocket are firmly threaded through the door panel into the metal door frame.

Air Dams and Spoilers

A number of front spoilers are available for the 914, but one of the cheapest and most popular is a fiberglass replica of the one the factory supplied for the 1974 Special Edition 914. It mounts easily below the bumper on all cars. It improves front end stability, yet has enough ground clearance to clear driveways and most parking lot curb stops.

Rear Valance Panels

Cars made prior to 1973 had a longer rear panel that extended below the exhaust pipe. In 1973 this panel was shortened to provide better engine cooling. At the same time, two air deflectors were mounted underneath the car to improve the flow of cooling air into the engine compartment. Both of these changes can easily be made to earlier cars. The valance panels are interchangeable.

The deflector panels mount at the rear of the floor pan with three mounting screws. Before drilling the mounting holes, make sure the panels are properly centered with 15.2 inches between them.

A Tale of Two Trunks

Having two trunks is extremely convenient in a small sports car. Until you can't open them. Porsche provided for this by hiding an auxiliary luggage compartment release behind the front bumper. You have to remove the front bumper to reach it, but once that's out of the way, you simply remove a rubber plug, then poke a screwdriver through the hole that held the plug and you should be able to release the lid.

Out back, things aren't as convenient. The simplest method — I won't say easiest because there is no easy method—is to go into the engine compartment and push up on either of the two plastic cups that are used to locate the front latches when the top is stored in the trunk. Once you pop these out, you can thread a long stiff wire through the hole into the trunk and try to spring open the trunk release. Another method suggested is to again go into the engine compartment and locate the bolts holding the trunk lid to its hinges. Remove the forward bolts first and then the rears. Now you can lift the trunk lid off.

One other trouble spot in the rear trunk is that the nylon rollers used in the rear hinge assembly do wear out, affecting the fit and closure of the trunk lid. Longer wearing metal replacement units are readily available. Replacing them is fairly straightforward but potentially dangerous. The hazard comes from the removal and reinstallation of the torsion springs that apply tension to the hinge assembly. Prying them in or out with a crow bar or similar tool is a two-man job that can generate tremendous spring tension. One slip can launch a steel rod capable of wreaking as much damage as any cruise missile. This is a job better left for people who have had prior experience and the proper tools to deal with these parts.

A restoration job that anyone can easily perform is the replacement of the plastic or rubber retainers that hold the top in place when it is stored in the rear trunk. The ones along the front edge of the trunk must be pop riveted in place, while the rear clips bolt in. The latter are a bit pricey but it pays to protect your top from damage by properly clipping it in place. The proper stowing of the top could also affect the ease of closing the rear trunk lid, reducing the stress on the trunk hinges and possibly avoiding the hassle and danger of replacing worn rollers. It's also a good idea to periodically oil the rear hinges to keep them from sticking and eventually seizing up and breaking.

Interior

The wide open spaces of the 914 interior is one of the car's best features, as evidenced by the fact that very few major changes were made to it through the years. The one big glitch was solved in 1972 when the passenger seat was redesigned to make it adjustable. Retractable seatbelts were also added during that model year in place of the older style belts.

Prior to 1972, you could say that Porsche really emphasized the 914 as a driver's car by offering only a tethered foot "stool" as a concession to the passenger's needs for individualized seating comfort. Legroom was not an issue. There may have been too much for the average person, so the movable upholstered wooden block served as an "adjustable" footrest. Today, the few surviving footrests are valuable primarily for scoring originality points in concours judging and as curiosity pieces. They prove that even German engineering departments are not immune to the Dilbert principle.

As roomy as it was, the original 914 interior was also pretty stark. Over the years improvements were made to the dash, seating materials, and door panels to make it look more inviting. The optional also added to the esthetics and functionality of the 914 cockpit.

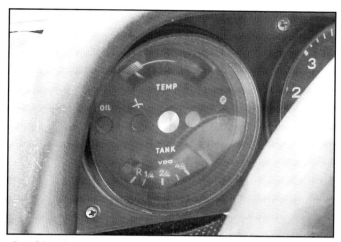

Combination gauge fitted to 914/6. www.pelicanparts.com

Before we get into specific repairs or improvements you can make to your 914's interior, let's review the changes that Porsche implemented over the midengine roadster's lifespan.

The dashboard is the first thing you see once you're seated in your car, so let's make it the starting point for our cockpit tour. Its construction is unique to the 914. Unlike the later 356s or the 911, the 914's entire dashboard assembly was removable from the car body. The dash's top cover, due to the arrangement of the air vents, was different for the early 914/4 and the 914/6. The difference was a center defroster vent on the early 914/4s, which was not on the six-cylinder cars. A third style dash top appeared in 1972 for the four-

Turn center pad on steering wheel counterclockwise to remove. www.pelicanparts.com

This photo illustrates the procedure for using a breaker bar combined with The Club to loosen the steering wheel retaining nut. www.pelicanparts.com

cylinder cars that was used until the end of production in 1976. The later dash also lacked a center vent, but fresh air vents were added at each end.

Another difference between the six- and four-cylinder cars was the placement of the ignition switch and the wiper controls. Most 914/6s had the ignition on the left side of the dash, like a 911, while the 914/4 had it mounted on the right side of the steering column. The last of the six-cylinder cars, built as 1972 models, used the steering column and ignition switch from that year's four-cylinder cars. Wiper controls were steering column mounted on the 914/6 from the beginning and on 914/4s from 1972 forward. Before 1972, the four-cylinder cars had dash-mounted wiper controls.

Instrument pod from a 1974 914. Note black plastic centers on gauge needles, and the owner-added temperature gauge along the top of the combination gauge. www.pelicanparts.com

Center console with gauges. www.pelicanparts.com

The turn signal and wiper stalks used on the 914/6 are not the same as those on the 911 or 914/4. Through the years, the 914/4 used control stalks and ignition switches that were adapted from items in the VW parts bin.

The steering wheels used on the 914/6 and the 914/4 are not interchangeable with each other nor do they cross fit any other Porsches or VWs. The standard wheels were hard

rubber, but leather covered rims were an option and standard on the 1973 2.0-liter cars. U.S. cars carried horn pads bearing an embossed Porsche crest; cars sold elsewhere had a VW "Wolfsburg crest" style emblem.

The dash for all 914s held three large gauges featuring a 115-millimeter-diameter tachometer in the center with slightly smaller (100-millimeter-diameter) gauges on either side. The gauge on the right was the speedometer, while various combination gauges were used on the left.

The 914/6 had a tachometer and combination gauge unique to its application. Its 150-mile-per-hour speedometer was the same as the 911 of that period. The combination gauge for a 914/6 had an oil temperature gauge at the top and a fuel gauge at the bottom. It also had warning lights for low oil pressure (green), hand brake (red), and generator charge (red). A fourth light was rigged to glow red, indicating high transmission fluid temperature for the rare Sportomatic-equipped cars. On manual shift cars, this light was replaced with a dummy white indicator light.

For the four-cylinder cars, only minor changes were made to the tachometer through the years. These included switching from a chrome center button for the tach needle to a black plastic center button and needle, and replacing twin turn signal indicator arrows with a single round light. The location of the high beam indicator light also moved. The material used for the gauge cover went from glass to clear plastic. All of these changes took place during the 1974 model year. All four-cylinder cars had 7,000-rpm tachometers with a red line area blocked out from 5,600 to 5,800 rpm. On six-cylinder cars, the tach went up to 8,000 rpm with a red zone at 6,400

U-shaped bracket that runs across the top of center console. www.pelicanparts.com

Center bracket for console. www.pelicanparts.com

Bracket that mounts the console to the floor between the seats. www.pelicanparts.com

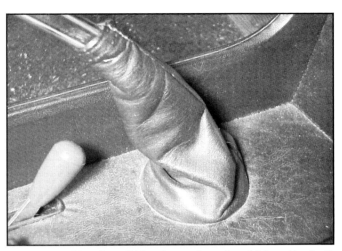

Close-up of leather shifter boot that should be attached to the center console when you buy one. www.pelican-parts.com

rpm. The 8,000 rpm tachometer used in the special 916 models had a red zone between 7,200 and 7,400 rpm.

Speedometers in U.S. cars varied, depending on model year and original equipment tire size. Before 1973, there were two 120-mile-per-hour speedometers used, one calibrated for 155 series tires, the other for the optional 165 series rubber. The latter was used in 1973 with the exception of 2.0-liter equipped cars, which came with a 150-mile-per-hour speedometer. From 1974 on, a 150-mile-per-hour speedometer was fitted to all U.S. models.

Things are even more complicated when it comes to the various types of combination gauges that sat to the left of the tachometer on the four-cylinder cars. Until 1973, the gauge fitted had a big red handbrake warning light stretched across the top and a fuel gauge along the bottom. It also had two small warning lights—a green one for low oil pressure and a red one for the generator charge.

This same gauge continued over to 1973 on cars with center consoles. Cars without a center console used a gauge that had a temperature gauge along the top, a fuel gauge along the bottom, and round warning lights for the handbrake (red), oil pressure (green), and generator (red). Similar gauges were used from 1974 through 1976, using a black plastic decorative center button that matched the needles of the tachometer and speedometer.

The center console that first appeared in 1973 had three gauges—a clock, oil temperature gauge, and a voltmeter. In 1974, the oil temperature gauge face was changed to show a smaller red zone, but otherwise all the gauges were identical.

One other cockpit feature of the 914/6 distinguished it from the 914/4. It had a hand throttle fitted to the center tun-

nel, just in front of the gearshift. The four-cylinder cars did not have this feature.

All cars had the handbrake located between the door sill and the seat, at the driver's left. Early cars had a handle that, once engaged, would drop back down to provide easier entry and exit. Releasing the brake required raising the handle again, then pushing and holding in the release button while lowering the handle out of the way. Despite the big red warning light used on the early-model combination gauges, there was, and is, a tendency to drive off with the brake engaged.

That's why a more conventional-operating handbrake, mounted in the same location but lower in the car, was installed in 1973. Porsche obviously felt this would solve the

Defroster lamp cover alongside slot for heater control handle on center console. www.pelicanparts.com

drive-away problem of the earlier unit, since the size of the handbrake warning light was also significantly reduced on the newer combination gauges introduced with the center console that same year.

We've already discussed the major change in the seating area that took place in 1972, but there were other interesting changes pertaining to carrying passengers. The standard plastic tray mounted between the seats that served as a center console for all models of the 914 could also be fitted with an optional padded insert ostensibly to carry a third passenger. In 1973, an upholstered console with a hinged lid became available to fit the space between the two seats.

Early cars had smooth, but Spartan appearing, vinyl door panels that were switched to a basket-weave pattern in 1972. In 1975, a wider spaced basket-weave pattern was used that continued through to 1976. More questionable was the move to save costs in 1975 by going from stitched seat pleating to heat-pressed pleats that tended to separate more easily. Leather seats and door panels were available on the 914/6. Seat patterns for all cars came in a variety of materials from smooth vinyl, basket-weave vinyl, corduroy, and Tartan cloth (1975, 1976) to hound's tooth check cloth (1970).

Window cranks and interior door handles went through minor changes over the years. The biggest difference was the switch from chrome to black plastic.

Radios were normally dealer installed options, mostly Blaupunkt units. Air conditioning was also a dealer option. Two types were used, DPD and VPC. The differences between the two types were in the shape of the vents and the control knobs. These were placed along the lower molding of the dashboard. Each air conditioning system had its own unique center console. The DPD console was the more attractive of the two, with the gauges all angled to face the driver. While the DPD console is not exactly rare, you're more likely to come across the factory style center console.

Sun visors had 901 part numbers (the prefix for 911 parts) but were unique to the 914. The gas, brake, and clutch pedals, however, along with the pedal assembly, are all 911 items.

The heater controls were similar to those in the 911, but not the same. They varied in appearance over the years with changes occurring in 1973 and 1975. Other controls were primarily VW parts, although, for some reason, the cigar lighter was a Porsche part. The original fog light switch was green in the center before later versions switched to gold. The headlight switch was another Porsche piece, but the knob came from VW.

The door threshold plates, like many trim pieces, went from chrome to black plastic in 1974. Three different styles of door latches were also used over the years.

Interior Redecorating

A Turn for the Best—Steering Wheel Removal/Replacement

One of the easiest ways to give your 914 interior a high dollar, high performance image is to replace the stock steering wheel with an aftermarket leather-wrapped steering wheel. Prices have come down quite a bit since airbag-equipped wheels on newer cars have cut into the market. Of course, like anything that sounds too good to be true, there is a hidden cost beyond the enticing price of the new steering wheel. You will need an adapter that matches the mounting spline of the 914. Unless you can find a used one, an adapter can be expensive, adding nearly 80 bucks to the cost of the new steering wheel itself. This is also a good thing to remember if you see a bargain steering wheel at a swap meet. Make sure it has, or you can easily get, the specific adapter for a 914. VW adapters won't work.

It should be mentioned that while the smaller aftermarket wheel will make entry and exit a bit easier for taller drivers, it will also make the car a little harder to steer. The tops of the tachometer and speedometer may also be obscured. This may be remedied by twisting the gauges slightly so the "more important" numbers are visible. I prefer the more modern look and thicker rim of the aftermarket steering wheels and don't feel they compromise steering effort to a great degree. Others prefer to keep their cars as stock appearing as possible. It's your call.

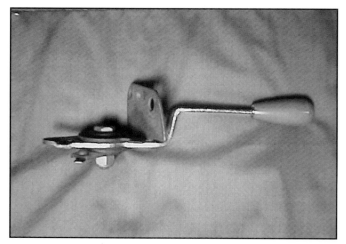

Heater control lever with proper offset to fit center console slot. **www.pelicanparts.com**

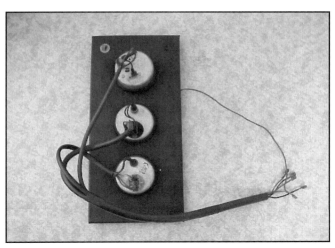

The back of the console gauge panel shows how the gauges are attached to the wire harness.
www.pelicanparts.com

Note how the gauges on a console in an air conditioned 914 are lower and angled towards the driver.
www.pelicanparts.com

Even if you aren't replacing the steering wheel, it's still a good idea to know how to remove it for any repairs on steering column–mounted controls.

Step one is taking a firm grasp of the rim with one hand while you turn the center pad in a counterclockwise motion with the other. It's a bit like unscrewing a big rectangular gas cap.

Once the center pad is free, don't just yank it away from the rest of the wheel. You must remove the horn signal wire that attaches to the wheel hub. You should be able to gently pull this wire from its connector.

Now you'll need a 29–30-millimeter socket to unscrew the large nut that holds the steering wheel in place. Before you start twisting on this nut, it's a good idea to center the steering wheel and mark the column and the wheel so you can line it up properly when you replace it. If you are putting on a new wheel, make sure that once you have the front wheels perfectly straight, you don't nudge them out of position. Otherwise, the coolness factor of your new steering wheel will take a big hit as your passenger notices the spokes don't quite correspond to the direction of the front wheels when you're driving in a straight line. This would also make things a lot more exciting than they ought to be as you negotiate your way around the race track.

OK, so all you need to do is to fit that big socket on your air wrench and loosen the steering wheel nut. What's that—you can afford a fancy Italian steering wheel, but you don't have an air wrench? Hopefully, you do have a long-handled socket wrench or a breaker bar. The trick is to hold the steering wheel steady while you break the nut loose. A tip passed on by Wayne Dempsey at Pelican Parts is to use an antitheft steering lock, such as The Club, to help you generate enough leverage. Clamp The Club onto the steering wheel close to the handle of the socket wrench and then squeeze the two together. Another option is to remove the ignition key and let the steering wheel lock hold the wheel in place. The problem with this method is not being able to center the wheel exactly when the lock clicks on.

After the nut is removed, you can slide the steering wheel off the spline. You may have to tug a bit or use a little spray lubricant to work it loose. When you replace the wheel, be sure that the grooves on the steering wheel center hole lineup properly with the splines on the steering column. Don't force it. It may be a snug fit, but the steering wheel should slide into place. Again, keep the wheels straight during the process of removing and replacing the steering wheel.

Once the wheel is in place, thread on the retaining nut and torque it down to about 40 lb-ft. Use The Club again for leverage when you apply the torque wrench. Hook up the

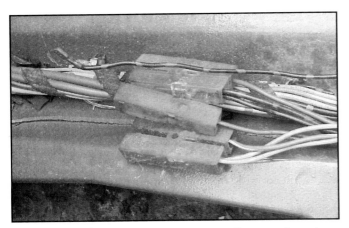

Main wiring harness with connectors for console as in later 914s. www.pelicanparts.com

horn signal wire, making sure it doesn't get crimped in the process of attaching the horn button assembly. The horn will be able to tell you if it's hooked up properly or not.

Console Counsel—Installing a Center Console and Auxiliary Gauges

The 914 center console was available as an option starting in 1973, and was standard on that year's 2.0-liter cars. It's a great way to overcome the barebones look of the basic 914 interior. You'll also be better informed about what's going on in the engine compartment, thanks to the oil temp and voltmeter gauges. And by having a clock, you can leave your

watch at home to avoid tan lines when you're cruising with the top off. At night, the warm glow off the extra gauges adds a romantic touch. All this for less than a couple hundred bucks and a few hours of work.

The first step in this process is to be a smart shopper and find a console that is obviously in good shape but, even more important, complete as to all the necessary hardware for a proper installation. That means a console with all three of its mounting brackets—a U-shaped top bracket to mount to the dash, a metal center bracket, and a rear mounting tab. You should have three working gauges and the wiring harness for hooking them up to the car's main wiring system. Worst case, you could go to Radio Shack and buy the necessary connectors and wires to make a wiring harness. Rebuilding a clock can get expensive, so make sure all the gauges work before you buy them.

Another item you'll need is an oil temperature sending unit that sends a signal from the engine to the temperature gauge. This should already be in place on cars from the 1973 model year and on. Certain sending units were calibrated for specific gauges. Make sure that the gauge you have matches the sending unit in the car. You may have to change one or the other for proper readings. If you have a pre-1973 car without a sending unit, get a sending unit off a later car (it's best to get the gauge and the sender from the same car) and install it in place of the plate on the driver's side bottom of the case, near the larger oil strainer cover plate. Aftermarket solutions have included sending units integral to the oil dipstick and units that had to be mounted through a hole drilled in the oil strainer cover plate. For adding an oil pressure gauge, replace the sending unit for the idiot light, which is on top of the case next to the distributor. Dual-function sending units are

Console must be twisted into position. www.pelicanparts.com

Wiring for center console must go under the center bracket for console. www.pelicanparts.com

Photo illustrates all the retaining rings and gaskets that keep the clear face of the gauge in place while sealing the dust boot. www.pelicanparts.com

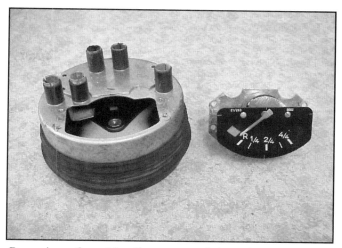

Rear view of combination gauge with module removed. www.pelicanparts.com

available if you want to keep the warning light as a backup to the pressure gauge. By the way, a leaky oil sender is a common source of oil leaks in 914s. It's a cheap and easy fix.

The center tray of the center console is equipped with its own specific leather shift boot. This tray also mounts the defroster lamp cover and has a slit for the heater control lever. The defroster lamp is the same as the one mounted to the floor of cars without a console, but the heater control lever is not the same as the standard unit. It has a special angle to clear the console. It's possible to bend the standard lever to fit, but the preferred method is to replace your original heater control with the console-friendly part. But we're getting

ahead of ourselves, so let's back up and start at the beginning of the console installation process.

Start by removing the defroster lamp cover and its holder from the center tunnel. Next, unscrew the red handle from the heater control lever. Then pull the shift knob off the shifter. When doing so, be careful not to lose the crush washer located inside the knob. You will need it to securely reinstall the shift knob after you have added the console and its leather shift boot. If your shift knob won't easily pull off, try sliding an open-ended wrench onto the shifter just under the knob for leverage, and gently tapping from below with a hammer. Be careful, those original shift knobs may look plain but they are incredibly expensive.

Now you can pull up and remove the carpeting covering the center tunnel. Taking out the driver and passenger side floor mats will make this job a bit easier. Once the carpet is out of the way, you will be able to see the shifter assembly and the connectors from the main wiring harness for the center console gauges. If you have a car that was made before 1973, these connectors will not be present so you will have to refer to the wiring diagram for your car as to how to tap into the wiring harness.

Before we can install the console and make any electrical connections, it is necessary to install the proper heater control lever. Unbolt the old lever and pull it out of the center tunnel. You will see a cable running through the center of the handle that runs to the rear flapper boxes on the heat exchangers. Now comes the dirty part. You will need to crawl under the car to loosen the barrel nuts on the left and right flapper boxes that hold the ends of the control cable in place. When the cable ends come free from the flapper boxes, you

Touching up nicks on outer ring of gauge with permanent black marker. www.pelicanparts.com

Removable gauge modules allow you to plug and play with different gauges and faces. **www.PELICANPARTS.com**

can pull the cable up through the center tunnel from inside the car.

Check the cable for wear and tear and get a new one if needed. Thread the cable through the heater lever that you will be using in conjunction with the center console. Now insert the two ends of the cable into the two tubes in the center tunnel, pushing them all the way through to the flapper boxes. Reattach the cable ends and tighten the barrel nuts. Head back to the cockpit and bolt the new heater lever in place.

With the new heater control lever in place, you can reinstall the center tunnel carpeting. Be sure to pull the lead wire (blue) and the ground wire (brown) for the defroster lamp through the carpet as you put it back down. You will also have to cut a slit in the carpeting to pull through the wiring connectors for the center console. Remember, if you have a pre-1973 car, you will need to tap into the main harness before reinstalling the carpet. Early cars might also need to have an additional wire running into the engine compartment to connect to the temperature sensor.

Once the carpet is back in place, it's time to install the console. Removing the U-bracket on the top of the console makes it easier to maneuver the console into position. It takes a bit of twisting and turning to wedge the console in place. Don't force it.

After the console is in position, it's time to hook up the wiring harness. Just match the color of the wires on the console harness to the corresponding colors on the connectors to the main wiring harness. When the wiring has been completed, it's time to bolt down the console. Attach the U-bracket to the console and then to the underside of the dashboard. If your car lacks the two mounting holes

necessary, you will have to drill them per the holes in the bracket. The same is true for the holes in the center and rear mounting brackets. There should be a hole in the chassis for each. Use sheet metal screws to hold the console in place.

Slide the lower console cover in place over the heater control handle and shift lever. Connect the wiring for the defroster lamp. Install the shift boot and red handle for the heater control. Press fit the shift knob, with its crush ring, onto the shifter.

Press the gauge panel in place. Go back to the engine compartment and bolt the temperature sensor into the bottom of the engine case. This involves removing two bolts and a plate, then bolting the sensor in its place. You may want to time the installation of the temperature sensor with your regular oil change since you must drain the engine oil before beginning this procedure. Plug into the sensor the green and black wire from the wiring harness. That should do it.

When checking out the operation of the gauges, don't be alarmed to see the voltmeter needle jump when you use the turn signal, tap the brakes, or turn on the lights. It's a common characteristic of these gauges even when new.

Stereo buffs might consider using the area behind the gauge panel of the center console for adding an amplifier or subwoofer.

By using a dash-mounted combination gauge that incorporates a temperature gauge, like those used in cars from 1974 on that did not have a center console, it's possible to replace the temp gauge in the console with an oil pressure gauge.

Tuning Up Your Instruments

Removing the gauges from the instrument panel of the 914 is fairly simple because, as on the 911, they are held in place by black rubber rings that can be pried out using your fingers or with the help of a screwdriver. Just be gentle when using the screwdriver, so you don't rip the rubber or mar the instrument panel. Unlike the 911, an alternative method is to remove the four screws that hold the instrument panel in place and then push the gauges out from the back. This requires removing the steering wheel.

Mounting the gauges in this way also makes it easier to twist the face of the speedometer or tachometer so that the important numbers on the top of these dials can be seen if an aftermarket steering wheel should obscure them in their normal position.

Glass lenses were used on the earlier gauges, but later 914s may have plastic in their place. If the plastic on your gauges is scratched or discolored, you don't have to buy a

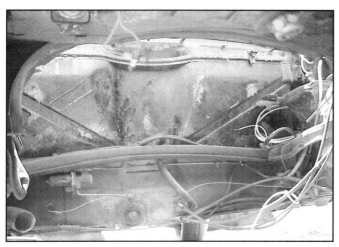

Bare metal firewall can add to cockpit sound level.
www.pelicanparts.com

Sound padding improves the looks of the engine compartment while lowering the noise level in the passenger compartment. *www.pelicanparts.com*

new gauge to remedy the problem. You can disassemble the gauge and replace the lens with a new one made of glass. All VDO gauges have the lens held in place by a retaining ring. Use a small screwdriver to gently pry this ring away from the outer wall of the gauge. Be careful, as you will need to have this ring in decent shape to reseal the gauge. It's a good idea, once you have a portion of the ring loose, to complete the removal using your fingers instead of the screwdriver.

Once this retainer is off, you can remove any other rings or gaskets surrounding the lens. Remember in what order these came off, as you will replace them in the reverse order when you put on the new glass. While you have the top off, a little blast of compressed air from a spray can like those used to clean computer keyboards wouldn't be a bad idea to whisk out the 25 or so years of dust that has accumulated.

After reassembly and cleaning, slide the retaining ring in position and bend its edge back in place for a nice tight fit. A little touch up from a permanent black marker should take care of any nicks or scratches.

Another interesting feature of Porsche gauges is that many have interchangeable modules that can be easily swapped out. Just unscrew the module from the rear of the gauge, lift it out, and put in another one. On the 914, this can be done to add a temperature module to a car that doesn't have one, or to add an oil pressure gauge to a combination gauge. Obviously, switching modules is a quick and dirty way to replace a broken gauge.

Not all of your gauge troubles can be internal problems. Before disassembling the gauges, check all wiring for continuity and test the sending/sensor units. If the speedometer suddenly quits working without warning, it's a good bet that

the fix is relatively simple. The culprit is usually a broken cable or the speedometer angle drive, located at the rear of the transmission.

Putting Engine Noise Behind You

While no serious Porsche driver will complain about having to listen to the sound of a well-tuned engine hard at work, even motorheads have their quiet moments. If you occasionally like to listen to the radio or hold a conversation while driving your 914, it's nice to have a little insulation between you and road noise.

Replacing worn, thin carpeting with something a little more plush can do wonders toward absorbing sound and improving the looks of your car's interior. There are a number

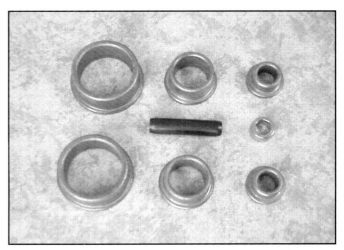

Bronze bushings replace the OEM plastic parts that leak and squeak. *www.pelicanparts.com*

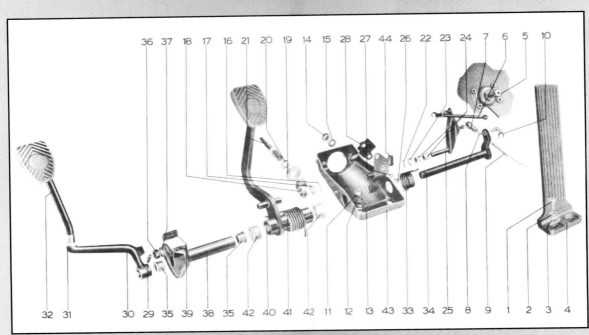

Diagram of all components of pedal cluster. Porsche AG

No.	Part Description
1	Screw M6X16
2	Spring ring
3	Washer
4	Accelerator pedal
5	Stop screw-accelerator pedal
6	Push rod for accelerator pedal
7	Ball socket
8	Nut M5
9	Throttle cable controls
10	Fork bolt
11	Nut M8
12	Spring ring
13	Washer
14	Nut M8
15	Spring ring
16	Cotter pin for actuating rod
17	Washer
18	Intermediate piece
19	Stop washer for brake light switch
20	Hex nut M10
21	Piston rod
22	Cotter pin for guide lever

No.	Part Description
23	Washer
24	Bushing
25	Guide lever
26	Oval head screw AM 4x10
27	Serrated washer
28	Brake light switch
29	Hollow set pin
30	Clutch pedal bottom
31	Nut M14x1.5
32	Clutch pedal top
33	Spring for clutch pedal shaft
34	Clutch pedal shaft
35	Bushing
36	Nut M8
37	Spring ring
38	Bearing tube
39	Rubber stop
40	Brake pedal
41	Return spring
42	Bushing
43	Mounting bracket
44	Rubber stop

Close-up of brake pedal spring. www.pelicanparts.com

Clutch pedal bottom and clutch pedal shaft after removal from pedal assembly. www.pelicanparts.com

of carpet kits available on the market in a wide range of prices, colors, and materials. If you're a concours competitor, you will try to match the OEM look and color that the factory fitted to your car. Everyone else can let their budget and their fashion sense rule their choice. Most suppliers will be happy to send you samples to assist in the decision making.

Putting down new carpet in a 914 is pretty straightforward work. Just work on one section at a time. As you remove the old pieces, match them up with the new ones for easy replacement. If you have the room, you may want to remove all the old pieces and set them down near the car in their proper order as a guideline. The adhesive of choice these days for interior carpet work is 3M Trim Adhesive. For really heavy-duty tasks, use 3M Super Weatherstrip Adhesive. Use it

sparingly around the edges and where the carpet bends. A little goes a long way. You may also need to pull up the carpet some day for repairs or adjustments, and you don't want to have to rip it out or ruin it.

Don't forget new carpet mats for the front and rear trunks. Another effective way to quiet down the cockpit of a 914 is to look in the engine compartment to check the condition of the sound pad that's glued to the firewall. If it's torn or loose, you may be able to glue it back in place. You definitely don't want loose or crumbling insulation to get caught in the engine fan spinning just a few inches away. If you can't find any sign of an insulation pad on the firewall in your car, your lifestyle will definitely improve by a few decibel levels after you install one. Cars made prior to 1973 did not come equipped with this pad.

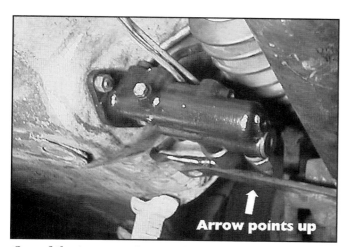

Arrow points up

One of the two nuts that need to be removed in order to disconnect the pedal cluster from the master cylinder. www.pelicanparts.com

Removing old bushing from the center shaft. www.pelicanparts.com

Brake pedal spring installed. www.pelicanparts.com

Clutch pedal spring installed. www.pelicanparts.com

Using a vise to install a new roll pin, when a press is unavailable. www.pelicanparts.com

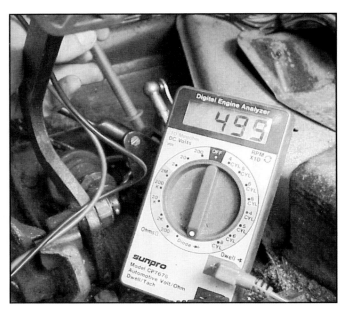

A multitester is used to check and adjust the brake switch, so the brake lights come on when the pedal is pressed. www.pelicanparts.com

You can buy a used sound pad, which is obviously precut to fit, or you can try to save a few bucks by cutting your own. If you can find a used one in good shape, the time you save and the fit you get is worth spending a few bucks. Gluing the pad in place is pretty straightforward. Apply the adhesive to the right side first and lay it up against the firewall. The pad is heavy but the 3M Super Weatherstrip Adhesive fixes it in place after a minute or two. Before then, you have time to position it correctly. The position of the relay board and its cover on the left side of the engine compartment may interfere with pad placement on that side. Feel free to unscrew the relay board and push it out of the way to enable the padding to snug down to the firewall properly. Be sure to bend the little metal tabs at the top of the firewall over the pad to further secure it.

With new insulation, carpets, and rubber seals for the windows and top, your 914 should be almost as snug as a VW Bug.

Pedal It

Sticky or squeaky pedals signal the need to rebuild the pedal cluster. This is a problem common to the 356 and 911 as well as the 914. In fact, the 914 shares its pedal assembly with the 911. For this reason, rebuild kits are available that make rebuilding and upgrading your pedal assembly a reasonable do-it-yourself project. The upgrade consists of bronze pedal bushings to replace the original plastic bushings. These bushings are more resistant to corrosion from leaky master cylinders and rust from errant water leaks. Working on the pedal assembly is also a good time to replace worn rubber pedal pads.

The first step to working on the pedal assembly is to remove the carpet on the driver's side footwell. Under the carpet is a wooden floorboard held in place by two hex nuts. Remove these and take out the floorboard to reveal the pedal assembly. Also revealed will be many years' worth of dirt and debris that needs to be vacuumed out before you do anything else. You should also inspect the floorboard for water damage and other signs of deterioration. Used boards are available if yours is damaged. Wayne Dempsey at Pelican Parts suggests spraying the floorboard with high tech sealant paint to protect it against future wear.

Once you have the area cleaned up, start removing the pedal assembly by disconnecting the clutch cable from the cluster. The cable is attached to the pedal cluster with a cup-in-ball connector that should snap apart. A similar connection attaches the accelerator pedal to its cable. This connection can be separated by pulling the gas pedal toward the rear of the car.

Now it's time to jack up the front of the car, safely support it with jack stands, and remove the metal cover that protects the steering rack. You need to locate the master cylinder and undo two nuts that mount it to studs from the pedal assembly.

After doing this, return to the footwell and remove the two bolts that mount the pedal cluster to the chassis. You should now be able to lift the pedal assembly out of the car.

After the pedal assembly is out of the car, you can begin taking it apart. If you didn't remove the rubber pedal pads when you were taking out the floorboard, do so now. Examine the springs that compress against the brake and clutch pedals. You will have to replace them if they are damaged. To disassemble the pedal cluster, you must remove the roll pin (29) that is inserted through the end of the clutch pedal. The easiest way to do this is by using a press. An alternative is to place a bolt on one end of the pin and tap it out with a hammer. Make sure the base of the clutch pedal is securely mounted in a vise when you do this to avoid damage to the pedal cluster. Another method is to drill the pin out.

Once you have succeeded in removing the pin, you can disassemble the components of the pedal cluster. First pry off the clutch pedal lever (30) and then slide out the clutch pedal shaft (34). Now remove the brake pedal by unscrewing the nut (36) that holds in the flange attached to the bearing tube (38). Once the nut is off, the bearing tube can slide out, freeing up the brake pedal.

Take the bearing tube and remove the plastic bushings from either end. Clean the tube by lightly sanding off any rust. Apply a small amount of lithium grease to the two medium-sized bronze bushings from the rebuild kit and insert them on each end of the bearing tube.

The accelerator guide lever (25) now must be removed from the pedal cluster base. This is done by removing the cotter pin that holds the lever in place. After sliding the lever out from the base, replace its plastic bushings with the appropriate bronze bushings. Remember to spread a little grease on the new bushings before inserting them. When you've completed this procedure, reinsert the guide lever shaft into the cluster base and reinstall the cotter pin.

Take the remaining small bronze bushing and insert it in the end of the clutch pedal shaft. All you should have left from the bronze bushing kit is the new roll pin. Reassemble all the parts of the pedal cluster, lubricating the parts with grease, and ensuring that the springs are installed properly. Remember that the brake pedal is sprung to come up off the floor while the clutch pedal goes in the opposite direction.

The final step is to press the new roll pin in place. Again, a press is preferred for this task, but a vise can be used satisfactorily.

All that needs to be done is to install the rubber pedal pads. A screwdriver should stretch them enough to pop into place.

Install the assembly back in the car, making sure that the master cylinder is bolted down tight and that the accelerator and clutch cables aren't wrapped around each other. An indication of the latter is a bit of unintended acceleration whenever you step on the clutch pedal. Make sure the brake light switch is reconnected and working when you tap the brakes.

Reinstall the wooden floorboards and carpeting. Now you have no excuses for not being able to smoothly heel and toe your way around corners.

5

Lighting/Electrical

We could subtitle this chapter on the electrics of the 914 with a warning that "where there's smoke, there's fire." The compact midengine location with a collection of wiring, cables, and fuel lines (some over 25 years old) vying for space increases the propensity for these cars to burst into flames. It's one thing to look out the rearview mirror to see how badly you've smoked the cars trailing you through the esses, and quite another to see smoke and flames trailing out of the engine grille. Just ask my neighbor, who had the misfortune of driving my 914 when the throttle cable completed its erosion of the insulation surrounding a coil wire that had strayed a bit too close. I strongly urge anyone with a 914 to make it part of a routine maintenance program to inspect and upgrade when necessary the fuel lines and electrical wiring and connections on their cars. The combustibility factor aside, it's always better to stop problems in the comfort of your garage, before they stop you on the side of a busy freeway in the rain. This would be an especially aggravating circumstance if you also failed to heed the instructions regarding weatherproofing your targa top.

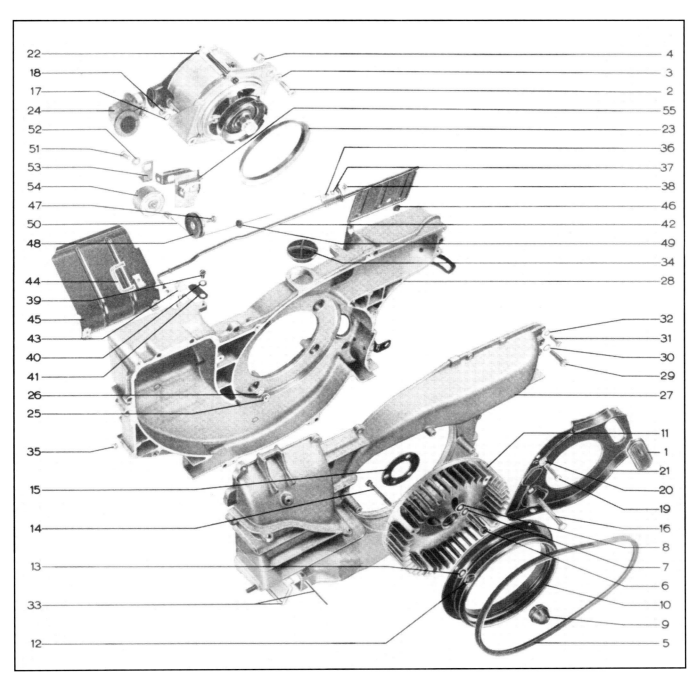

Key components of the 914 alternator and cooling system are V-belt (5); pulley (10); cooling blower impeller (11); alternator (22); rear and front half of cooling blower housing (27, 28); throttle valve left and right (42, 45); and thermostat (54). Porsche AG

Plastic ignition switch can develop cracks after years of daily abuse. www.pelicanparts.com

Removing the steering wheel allows access to inner part of steering column. www.pelicanparts.com

OK, let's charge forward with our look at the electrical system. We've already discussed the location of the battery and the importance of keeping it in good shape for anticorrosion reasons. Obviously, doing so will also pay off in avoiding electrical problems. Check the water level on a monthly basis. Fill it with distilled water as needed. Keep the cables clean and corrosion-free. Get a battery cover and install a battery mat as added protection in case of leakage.

The miracle of modern chemistry has brought to market various sprays to clean and protect the terminals. Those of you preferring a holistic treatment can fall back on a low-tech home remedy and apply a coating of petroleum jelly.

New battery cables and ground straps can also make a big improvement to your car's performance. Don't forget to inspect, and replace if necessary, the ground strap at the rear of the car that attaches to the end of the transmission. A battery disconnect switch installs easily to your battery's negative terminal. You can use it as an antitheft device, but more importantly, it will keep your battery from discharging over extended periods of downtime or storage. Units are available that will allow a trickle of voltage to maintain clock and radio settings.

Underside of the passenger seat from 1974–on 914 shows Big Brother device to ensure seatbelt use. Smaller box is the buzzer for the larger box that controls seatbelt ignition interlock. www.pelicanparts.com

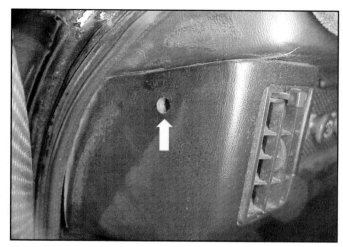

Left side retaining screw that, along with its mate on the right side, must be unscrewed to remove the kneepad of dashboard. www.pelicanparts.com

With kneepad removed, you can access the wiring for the wipers and turn signals. Note fuse box on lower left. www.pelicanparts.com

Removing the four screws that hold the wiper and turn signal switch assembly. www.pelicanparts.com

Spending about twice the cost of a standard replacement battery will get you a sealed, dry cell battery, like the Optima. It's more expensive up front, but it will avoid acid leak worries and also improve cranking ability in cold weather. It should have a longer life span as well.

The Buzz on Alternator Problems

The alternator on the 914/4 is a 50-amp Bosch unit that is fairly reliable. Its removal, while conceivably a one-person job, does require disassembly of a part of the engine's cooling tin and the need, at one point, for a pair of hands at the top and bottom of the engine compartment. Even if you do get it out of the car, repairing the alternator may be some-

thing better left to an expert. There are, however, a number of things that can be checked before resorting to alternator removal and repair.

We already mentioned checking all the ground connections, including the transmission ground strap. A worn or loose alternator belt will contribute to charging system woes. By the way, Brian Kumamoto, who has been driving 914s for many years, passes on a tip about a quick way to replace the alternator belt. He says to put the car in second or third gear, and working from the driver's side of the engine compartment, place the new belt on the alternator pulley and then stretch it over to the fan. Start at the top of the fan pulley and work the belt as far as you can toward the bottom. Then roll,

Better view of wiper and turn signal electrical connections. The large bolt holds the steering column housing in place. www.pelicanparts.com

Two screws hold the housing together that contains the ignition switch. www.pelicanparts.com

Use the key to pull out the old ignition switch.
www.pelicanparts.com

New switch in housing, ready to go back into steering column. www.pelicanparts.com

or push, the car backward. The belt should pop into place. He says he has followed this procedure for years. A good thing to remember the next time that red light comes on, assuming, of course, that you remembered to pack a spare belt.

A failed or deranged voltage regulator can also be the perpetrator of alternator problems. The best way to check the status of the regulator is to measure the voltage output to the battery while the engine is running. You can also remove the suspect voltage regulator and replace it with one that you know is properly working and note any changes. The voltage regulator resides on the relay board in the left side of the engine compartment. To replace it, disconnect the battery ground cable before removing the cover over the relay board.

Unbolt the old regulator and disconnect it. Plug in the replacement and bolt it in place. By the way, when shopping for a new regulator, an electronic regulator should prove to be a lot more reliable than the OEM unit. The final steps to this procedure are to replace the relay board cover and reconnect the battery ground.

Here are some other indications of alternator trouble and what they mean:

Alternator warning light on and ignition key is off.

- Not a good sign. Your alternator has failed. The diodes have shorted out. Disconnect the battery until the alternator is replaced.

Alternator light does not come on when key is turned on.

- Good news would be that it's a burned out bulb.
- Bad news would be that the voltage regulator has failed.
- Worse news is that the alternator has failed and the internal slip-rings are open.
- Other possibilities include a dead battery, loose battery connections, other broken wires or defective connections.

Alternator light remains on after engine starts and is running above 2,000 rpm.

- Fan belt broken or slipping.
- Regulator has failed.
- Alternator is bad or dirty.
- Alternator not firmly grounded or battery lead to alternator disconnected.

Close look at set screw that holds ignition switch in its housing. www.pelicanparts.com

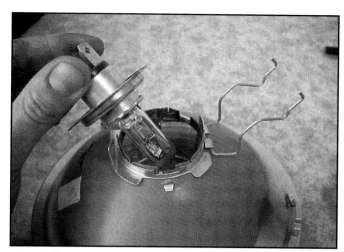

Carefully install the lamp inside the headlight without touching the filament. Any finger smudges will reduce light output. **www.pelicanparts.com**

Plug the new headlamp into the connector. Make sure the connection is tight. **www.pelicanparts.com**

Alternator light is dim after starting, but gets brighter as engine rpm increase.

- Battery lead to alternator is loose or broken.
- Ground connections are bad.
- Battery is dead.
- Alternator has suffered diode failure.

Alternator light is dim after starting, but gets dimmer and goes out as engine rpm increase.

- Battery charge is low.
- Battery connections are loose or corroded.

Alternator light is dim after starting, gets dimmer as rpm increase, but stays lit.

- Regulator has failed.
- Alternator is failing.

Stop Jiggling Your Keys—Replacing the Ignition Switch

Starting problems caused by the electrical system can be the result of a bad battery, loose wiring, or a problem with any of the following: starter, solenoid, or ignition switch. Cars equipped with the Orwellian "seatbelt interlock" system (1974–on), which employs seat sensors to detect whether the seats are occupied and then requires the seatbelts to be fastened before allowing the engine to start, may also suffer starting problems, should Big Brother fall asleep at the switch.

Before tearing into the steering column to replace the ignition switch, it's wise to perform a few tests to make sure that one of the other components mentioned above has not failed. With the headlights on, turn the key and see what happens. If the lights go out or significantly dim and the starter doesn't turn over, then the problem is related to the battery or its connections.

If you know the battery is strong, but the starter barely turns over, the latter has problems. If the lights stay bright or dim slightly when you turn the key, the problem is either in the solenoid or the starter. Test the starter switch to see if current is being sent to the solenoid.

If you have a later car, check the seatbelt starter relay under the passenger seat. You will see two boxes, the larger is the starter relay and the smaller is the warning buzzer. Because it is located on the floor, the wiring to this relay is subject to corrosion and damage. The simplest way to fix any

Clear plastic fuse box cover has descriptive markings indicating what fuse controls what system. **www.pelicanparts.com**

Battery disconnect switch comes in handy for working on car, prolongs battery life, and works as simple antitheft device. www.pelicanparts.com

problems with this relay is to bypass the entire system. You will have to locate the wires connected to the seats and the seatbelts and unplug them. Then locate the two large wires (usually yellow w/red stripe) going into the relay and securely wire them together. Use a plastic connector and electrical tape to avoid future problems with this connection. Then sit down and congratulate yourself for being someone who uses his own internal warning buzzer, a.k.a., common sense, to make sure that he and his passengers are properly buckled up before driving away.

Once you have determined that the ignition switch is the culprit to your starting woes, and you have gone beyond the stage where creative key jiggling no longer works, it's time to replace the offending part. The switch is made of plastic and

prone to cracking and just plain wearing out after all the use it gets. A major culprit is carbon build-up on the contacts over the years. Just think about the number of times you turn your car on and off in the typical week. Even a "flick of the wrist" can inflict damage over time.

After getting a new ignition switch, your first job in the replacement process is to remove the steering wheel, as we noted in chapter 4. Next up is the removal of the kneepad along the bottom of the dash. This is held in place with a screw on either end and five Phillips head screws along the bottom. The end screws should have plastic caps covering them. Carefully pry these off with a screwdriver to get at the recessed screws.

Once the kneepad is out of the way, you can reach under the dash and unplug the wiper and turn signal switch from the wiring harness. A hex head bolt holds the steering column housing in place. Remove this housing to gain access to the four screws that mount the turn signal and wiper switch assembly. Take out these screws and carefully pull out the assembly. Let it hang by the rubber hoses that lead to the windshield washer. Don't lose the mounting screws.

Next, remove the two screws that attach the housing cover for the ignition switch. As you remove this piece, be wary of a small spring that is part of the steering wheel lock. It resides in a small recess on the ignition switch housing. Reach in to the rear of the ignition switch and unplug its electrical connection. Insert your key, give it a twist, and pull the assembly free. You will notice a setscrew that holds the white plastic switch inside the metal housing. Remove this setscrew to withdraw the old switch and replace it with a new one.

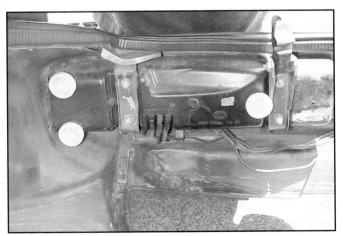

Large, round white plastic bolts inside the trunk hold the taillight lenses on. Also visible is one of the targa top retaining clips used to store top in trunk. www.pelicanparts.com

Each headlamp door is controlled by its own motor, with a knob for manually raising lamps in case of failure. www.pelicanparts.com

Regulator, in silver box, sits on the cover of the relay board on the left side of the engine compartment. www.pelicanparts.com

Tighten down the setscrew and put the entire assembly back in place. Plug in the electrical connection. Reattach the housing cover, making sure that the steering wheel lock spring is in place. Before going further, check the new switch by turning the ignition on. If everything works, continue with the process of reinstalling the wiper/turn signal assembly, steering column housing, kneepad, and finally the steering wheel. Humming the Rolling Stones' "Start Me Up" is considered a good mantra during this process.

A Simple but Not Petty Theft Prevention Device

We've focused on getting your 914 to start when you want it, but there may be a time when you're hoping for the opposite. Wayne Dempsey of Pelican Parts passes on a simple solution to prevent a thief from making off with your 914.

Wayne noticed that the electric tachometer line connects to the output from the points that drive the ignition coil. He realized that the points that trigger the coil would not work if the tachometer cable was accidentally grounded. By accidentally grounding the tachometer signal with an in-line switch he could protect his car from being hot wired by a potential thief.

He wired in an SPDT (Single Pole Double Throw) switch from Radio Shack that grounds the tachometer signal and prevents the coil from firing. Basically, he was achieving the

same effect as disconnecting the coil. The switch is mounted up behind the dashboard so it is not easily seen.

Illuminating Discussions and Headlight Reflections

With the obvious exception of the retractable headlight doors, maintaining or upgrading the running lights of your 914 pretty much follows standard automotive operating procedure. Removing the rear taillight lenses requires opening the rear trunk and unscrewing the large knurled plastic knobs that hold the lenses in place from the inside. If you're doing more than a simple bulb replacement, the reflector assembly can be removed by loosening the four bolts that are visible and then pulling it out a bit before unplugging the wiring.

The side marker lights have lenses that are held in place by two external screws. To remove the entire assembly, the attachment nut is inside the fender. Loosen it without losing the accompanying washers, pull out the lamp assembly and unplug it. Front marker/signal lamps follow a similar procedure.

To work on the headlights, pull out the dashboard switch to turn on the main beams and raise the doors. Disconnect the battery ground to maintain the upright position and eliminate the possibility of the doors closing while your fingers are busily working on the light assembly. This could not only be

Cover removed to display important fuses and three round relays that control most of the 914's vital functions. The fourth relay socket is for the option rear window defogger. www.pelicanparts.com

physically painful, possibly breaking a finger or two, but cause serious long-term bruising to your ego when your friends or significant other responds to your whelps as you struggle to free yourself from the grip of the 914. The fingers will heal and only twinge a bit on damp nights, but the mental anguish will remain an open wound, causing you to grimace at the words, "Remember the time you. . . ."

That point soundly made, let's resume with the headlight removal/replacement process. Remove the plastic headlight surround by undoing the three Phillips head screws. Wiggle it out of place and set it aside. Now remove the three small screws that attach the chrome retaining ring to the headlight. Take care not to strip these screws as you remove them. Make sure you are working with the screws holding the tabs of the retaining ring and not the two headlight aiming adjustment screws. Once the chrome ring is loose, you can pull out the headlamp and unplug it. Another word of caution: Many of the white plastic electrical connectors used on the 914 get brittle over the years and will crumble apart if you yank too hard when unplugging them. Make sure you replace any broken or cracked connectors properly.

By the way, instead of merely replacing the stock sealed beam units, this would be a good time to upgrade your night vision with a set of H4 quartz halogen headlights. Check your local lighting laws before doing this. Federal law still requires that to be legal in the United States all headlight lenses must have the little external nubs that fit headlight aiming equipment. It's an old and odd law, but I wouldn't flash my lights at a passing state trooper to protest it. Hella has recently made available an HB-2 light with a lens that is 50-state legal. I do not know if this light matches the H4's performance but it is significantly better than the OEM 914 lights and it is legal. Either the H4 or the HB-2 will install the same as a standard light with one exception. Because they use replaceable bulbs, you must first install the bulb into the headlight unit (follow the manufacturers instructions) and then plug it into the proper connector on the car. The H4s may cause a power surge on your car's 20-something wiring, so installing a relay wouldn't be a bad idea. You definitely need a relay if, after the H4s are in place, the ignition switch becomes very hot.

Place the chrome retainer ring, which only fits one way, on the new headlight, put the light in position, and tighten the screws. Reinstall the plastic surround. Hook up the battery and stand back to see your car in a new light. Make sure that both high and low beams work.

You will also want to check that the headlights are properly aimed for your safety and that of oncoming traffic. Those of you brighter than your lights will also come to the conclusion that flaunting illegal H4s in the face of an approaching police car is not a good idea. A quick and dirty way to aim your headlights is to find a level spot about 30 feet away from a wall or garage door. Make sure the car is level. Adjust the headlights to point straight ahead and a little below the centerline of the headlight if you were to draw a line from the headlight to the wall. If you're very conscientious, you can measure the distance from ground to the center of the headlight with a tape measure and then use it to make a reference mark on the wall. The adjusting screws are at the top and outer side of each headlamp assembly. It's easier to do this before you replace the plastic shroud.

Installing fog or driving lamps requires removal of the front bumper to reach the mounting brackets. To simply replace the bulbs, it is not necessary to remove the bumper.

The trickiest part about backup light repair is knowing where to look for the switch. It's mounted on the left side of the transmission. To replace this switch, unplug the wiring connector and unbolt it. Because of its location, before resorting to removal, make sure the connections are solid and the wiring/contacts are not corroded.

As for the headlight doors and the electric motors that raise and lower them, most problems can be solved by replacing or checking the connections of the plug in relays located inside the front trunk. The headlamps can be raised by hand if necessary, using a tool that was supplied as part of the standard tool kit.

Fuse Box

The fuse box is located under the left side of the dash. The cover is cracked or missing on many cars. Make sure your car has a decent cover to prevent corrosion of the fuses and to keep an errant kick when entering or exiting the car from knocking a fuse loose. Another good reason to have a cover is that the cover tells you which fuse does what. This information is also in the owner's manual, but how many 914s do you come across that still have an owner's manual in the glove box? If you don't have a manual, it's a good item to put on your swap meet "to do" list. They can be pricey, but sometimes you can find a tattered but readable one for a few bucks. Just make sure it matches your car's year.

While we're talking about the contents of your glove box, make sure you have enough extra fuses in there. The older style "bullet" fuses are getting harder to come by, so stock up when you can. Obviously, if you keep blowing fuses you need to do more than buy replacements. Check the source of your problem before you have to reach for the fire extinguisher instead of another fuse.

Suspension

If you look under the earlier versions of the 911, you'll find a lot of similarities between its suspension setup and the one in a 914. In fact, all the way up to the 1989 model, the 911 front suspension is a bolt-on replacement for the 914 front suspension. We'll talk more about this later. The point we want to make right now is that when Porsche designed the 914, it applied what they felt was the best suspension setup around, that of the 911.

The basic components of the front suspension are the shock absorber strut assembly, the lower control arm, the torsion bars, and the steering rack. While the length of the torsion bars, 24 inches, is the same for the 911 and the 914, the diameter used for the 914, 17.9 millimeters, is different. The 914/6 also uses a 17.9-millimeter torsion bar, but it differs from the four-cylinder bars. This is important to remember when you replace the torsion bars. Make sure you get the correct torsion bars for your application. The end splines on a four-cylinder torsion bar are different from the ones for a 914/6. Neither will accept 911 bars.

Another difference between the four- and six-cylinder cars is that the 914/6 was equipped with five-lug wheels from the 911.

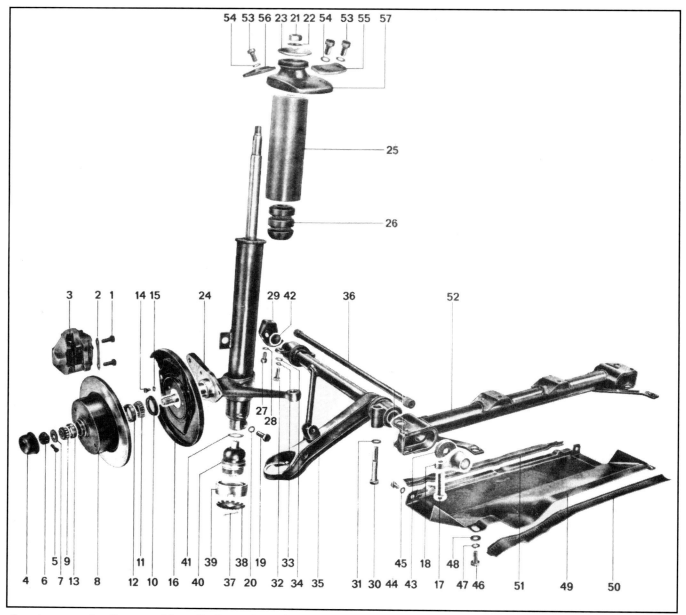

Front suspension borrowed heavily from that of 911. Major parts include brake caliper (3); brake disc (8); torsion bar adjusting screw (17); shock absorber strut (24); protective tube for shock (25); transverse control arm (35); torsion bar (36); and ball joint (40). Porsche AG

There are a number of ways to adapt five-lug wheels to the four-cylinder cars. That's a topic we'll cover in chapter 11, when we look at wheels and tires.

While the front suspension on the 914 mimics that of a 911, the rear suspension is different. It still uses trailing arms, but the torsion bars of the 911 are replaced with coil springs. This is because the 914 is a midengine car as opposed to the 911, which has its motor mounted behind the rear axle. Torsion bars couldn't be used on the 914 because the engine sits where the

torsion bar tube is located on the 911. Another consideration was having a rear suspension that could accommodate the mounting of both the four- and the six-cylinder engines.

Anti-sway bars were not considered necessary by the factory when the 914 came out. Over the course of production, that thinking changed, and various combinations of front and rear anti-sway bars were fitted. The 15-millimeter front bar is the most common. Rear bars, when fitted, were 16-millimeter.

Rear springs come in a variety of stiffness rates to match your driving preference, from street to track. www.pelicanparts.com

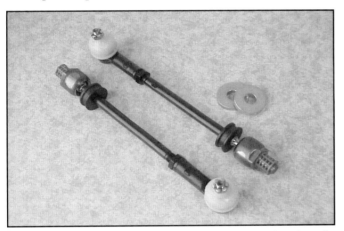

Originally designed for the 930 Turbo, the turbo tie rod kit fits all 911s and 914s, to make steering more responsive. www.pelicanparts.com

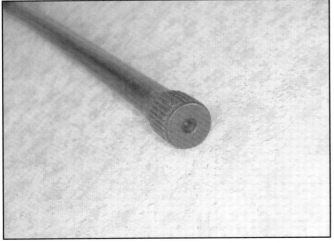

The splined end of a 914 is unique to that car. The 914/6 splines are different, although the bars are the same size for both types of car. www.pelicanparts.com

OEM rubber bushings wear out and cause the 914 to have sloppy reflexes. Aftermarket polygraphite parts are much stiffer and last longer. They provide tremendous improvement in handling, but the ride becomes harsh and noisy for a daily driver. www.pelicanparts.com

Repairs and Maintenance

Springtime

The 914 was designed with a wheelbase longer than the 911's and long suspension travel for a comfortable ride; Yet most 914s that you ride in today tend to have a harsh ride. Stiffer springs, shocks, torsion bars, and anti-sway bars may improve a car's handling but take a toll in ride quality. The original rear springs were relatively soft with a rating of 60 pounds/inch. Over the bumpy course of time, the tension in the coils weakens, causing the springs to sag. If your 914 has a droopy rear end, chances are it needs new springs. Later in the book, in chapter 12, we'll discuss changes to the suspension aimed at improving handling for autocrossing and track driving. For now, if you need to replace the rear springs and are looking for a comfortable daily driver as opposed to a track demon, rear springs rated at 100 pounds/inch would be a good compromise.

Over the years, rear springs have become available in a number of sizes from the OEM 60 pounds/inch to 100 pounds to 140 pounds to race track–only 180 pounds. One of these sizes should meet your needs. There is no need to experiment by cutting coils. Cutting out a coil or two from a spring will not only make it shorter, it will make it much stiffer. There has been a vast amount of experience built up over the years concerning the current aftermarket offerings. It's much easier to use that data to balance out your suspension needs than to become the mad professor of coil-cutting. Furthermore, the cost of new springs is fairly low.

For safety's sake, when changing the rear springs or shocks, a spring compressor is advisable.

Shock Treatment

The major brands of shocks fitted to 914s are Koni, Bilstein, Boge (pronounced Bogey), and KYB. They can be identified by their color. Boge is black, Koni is red/orange, Bilstein is green and sometimes yellow, and KYB is white. Opinions vary as to which is the best shock for a 914. Konis are expensive but have the advantage of being adjustable, allowing you to tailor a combination of ride and handling to suit your personal preferences or need. Chiefly, Konis are preferred for the way they improve a car's handling. Bilsteins also receive high marks. They provide the best combination of ride and handling. Over the years, Porsche chose Boge shocks as original equipment on many cars. KYB offers a price advantage, but many 914 owners consider it to be the hardest riding of all the shocks. Long-term durability tends to be an issue, along with occasional lapses in quality control.

Poor handling and excessive vibration or feedback through the steering wheel on bumpy roads can be indications of worn shocks. Having your 914 do a nose dive under braking is another symptom. It's a good practice to periodically inspect your shocks for signs of leakage and loose or missing mounting bolts.

Twisted Tale

Torsion bars are generally fairly hardy, but they are subject to rust and can weaken or crack over the years. If the front of your 914 lists to one side, you may need new torsion bars. You may also experience odd cornering behavior, like excessive tilting or pitching, when good bars turn bad. Torsion bars are marked right and left. They should always be replaced in pairs.

Removing and installing torsion bars is a fairly simple process. Raise the front of the car and support it using jack stands. Remove the wheels. At the rear end of the A-arm you will see the adjusting screw that sets the ride height. Unscrew the adjusting screw and pull off the adjusting lever and the seal. Go to the front mounting point for the A-arm and remove the single screw that holds on the dust cover plate. Carefully pull or tap out the torsion bar toward the rear. Check for any cracks or damaged end splines. Installing is the reverse process. Make sure that you don't mix up the left and right side torsion bars. They should be marked on the end. The bars should be clean and free of rust. Coat them lightly with grease, especially the splines. Insert the bar from the rear. Install the seal. Now use a pry bar on the A-arm to pull it down until the shock absorber is fully extended. Insert the

adjusting lever over the torsion bar spline. Lubricate the adjusting screw with a bit of grease and screw it into place, making sure that the adjusting lever is as close as possible to the stop located on the support brace. A good way to ensure this is to have only a bit of the adjusting screw sticking out the top of the adjusting lever. Attach the front cover and then the dust cover plate. Adjust the ride height and then take the car to an alignment shop.

Feeling Bushed

Since all 914s are over 23 years old, it's a good possibility that the rubber bushings in the suspension have become worn or mushy and need replacing. This is a repair that can do wonders to bring back a solid, new car feel to the ride and handling of your car. It will feel more responsive to steering input. You can buy aftermarket bushings in sets to replace the stock bushings in the front A-arms and the rear suspension arms. There are also bushings available for the drop links of the factory anti-sway bar. Replacing the bushings is not hard but very time-consuming, as it requires disassembling the major parts of your suspension to get at the bushings.

Removing the old bushings may be difficult, as they are pressed in place. The ideal way is to use a press to remove them. If you don't have access to a press, you can try prying them loose with a screwdriver. Burning them out with a torch is the quick way. Because of the danger of fire or explosion from gasoline fumes, it is advisable to completely remove the suspension arms from the car and take them to a safe, well-ventilated area when using the torch.

Chapter 12 will address the subject of performance bushings. Performance bushings are very hard and not recommended for daily street driving for all but the hardcore handling fanatics. Slightly softer "street" suspension bushings are the preferred choice for those who value a comfortable ride or have loose fillings. Whichever type you choose, be sure to apply a waterproof, nonmelting bushing grease when you install the new bushings. Otherwise, your 914 will sound like a haunted house full of creaks and groans.

Steering a True Course

An upgrade that is very popular with 911 owners is also used by many 914 fans to improve the feel and response of their car's steering. Turbo tie rods were developed by Porsche for the 930 turbo cars. Metal balls replace the rubber used in all other applications. These tie rods are direct replacements for the stock tie rods. If your car's steering feels loose or sloppy, new tie rods will make a big improvement. This is considered a must for anyone who uses their 914 in competition.

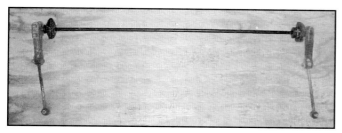

Front anti-sway bar assembly. www.pelicanparts.com

U-tab for mounting anti-sway bar is attached to A-arm. www.pelicanparts.com

The Princess and the Pea

A final comment on suspension upgrades. Remember that all this talk about ride comfort versus cornering capabilities is all subjective. Some of us have backsides that are a bit more tender than others. The conditions of the road surfaces where you live are also a big factor. How far and how often you drive your 914 is another consideration. A stiffer ride is easier to live with in a weekend tourer than a daily driver. Commuting to work is tough enough without your own car committing road rage against you.

One of the 914's key attributes is the handling prowess built in when it left the factory. Just getting everything back to OEM specs will give you a proper sports car. Use that as a baseline. Talk to people who have made the changes you are considering before making a commitment to your car. If you can, the best course would be test driving modified cars to see how they handle and feel in the real world. I tend to prefer a stiff ride and usually don't experience the discomfort others may feel, as long as a car is responsive and handles well. That said, I have driven in 914s that I wouldn't drive anywhere other

than a smooth race track. So listen to what people say about setting up your car, but before you get down to spending time and money on changes, make sure that those "changes" will end up being improvements when all is said and done.

Balance is the key. Running stiffer rear springs with an otherwise stock suspension setup will lead to oversteer, or a propensity for the tail to break loose when rounding a bend. Ways to tone this tendency down, or eliminate it, are to make changes up front. Heavier torsion bars, a thicker or stiffer anti-sway bar, and harder shock settings, or combinations thereof, will counteract the stiffer rear springs. They all work toward an understeer condition where the front end of the car is reluctant to go round a corner. In an extreme situation of understeer, the car prefers a straight path, even when the wheels are turned in the desired direction. We'll go into greater detail in chapter 12 about how all this can be adjusted for autocrossing and other track events. The important point to remember is that any change to a specific part of the suspension, front or rear, will have an effect on all the other suspension parts.

If you are looking for a good compromise in a daily driver between handling and comfort, a good combination would be Bilstein shocks, 100 pound/inch rear springs, a stock front anti-sway bar and the stock torsion bars. You can lower the car a bit, but avoid cranking it down too low. You'll have trouble clearing driveways and speed bumps, and the ride will be too stiff.

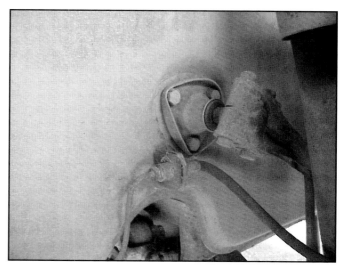

Front anti-sway bar passes through the inner fender wells. Triangular bracket stiffens surrounding area where bar passes through. www.pelicanparts.com

Straight Facts About Alignment

Any time you make changes or adjustments to the suspension of your 914—installing shocks, springs, adjusting the ride height—you should have the alignment checked immediately after you are done. You can spend a lot of time and money on upgrading the suspension parts, but it's all a waste if the car is not properly aligned front and rear. This is a job better left to professionals with the proper equipment. Misalignment can create abnormal and accelerated wear to tires and suspension pieces. It can lead to unsafe handling or equipment failure.

On the other hand, a proper alignment can improve the way your car handles. Just make sure you take it to a shop that knows how to properly align a 914, especially the rear suspension. A set of shims located outboard of the trailing arm where it is attached to the chassis is used to adjust rear camber settings. Running too much negative camber in the rear, a byproduct of lowering the rear suspension, can cause excessive tire wear.

Following is a list of terms and their definitions to help you understand what you may hear at the alignment shop:

Camber: The tilt of a wheel in relation to a vertical line down the center of the car when viewed straight on. Positive camber means the top of the wheel tilts out. Negative camber means the top of the wheel leans inward.

Caster: The axis about which the wheel turns during steering. Positive caster means the wheel leans backward. This is the angle you need to have the wheels return to after a turn. It also keeps a car from wandering on a straightaway.

Toe-In: Making the front edges of the wheels point inward when the car is at rest. This actually keeps them pointing straight once the car is in motion.

Mounting bracket for rear anti-sway bar. **www.pelican-parts.com**

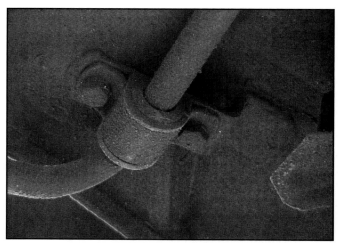

Rear anti-sway bar bracket mounted in car. **www.pelicanparts.com**

Adjusting Ride Height

The front ride height can be adjusted by turning the adjustment screws at the rear of the torsion bars on either side of the car. The factory way to set ride height is to park the car on a flat surface. Push down on the bumper a few times to settle the suspension.

Measure the distance from the ground to the center of the dust cap on the wheel bearing. Subtract 90 millimeters (3.54 inches) from this distance. Now make another measurement from the floor to the center of the torsion bar. This second distance should be 225 millimeters (8.85 inches) plus or minus 5 millimeters. Do the same for the other side of the car. The distance you come up with on the other side should be within 5 millimeters of that on the first side you measured.

Setting your ride height too low will result in a condition known as "bump steer." When you go over a bump, the steering wheel will jar your hands. Because of the location of the steering rack on the 914 and 911, lowering the car throws off the geometry between the steering rack and the tie rods. The rack becomes lower than the tie rod ends. An inexpensive set of spacers is available that will not alter the lower ride height but will shim up the steering rack, raising it to a level position with the tie rods.

The rear ride height can be adjusted by changing the rear springs. If you have Bilstein shocks, the spring perch can also be adjusted to alter ride height.

A quick and dirty method of setting ride height used by 914 owners, especially those who autocross, is to set the rear height so that the distance between the fender lip and the wheel rim is 1.75 inches. Set the front so that it sits a half-inch lower than the rear.

Installing a Front Sway Bar

Sway bars are actually anti-sway bars since they inhibit the car's body from leaning, or heeling over, around turns that could cause it to sway. They add stiffness to the suspension by coupling the spring effects of one side with the other. When one side of the car starts to dip, the torsion acts to pull it back up. Leveling out the car's attitude gives the driver a better sense of control and allows safer and faster cornering. The front sway bar cuts down on a car's tendency to slide out its tail, or oversteer, when turning. Rear sway bars have the opposite effect. Most 914 drivers feel safer and more confident having a stock-sized 15-millimeter-front sway bar and no rear sway bar. A smaller number like the combination of a front bar combined with a rear bar of equal or slightly smaller size. No one recommends adding just a rear bar, as this would create dangerous handling characteristics.

The front sway bar on the 914 passes through the inner fender bulkhead. In order to prevent cracking or tearing of the inner fender, a triangular reinforcement must be used where the sway bar passes through the bulkhead. To do this properly, the gas tank must be removed. Refer to chapter 9 for the procedure for removing the fuel tank. There are kits available to bypass the need for removing the gas tank, but they are not as suitable. Cars that were equipped with sway bars from the factory do not need to perform this step.

A complete sway bar setup will include the sway bar, drop links and bushings, the bulkhead reinforcement kit, a U-tab mounting kit for the A-arms, and bushings for the sway bar mounts. Substituting adjustable drop links will allow you to fine-tune the distance between the sway bar and the A-arm for specific driving conditions.

The first step is to install the U-tabs to the A-arms. Two holes must be drilled in the A-arm to mount the U-tabs. It is important to drill these holes straight through and not at an angle.

Now comes the hard part, if your car doesn't have factory sway bars. You must remove the gas tank before mounting the reinforcements for the inner bulkheads.

Assuming the gas tank has been removed, you are ready to drill three holes needed to mount the reinforcement to the bulkhead. Securely place the car on jack stands and remove the front wheels for access to the bulkhead. Use the diagram that came with the reinforcement kit as a template for drilling the three necessary mounting holes. It's a good idea before you start poking holes in it to make a few copies of this template. Drill the top forward hole first from the outer side of the bulkhead. This will let you bolt the reinforcement bracket in place as a guide for drilling the remaining holes.

Good view of how anti-sway bar is mounted to curve around transmission. www.pelicanparts.com

Additional support for rear anti-sway bar is provided by welding reinforcement plates in trunk. www.pelican-parts.com

After the holes are drilled, put the other top bolt through the bracket. It's time to take a 1-inch hole saw and drill out the center hole of the bracket through which the sway bar passes. Drill slowly and with slight pressure. Let the saw do the work. Repeat the entire process for the other side of the car.

Although you used the bracket as a drill guide on the outer side if the bulkhead, it actually mounts on the inside. To make it fit properly, you will need to grind away a bit of sheet metal from the gas tank area. You will create a tiny notch that the bracket fits into in order to lineup with the holes you made. This is something you will have to eyeball for the proper fit.

Once you have both brackets installed, before you remount the gas tank, you need to install the bushings where the sway bar passes through the brackets. Keep the mounting bolts on the brackets loose to help you slide the bar through and seat the bushings. Use new bushings, because you don't want to go through this process again for a long time. Once you have the bar through both sets of bushings properly in place, tighten down the reinforcement mounting bolts.

If you removed the gas tank, now is the time to put it back in place. If you haven't done so, this would be a good time to replace your old fuel lines.

Install the drop links on the sway bar and then to the U-tabs on the A-arms. Make sure the sway bar is properly centered in relation to the left and right A-arms. You don't want any "preloading" of the sway bar. Also check that the drop links clear the brake lines and the strut. When you're satisfied that everything fits nice and proper, put on the wheels and check out the handling. I won't say "go for a spin" because that shouldn't happen if your installation is right.

Installing a Rear Sway Bar

Adding a rear sway involves some welding both inside (top of floor) and outside (bottom of floor) the rear trunk. You may want to drive your car with only the front bar for awhile to see if you really need and want a rear bar. Getting your hands on a car with a rear bar installed would obviously be a big assist to your decision-making process. Most 914 owners choose not to use the rear bar. Dedicated racers will install it just to have it in case they visit a track where it may prove to be an advantage. The majority, however, won't run a rear bar.

For those of you who already know what you want and don't mind a little welding, here we go. Your shopping list should include a sway bar (duh), four droplink bushings, two sway bar "running" bushings, two sway bar brackets, and two reinforcement plates.

The sway bar brackets fit on the underside of the trunk. They are L-shaped to fit around the transmission support bar. They also attach to this support bar. Besides being L-shaped,

the bracket comes with two nuts welded in place. One of these fits into an existing hole countersunk in the bottom of the transmission support bar. Placing the nut into the hole allows you to align the edge of the bracket with the edge of the trunk. Once you have the bracket in place, scribe locating marks into the sheet metal. Before you weld it in place, it's a good idea to put the entire sway bar assembly together to make sure that everything fits properly.

You may have a problem on the left side of the car with a U-shaped sheet metal brace that interferes slightly with the bracket for that side. Removing a bit of the brace should cure this problem. Whatever you do, don't try to enlarge the existing countersunk hole in the transmission support bar in an attempt to force the bracket in place. This will cause the sway bar to be misaligned.

The droplinks attach to special bolts that replace the ones locating the shocks to the bottom of the trailing arms. You will need to have the car on a lift or supported by jack stands to put the special bolts in place. Once the car is up in the air, put a floor jack under the trailing arm and jack it up to the point where the shock assembly is relieved of tension. Loosen the exiting shock mounting bolt and wiggle it free. If you're lucky, it will easily slide free. The rest of you, keep wiggling. Once you have it out, replace it with the new bolt that has the droplink mount. Repeat on the other side.

Now more wiggling will get the sway bar into proper position so it isn't contacting the transmission mounts. Once the sway bar is in place, bolt a U-clip retainer, with a running bushing inside, to the sway bar bracket. Make sure the bracket lines up with marks you made earlier. If it does, weld it in place. Attach to both the trunk floor and the transmission support bar. Further support for the sway bar bracket comes from reinforcement plates that are welded, from inside the trunk, on the opposite side of the trunk floor. These will be covered by the trunk carpet.

Make sure that the sway bar and droplinks do not contact or interfere with anything. Find a twisty road and have fun.

Brakes

How can I put this delicately? A good many people, myself included, think the braking system on the 914 sucks. Step on the brake pedal and both your confidence level and your foot sink. The car seems to stop OK, but you're never comfortable with late braking maneuvers in traffic. The 914 brake system also has certain design oddities, most significantly the rear calipers, that add mechanical complexity to its questionable performance.

OK, let's pause a few seconds to give the hardcore 914 purists a chance to regroup from my initial attack. Defending the faith is the purist's prerogative. Just remember that very few of these purists drive around in 914s that maintain the stock brake system. Those who do keep their systems stock follow a meticulous maintenance schedule and, most importantly, use high quality brake pads.

I must admit that I am a bit prejudiced. We won't call it a brake bias, to avoid confusion with the role of another of the system's anomalies, the brake proportioning valve. My intolerance for the stock 914 brakes is rooted in the outstanding stopping qualities of the Porsche 911.

Anyone who has driven a 911 and had to rely on the capabilities of what are lovingly referred to as "Porsche brakes" to get them out of some very close calls is prone to expect that philosophy and performance to have trickled down to the 914. The firm pedal feel and excellent stopping that are trademarks of the 911 were somehow lost in translation to the 914. The weak, spongy feel of the 914 pedal does little to inspire confidence. Overall stopping ability can at best be rated as adequate, especially for a car that can generate such outstanding speed through the corners.

The theory of a light car with four-wheel disc brakes is obviously a good one, and, as we have pointed out, the 914 was one of the first lower priced cars to offer this system. The good news is that over the years a number of techniques have been devised to improve the 914's braking prowess. Even better news is that some of them do work. The bad news is that some of the more popular tweaks, while certainly contributing to the overall quality of the system, have become the 914 counterparts to urban legends. It's a case of good intentions missing their specific targets but still providing

value. We'll examine these improvements more closely a bit later. I'm specifically referring to the ideas that a larger master cylinder and stainless steel brake lines will cure the 914's spongy pedal feel. Before we go more in-depth on this and other performance changes, let's review the basics of the stock 914 brake system.

A Breakdown of the Basic 914 Brake System

The 914 brake system consists of disc brakes with fixed calipers at all four wheels. The brake pedal moves a push rod to actuate the dual-circuit master cylinder. The main system is hydraulic, while the emergency brake is mechanically operated by two cables that apply pressure to the inner brake pads on each rear caliper. A brake pressure regulator mounted in the engine compartment controls the pressure sent to the rear calipers to guard against the rear brakes locking up and causing the car to spin. The brake lights are activated by a mechanical switch mounted on the pedal assembly.

The 914/6 differs from the rest of the 914s by having ventilated front brake rotors, a 19-millimeter as opposed to a

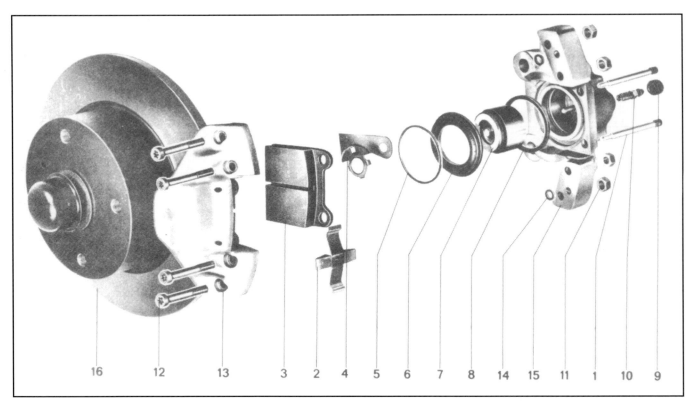

View of front caliper, showing brake pad retaining pin (1); spreader spring (2); brake pad (3); piston retaining plate (4); clamp ring (5); seal (6); piston (7); bleeder valve (10); and brake disc (16). Porsche AG

17-millimeter master cylinder, and slightly larger rotors and calipers all around. It also stops better.

Brake Work

Before discussing how and why to modify the 914 brake system, let's cover some aspects of routine maintenance that aren't quite as routine when dealing with our little twin trunk vehicle. Because I think that even a person who just uses his 914 as a daily driver needs to upgrade the performance of the braking system, I am deviating from my plan to group all racing and track related improvements in the chapter on competition—chapter 12. I have decided to include all braking modifications in this chapter.

This is also a good time to issue a warning that safety should be a major concern whenever you are working on and around your car. This is especially critical when working on the brake system. Remember, if your brakes are not working properly you are not only putting your life at risk, you are endangering the lives of anyone who rides with you along with anyone else on the highway.

Installing New Brake Pads

Even if you think you can change brake pads in your sleep, the 914 has enough idiosyncrasies to keep you up nights trying to make sense of what Porsche was thinking when it designed the rear calipers. Before working our way back to introduce you to the weird science of the rear brakes, we'll start our installation procedure with the front pads.

Indications of worn or abused brake pads include squealing or grinding noises when the brakes are applied, veering to one side or another under braking, a spongy or soft brake pedal (a bit tricky to diagnose since stock 914 brake pedals

914 rear caliper. www.pelicanparts.com

always feel spongy), and longer stopping distances than normal. Any of these symptoms should prompt you to remove the wheels and visually inspect the brakes, specifically the pads. Check for unusual or uneven wear. Porsche says pads should be replaced when they are worn down to 2 millimeters, about .08 of an inch. Many pads have indicator grooves cut into them that make it easier to determine when it's time for replacement. As this groove begins to disappear it's time to start shopping for new pads.

Always purchase and install new pads as a complete set for each axle. In other words, you may not have to do both the fronts and the rears at the same time, but you should do all the fronts, or all the rears, at the same time. The front and rear pads are not interchangeable. Remember that if you do plan to reinstall used pads, make sure you mark them as to where they originally were located so that you can put them back exactly the same way. Pads develop wear patterns over use and switching their location can cause uneven braking applications that lead to vibration and pulling to one side or the other.

There are a number of options available when choosing a brake pad. If you will be doing most of your driving on the street with an occasional autocross or time trial, don't go overboard and get a set of pads that are designed for heavy racing use. The problem with many pads developed for the track is that they need to heat up thoroughly before they work well. Normal street driving may not heat them up enough to be effective. Driving for miles on the freeway without having to apply the brakes and then suddenly having to

Front caliper piston retaining clip. www.pelicanparts.com

Note ends of brake pad retaining pins on right edge of caliper. www.pelicanparts.com

make a panic stop from 70 miles an hour is not the kind of application racing brakes were designed to handle.

Another disadvantage of the pads directed more for track use than the street is that they tend to squeal. Some more so than others. The carbon compound pads also throw off a good bit of black dust. This can discolor your wheels if you neglect to clean them on a regular basis. The black powder will bake itself to the wheel surface, making removal very difficult. There are a number of sprays, lubricants, and rubberized pad liners that are sold to reduce or stop squealing pads. Most work to some degree, and you will have to

experiment to determine which solution works best for the pads in your car.

Pagid and Porterfield have earned the respect of many 914 owners who participate in some form of competition. They offer a range of pads that should meet your needs for track or street use. There are a number of other suppliers that provide reliable and high quality products. The best way to find the pads that fit your needs and price range is by talking to other 914 owners about how they use their cars and their experience with various pads. A parts supplier who offers more than one brand will also be able to help you choose which is best for your use. You will be surprised how much difference a capable set of brake pads can make to the stopping prowess of an otherwise stock 914 brake system. If you only had to make one improvement to your 914's brakes, a quality set of new pads would be your best choice. Also keep in mind that since the front brakes do most of the stopping, if you need to watch your pennies, you can still increase a car's braking effectiveness by installing the high performance pads up front while sticking to a cheaper but still high quality set in the rear.

Once you have settled on a new set of front pads, it's time to remove the old ones before you can install the new ones. After securely setting your car up on jack stands and removing the front wheels, direct your attention to the calipers and drive out the brake pad retaining pins, using a punch or small screwdriver. The spreader spring that keeps the pads apart can now be removed. Pull out the pads. You

Arrow shows cover over adjusting screw that retracts pistons. www.pelican-parts.com

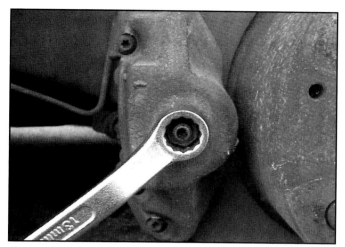

Loosening the outer retaining screw to retract piston on rear brakes. www.pelicanparts.com

Venting rear rotors by adjusting clearance between pads and piston. www.pelicanparts.com

may have to wiggle them a bit to free them up. A wire hook, made from a coat hanger, may be inserted in one of the holes in the back of the pad to pull it free.

Take a flat block of wood or plastic and use it to press the front pistons back into their housings. Make sure the wood rests flat against the entire surface of the piston before you begin pushing. If your brake reservoir is pretty full, you may want to siphon off a bit of brake fluid before pushing on the pistons to compensate for the fluid that will be forced back through the system into the reservoir.

Now pry out the piston retaining plate. Use compressed air to blow out any dirt on the inside of the caliper. Be careful, since many brake pads contain asbestos you don't want to touch or inhale any brake dust. Check for any signs of leakage around the rubber seal of the piston. If everything looks good, rub down the surface with isopropyl alcohol to clean it up. Using anything other than the isopropyl alcohol might harm the rubber seals around the piston. Replace the piston retaining plate by firmly pressing it down onto the head of the piston.

Before inserting the new pads, check the rotor for signs of wear. Take a micrometer and measure the thickness of the rotor. Its minimum thickness per the Porsche factory is 10 millimeters. Any thinner than that, it should be replaced. Also check to see if it is warped or shows signs of abnormal wear. If you're not sure, get a second opinion. Replacing the rotors is pretty straightforward, but it does require the removal of the calipers. The brake hose to the front caliper must be disconnected and plugged up. Then you can unbolt the caliper. Before you can detach the front rotors, you must also remove the clamp that holds on the outer wheel bearing. This is a good time to inspect and repack the front wheel bearings.

After installing the new front rotors and wheel bearing assembly, it is necessary to adjust the endplay of the wheel bearings. You must also bleed the brakes after this job. At the rear, there is no need to disconnect the brake lines before unbolting the calipers as long as you support the calipers and keep it from hanging by the brake line. Remember to unhook the emergency brake cables prior to removing the rear calipers. Removal of the rear disc simply requires unscrewing two bolts and pulling off the disc. Replacement is the reverse procedure of removal.

If everything checks out with the rotor, it's time to install the new pads. Slide them in place, then reinsert the retaining pins and the spreading spring that keeps the pads separated from each other. Use a hammer to gently tap the retaining

Removing the rear cover of inner adjusting screw is accomplished by reaching through hole in trailing arm. www.pelicanparts.com

Brake fluid reservoir should be watched during brake bleeding process so that it doesn't run dry. www.pelicanparts.com

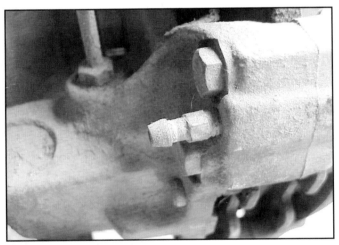

Close-up of brake bleeder on caliper. www.pelicanparts.com

pins in place. Install the retaining clips for the pins. Depress the brake pedal a few times to seat the pads.

You should have some space between the pads and the rotors. This distance is called the venting clearance. This should measure about .05–.20 millimeter (.002–.008 inch) for proper clearance. If the distance is larger than the acceptable limits, this could be an indication that the rubber O-ring inside the piston has become stuck. To remedy this, replace the brake pad with a wooden block at least 0.2 inches thick. Step on the brake pedal as hard as you can several times to free up the stuck piston. If you are successful, reinstall the brake pads and check the clearance. If you still can't come within the tolerance limits, it may be time to remove and rebuild the caliper.

Before you resort to this, it's a prudent idea to bleed the brake system and recheck the venting distance.

Now you're ready for new adventures with the 914 rear brakes. The parking brake system that works off the rear brake pads necessitates manually setting the venting distance when replacing pads. You should get better wear out of the rear pads than the front ones unless you are the absent-minded sort who drives off with the handbrake partially engaged. Removing the pads and inspecting and cleaning the rear calipers is pretty much the same drill as for the front brakes. Now things get ugly. Maybe that's being a bit too harsh for the 914 purists, so let's say "quirky."

Before installing the new pads, you must move the pistons back inside the calipers. This is done by adjusting screws on either side of the rear caliper. Usually, there are protective caps that must be removed to reach these adjusting screws. A black plastic cap is used for the outer adjusting screw. It should easily twist off with a gentle application of a wrench. Once the cover is removed, take a 13-millimeter wrench and loosen up the retaining nut for the adjusting screw. Now push on the piston with a flat object, while turning the adjusting screw clockwise with a 4-millimeter Allen wrench. This should get the piston to move back into position. For the inside adjusting screw, you will need an extension to reach through the access hole in the rear trailing arm to enable the 4-millimeter Allen wrench or hex key to remove the aluminum cover over the adjusting screw. Turn counterclockwise to remove this cover. Be careful. If the cap is stripped, it may be necessary to dismount the caliper to remove the cap. If this happens, take out the two bolts that hold the caliper in place. This should give you the room necessary to use needle-nose pliers to remove

The source of all your spongy pedal problems, the 914 proportioning valve. www.pelicanparts.com

the cap. Once you have access to the adjusting screw, use a 4-millimeter Allen wrench, turning in a counterclockwise direction to cause the piston to retract.

Insert the brake pads and replace the retaining pins without installing the spreading spring between them. Now you must set the venting distance. Insert a feeler gauge between the pad and the disc and tighten the adjusting screws until the clearance is .20 millimeter (.008 inch) on either side. Remember to turn the adjusting screws in the proper direction. Outside goes counterclockwise to tighten, inside is clockwise.

Once you have the proper clearances, remove the retaining pins, and install the spreading springs. Replace the retaining pins and secure them with the appropriate spring clips. Recheck the venting distance and make sure that you tighten down the retaining nut on the outside screw. Replace the inner and outer covers and you're done.

Bleeding the Brakes

Removing any air that has worked its way into the brake system is the first step toward eliminating the spongy brake pedal in a 914. There are brake bleeding tools on the market that make bleeding the brakes a one-person job. These tools either work as vacuums to suck the air out of the system or by pressurizing the system and forcing the air out. The standard brake bleeding procedure requires two people to carry it out properly. One person pushes on the brake pedal while the other opens and closes the bleeder valves on each of the brake calipers. No matter what method you use, there is a certain sequence as to which brake gets bled before another. The rule of thumb is to start with the brake farthest from the master cylinder and do each brake in turn until you finish with the brake that is closest to the master cylinder. Simply stated, start at the right rear, then left rear, right front, and finally, the left front.

Starting with the right rear caliper, have your assistant step on the brake pedal several times and then hold it down. While they hold the pedal down, open the bleeder valve, allowing any air and the old brake fluid to come out. You should have a large container for the fluid to drip into. (Remember brake fluid is highly corrosive. Protect yourself and your car's paint from the fluid. Use plenty of water to wash off any fluid that may come in contact with the paint. Do not rub it with a rag.) Close the valve. Have your helper pump the pedal several more times and then hold the pedal down while you again open the bleeder valve. After more air and old fluid come out, tighten the valve. Keep repeating the process until the fluid coming out is clear. Pedal feel should also be improving each time more air is purged from the system. Keep your eye on the brake reservoir and make sure you add new fluid as needed. If your 914 has two bleeder valves per caliper, bleed the bottom one first before doing the upper one.

Always use fresh brake fluid whenever you are working on your brakes. Brake fluid is adversely affected by moisture. It absorbs water from the air, so any containers that you have had sitting around, even if you tightly recapped them after opening, will have a very short shelf life. The fluid in your system can also draw water from the air, which is why Porsche recommends flushing the system every two years. Your 914 should use either DOT 3 or DOT 4 brake fluid. These will sufficiently meet the needs of daily drivers and the street/track

Master cylinder from 911 will cause a slight increase in braking performance but won't cure spongy pedal.
www.pelicanparts.com

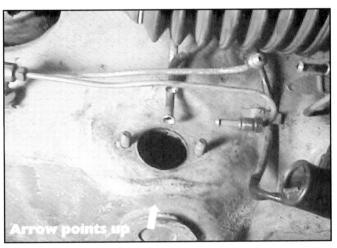

All that's left of the 17-millimeter unit is a hole and the disconnected lines. www.pelicanparts.com

cars. Silicone brake fluid has both its proponents and detractors. Porsche does not recommend silicone brake fluid. The safe call is to avoid it for any car driven on the street.

Installing a 19-Millimeter Master Cylinder

Over the years, one of the "urban legends" surrounding the 914 has been that the spongy pedal feel could be eliminated by switching to the 19-millimeter master cylinder that came on 911s and the 914/6. While the larger unit will give you a slightly firmer pedal, its main advantage is to increase the brake pressure of the system. If your 17-millimeter cylinder is leaking, the 19-millimeter unit costs about the same as rebuilding the smaller one, bolts right in, and does provide a slight performance improvement.

The first step in replacing the master cylinder is to bleed the brake system dry of fluid. Use a suction pump to remove fluid from the reservoir. Make sure the brake reservoir is completely empty.

Once this is accomplished, head under the car to remove the panel that protects the steering rack, fuel lines, and brake cylinder. Once you get this cover off, disconnect the wires for the brake pressure warning switch where they attach to the master cylinder.

Now remove the brake lines from the master cylinder. Be careful when loosening the nuts surrounding these lines. A crows foot wrench is recommended. After the brake lines are off, pull out the reservoir lines from the top of the master cylinder. The only thing left is to remove the two nuts that

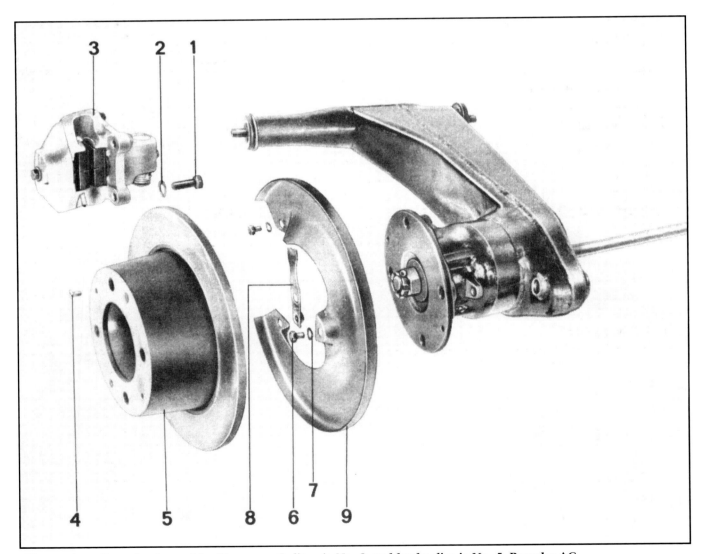

Illustration of rear brake and trailing arm. Caliper is No. 3 and brake disc is No. 5. Porsche AG

hold the master cylinder to the mounting studs from the pedal assembly. Remove the old master cylinder.

Installing the new master cylinder requires that you first attach the lines from the brake reservoir. Make sure these lines are properly attached before moving on. The next step is to mount the master cylinder on the two studs from the pedal assembly. Finally, reattach all the brake lines, followed by reconnecting the brake pressure warning switch lines.

Add brake fluid and bleed the brakes. Make sure everything is working satisfactorily before replacing the bottom protective panel.

If after bleeding the brakes, the brake pressure warning light on the dash remains lit and you know that everything is working properly, you may have to manually reset the switch. As stated above, the switch is connected to the master cylinder. If you remove the protective rubber boot where the connection is made to the master cylinder, you should see a reset button. Push it and the light should go out. It's the same principle as the little button on the kitchen garbage disposal that needs to be pressed after your unsuccessful attempts to grind up items like corn cobs or errant beer bottle caps. You may also want to check that the brake lights are working. It's possible that the brake light switch may have been knocked awry while you were working around the pedal cluster.

The Racer's Edge—New Brake Lines and Proportioning Valve Modifications

The 914 has more urban legends, especially when it comes to braking improvements, surrounding it than the Candy Man. One is the replacement of the OEM rubber flexible brake lines with stainless steel units. This is said to improve pedal feel. Again, this is one of a set of modifications (bigger master cylinder, high quality brake fluid, high quality brake pads, caliper rebuilding) that work together to improve the quality of the system. Just replacing the OEM brake hoses every couple of years will do as good a job. Brake hoses wear from the outside (abrasion, environmental erosion) and the inside. The insides suffer a form of mechanical arteriosclerosis where dirt and debris build up and shrink down the passage for flow of brake fluid. In short, they get clogged up with crud. Replacing them solves this problem.

If you do use the stainless steel lines, actually a Teflon/nylon tube with stainless steel braiding on the exterior, insist on the DOT-approved type. Make sure that they are long enough so they don't get stretched to the limit when you turn the wheels. Be wary of contact with any suspension parts or the wheels. Carefully check all clearances. Rubbing brake lines quickly become cut brake lines. That's not something you want to happen on the road or the track.

Now we get to the prime suspect in the case of the missing pedal pressure—the brake proportioning valve in the lower part of the engine compartment. A malfunctioning valve or one that has had air enter it is the biggest source of the 914's "soft" pedal. Some 914 drivers and racers simply remove it and replace it with a T-fitting from the hardware store. They consider it to be a quick and cheap solution to the spongy pedal problem. Before doing this on a street car, remember that the purpose of the stock unit was to prevent premature lock-up of the rear brakes under various road and weather conditions. Removing this valve could have an adverse effect on the car's ability to handle a variety of conditions.

There are also adjustable proportioning valves available to allow you to adjust the brake bias from front to rear. Many experienced 914 racers use these devices. The problem is, of course, being able to fine-tune the system to brake evenly under all situations. What works on the track may not be the best solution for the street.

Another alternative is to bleed the proportioning valve as you would the brakes. Do the inlet line first, having an assistant pump the brakes then hold the pedal down while you loosen the line. Once the flow of fluid stops, reconnect the line and repeat the procedure for the outlet side. This should remove any air that was trapped in the valve.

Installing Bigger Brakes

Another alternative to improving the 914 brake system is to install larger brakes up front. There are two common methods for doing this. The first goes hand in hand with improving the front suspension by installing the entire suspension/brake assembly from a 911. This is essentially a bolt-on replacement that also has the advantage of adding the five-bolt wheels from the 911. Obviously, you would have to convert the rear wheels to the five-bolt pattern as well.

Another alternative that is gaining in popularity since an aftermarket kit from GPR has been made available to take all the guess work out of the process is switching to the front brakes used on the BMW 320i. The advantages of the kit are that it includes new, as opposed to the used, parts you would acquire from a wrecking yard and that the minor clearance adjustments that are necessary have been engineered into the kit.

Of course, anyone building the ultimate track car or a "money isn't everything" street car can choose high tech racing brakes that cost more than a decent 914 daily driver. You just need to know when to call it quits as far as how well you want to stop your 914.

8

Engine

The difference between the 914/6 and the four-cylinder 914s is more than the additional two cylinders. The engine in the 914/6 is from a Porsche 911 while the four-cylinder cars used powerplants originally developed for use in a succession of Volkswagens—the model 411, model 412, and the Bus. That's not an indictment against the four-cylinder cars, but it does point out a fundamental philosophical and engineering difference regarding the origins and design between the two main types of 914 motive power. The 911 motor has its roots in racing. The four-cylinders were designed as daily drivers. Of course, many of the popular British sports cars were also built around working-class motors. Despite its humble beginnings, thanks to the popularity of VW engines in off-road racing and drag racing, the 914 four over the years has been able to overcome its ordinary roots and can be made to develop significant amounts of power and performance.

This book is not intended as a high performance tuning manual for the 914. There has been a lot of information written about rebuilding and improving Volkswagen and Porsche 911 engines. I have included references to some of that material in the appendix.

914 six-cylinder was the 2.0-liter from 1969 911T. It's shown here with the heater boxes attached. **Porsche AG**

My goal is to provide enough general information and maintenance tips for you to establish a comfortable relationship between you and your 914 in day to day driving.

914/6

The six-cylinder engine used in the 914/6 was the same 2.0-liter engine used in the 1968 and 1969 versions of the 911T, the lowest priced 911 in the line-up. It measured 80x66 millimeters (bore x stroke) for a true displacement of 1,991 cc. Compression ratio was 8.6:1. For 1970, the 911T used an engine that was bumped up in displacement to 2.2 liters but the 914/6 stayed with the smaller engine. It did benefit from a capacitive-discharge ignition system, a feature not found on the 911 versions of the 2.0-liter.

Comparing it to the four-cylinder 914 engines, the six could rev much higher and produce more power and torque. It was rated at 110 DIN horsepower at 5,800 rpm and produced 116 lb-ft of torque at 4,200 rpm. Other major differences from the fours include overhead camshafts, dry sump lubrication (separate oil supply tank), and 40-millimeter Weber triple-throat carburetors. It also weighed about 110 pounds more than the 277-pound four-cylinder of the 1970 914.

According to numbers recorded in *Road & Track* test reports for 1970, the six was about 5.2 seconds quicker from 0 to 60 miles per hour than the 1.7-liter four. Comparing *Road & Track's* 8.7-second reading for the 914/6 against a test it did of the 1973 2.0-liter four-cylinder, the Porsche engine still held a significant edge, as the later car could only do 0 to 60 in 10.3 seconds. That the 2.0-liter was 3.6 seconds faster than the 1.7-liter was still obviously a major improvement.

Overview of the engine compartment of the 914/6 lets you look down all six throats of the Weber carbs. **Porsche AG**

In addition to the quicker acceleration, anyone who has driven a 914/6 will also notice that the sound and power delivery of the engine feels more substantial than the 2.0-liter four-cylinder.

The Four-Cylinder Engines

For 1970 through 1972, the 914 was offered with a 1.7-liter engine (Code W) that was essentially the same engine that VW offered in its 411E. The E designation after the 411 signifies that the engine had fuel injection. This was the D-Jetronic electronic fuel injection that is also referred to as the MPC injection since it read manifold pressure to mete out the fuel. Compression ratio of the 1.7 was 8.2:1. Bore and stroke measured 90x66 millimeters for a total displacement of 1,679 cc. The horsepower was rated at 80 DIN at 4,900 rpm.

In 1973, the original 1.7-liter went under the EA code designation, while engines with additional emissions controls for California were designated EB. California-bound motors had a 7.3:1 compression ratio and put out 72 DIN horsepower at 5,000 rpm.

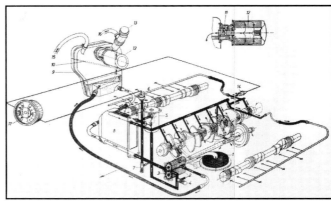

Drawing illustrates dry sump lubrication of the 911 engine used in the 914/6. Oil tank, No. 9, holds most of the oil, which is circulated by the pump, No. 3, and the return pump, No. 2. Oil filter, No. 12, is easily accessible in its location on the top of tank. Porsche AG

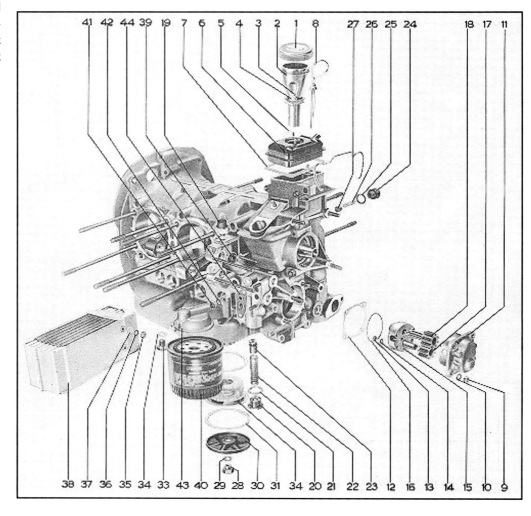

Four-cylinder engine uses a more conventional wet sump system, in which oil is stored within the engine (at least until it leaks out). Oil cooler is No. 38 and oil filter is No. 40. Oil pump assembly is at the front of engine, lower right in diagram. Porsche AG

The year 1973 also saw the engine line-up for the 914 change with the introduction of the 2.0-liter (GA) engine which was adapted from the Type IV VW bus motor. In the 914 version, Porsche designed special cylinder heads with bigger valves and other improvements to increase the flow of fuel and air. Bore and stroke were 94 and 71 millimeters respectively to achieve a total displacement of 1,971 cc. Because of the improved breathing capability of the heads, horsepower was 95 DIN at 4,900 rpm despite a compression ratio of 7.6:1. Engines for the rest of the world had a higher, 8.0:1 compression ratio, and flat-top pistons to produce an additional 5 horses. The reason U.S. cars had the reduced compression ratio was to accommodate the change in this country to the use of unleaded gasoline. The new 2.0-liter weighed 44 pounds more than the 1.7-liter.

The 1.7-liter engine was replaced by a 1.8-liter (EC) unit in 1974. The new engine featured the newer L-Jetronic fuel injection which you will sometimes see denoted as AFC, because it used an air flow meter in the air intake stream. Compression matched that of the previous year's California-only 1.7-liter at 7.3:1. Bore was increased to 93 millimeters while the stroke remained at 66 millimeters. Total displacement was 1,795 cc. Horsepower was right in between the two versions of the late 1.7, with a rating of 76 DIN at 4,800 rpm. Valve size was increased by 1 millimeter for both intake

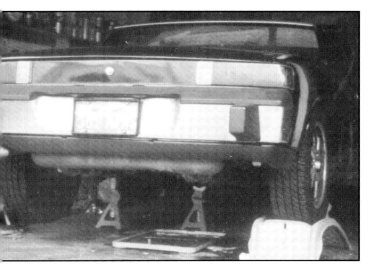

This photo shows the method for raising a car, suggested by Wayne Dempsey of Pelican Parts, to keep one rear wheel fixed so that the other could be turned during the valve adjustment process. Drive the car on ramps, then use jack stand to support one side so ramp can be removed. Make sure the car is secure. **www.pelicanparts.com**

and exhaust from the old 1.7 engine to improve breathing. The L-Jetronic allowed the EC engine to be considered emissions legal in all 50 states. It continued as such for 1975 and 1976 with the addition of an exhaust gas recirculating system for California.

Additional emissions controls including air injection and EGR knocked seven horsepower off the 2.0-liter in 1975. This engine now carried the GC designation. Catalytic converters appeared in cars bound for California. For 1976, the engines retained their 1975 configurations.

The biggest differences between the engine cases used in VWs versus the Porsches is that the Porsches have the dipstick tube on the top of the case. The heads for the 1.7 are the same for VW or Porsche, although emissions controls may have required air injection ports in some heads. The same is true for the 1.8-liter engines. All 1.7- and 1.8-liter engines share the same crank. The same is true for the 2.0-liter VW and Porsche engines. All the fans are the same.

Differences occur in timing mark placement, distributor types, and style of cooling sheet metal. The 914 2.0-liter also has its own unique heater boxes and exhaust.

Care and Maintenance

The four-cylinder engines in the 914 may not have the racing history or mechanical sex appeal of the six-cylinder but, if maintained properly, they are reliable. As with any VW, the key is to change the oil at the prescribed intervals and make sure that proper valve clearance is maintained. Other routine tune-up items include changing the spark plugs, plug wires, and points, plus setting the timing.

The ignition system is what was once considered a conventional breaker points system that is reliable and works well in the relatively low rpm range for which the engine was designed. I say once considered conventional because setting and replacement of points is almost a lost art due to today's distributor-less engines. Remember we are going back in time to the "flower power" era, and that means checking the point gap and replacing the breaker points on a regular basis.

To assure maximum performance, the point gap must be set with the assistance of a dwell meter. The dwell angle (gap) should be somewhere between 44 and 55 degrees for all rpm on 914s. Longtime 914 racer Lars Frohm suggests setting the dwell within its specified limits at 1,000 rpm and then revving the engine to check the dwell angle at 2,000 to 2,500 rpm. The reading at this rpm must not vary by more than plus or minus 1 degree. If the variance is greater than 1 degree it indicates that the bearings in the distributor are worn or that the cam profile that activates the points is worn. If there is any wear in the distributor, it must be either rebuilt or replaced for optimum performance. If there is a change of 0.004 inch (0.1 millimeter) in the points gap, it is the equivalent of approximately 3 degrees change in timing at the crankshaft.

For those of you who paid your dues and don't care to relive the point-setting days of the past, a number of breakerless systems are available in the aftermarket. As long as they are installed properly, they offer an improvement in reliability and performance. These systems have a high-capacity coil, a control module, and either an optical or a magnetic unit replacing the conventional breaker points. Lars equipped his car with an Allison system, and he is highly pleased with its performance. He cautions that if you decide to use one of these systems, or if you have a car that already has one of these systems, pay very close attention to the way it is installed. A poor installation could do more damage than good. For optimum results, all electrical connections should be soldered where they splice into the original system. Additionally, these connections should also be reinforced with a wire nut or other secure splicing device. This will prevent any loose wiring joints and voltage loss or power drop in the ignition circuit.

Lars points to another problem area in the distributor, the vacuum-activated timing advance. A clear indication of problems with this is that the car lacks power under full throttle. The operation of the vacuum advance can easily be checked with a timing light. You want to be sure that this system is moving all the way to its prescribed full advance. The timing specifications vary from model to model, so consult your service manual or mechanic for the correct specifications.

A good place to look when problems affect the timing advance would be the mechanical weights incorporated into the distributor that assist with advancing the timing at higher rpm. These weights must move freely to do their job. Dirt and dust may have collected on the plate or pins that support the weights, preventing their moving as freely as they should. Another trouble spot is that the vacuum unit itself may have developed a leak. Vacuum units, on any car, incorporate a rubber diaphragm that can crack from heat and age. The fix is to replace the vacuum unit.

There seem to be as many theories on valve adjustment for 914s as there are valves. Everyone has a preferred method of doing it. The important thing to remember is that no matter how you do it, it should be done every 3,000 miles to make sure that you are getting all the performance you can out of your car and to avoid burned or damaged valves. Of course, improperly adjusting valves can be worse than letting them fend for themselves.

Rotor pointing at mark on distributor housing to indicate TDC for No. 1 cylinder. www.pelicanparts.com

How do you know when a valve is properly adjusted? First make sure that the valves are cold before you start checking clearances. When checking the valve clearance, a properly set valve will put a slight bit of resistance on the feeler gauge as you slide it in or out. If you have to jam the feeler gauge into position, the valve is too tight. If you don't feel any drag on the gauge, then it's too loose.

A method for adjusting valves that you may want to try goes as follows. Locate Top Dead Center (TDC) for the No. 1 cylinder by removing the distributor cap so that you can see the position of the rotor. Place the car in fifth gear and roll it back until the rotor points at the notch on the distributor housing. As the rotor begins to move into this position, look in the timing port of the fan housing to see if the white tim-

Location of cap covering timing mark inspection hole in top of fan shroud. www.pelicanparts.com

Looking through hole on top of fan shroud at TDC mark on fan impeller. www.pelicanparts.com

ing mark on the fan is also lining up with the mark on the fan housing. When both the rotor and the fan marker align with their appropriate indicators, you have arrived at TDC for cylinder No. 1.

Leave the car in fifth gear and jack up the car. Make sure it is secured on jack stands. Once it's safe and secure, look under the car where the engine and transmission meet, and you will find a hole that will allow you to see the flywheel. After lining up the marks as described previously to locate TDC for cylinder No.1, place a white mark on the flywheel to indicate this point. As you rotate one of the rear wheels it will

Hole at bottom of transmission allows you to see mark made by factory to indicate TDC for piston No. 2 and No. 4. You will make a mark at the opposite side of the flywheel to indicate TDC for No. 1 and No. 3. Line up appropriate mark in this hole to adjust valves. www.pelicanparts.com

cause the flywheel to turn. As the flywheel turns you will see a notch that the factory put on the flywheel to indicate TDC for cylinders No. 2 and No. 4 come into view. It will be 180 degrees from the mark you made on the flywheel to indicate TDC for cylinders No. 1 and 3.

Now you're ready to adjust the valves. Remove the valve covers, having a rag or towel handy to catch whatever oil may drip when the covers come off. Hold one rear tire stationary while moving the other in a clockwise direction, as if the car were traveling in reverse. Stop when your white mark on the flywheel appears in the inspection hole and the rotor aligns with its mark on the distributor. This will be TDC for piston No. 1. Adjust the valves for cylinder No. 1. Use a 13-millimeter wrench to loosen the lock nut for the adjusting screw on each valve. Insert the proper size feeler gauge in the valve gap and turn the adjusting screw so that there is a slight drag on the feeler gauge when you pull it out. Once you have this setting, tighten the lock nut with the wrench while you hold the screw steady with the screwdriver. After tightening, measure again with the feeler gauge to be sure to gap hasn't changed. When you are done, rotate the rear wheel about 90 degrees and the notch on the flywheel should appear indicating TDC for cylinder No. 2. Adjust the valves for that cylinder. Keep going in a clockwise direction to adjust the other two cylinders. Remember that with one rear wheel stationary, for every 90 degree rotation of the other rear wheel, the crankshaft rotates 180 degrees.

Engine Rebuilding

Because of its VW roots, a wide variety of aftermarket options exist for anyone considering rebuilding a 914 engine. The dividing line seems to be those people who want reliability

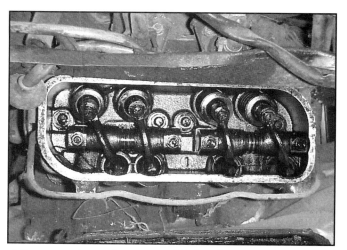

After removing valve cover, this is what you should see. www.pelicanparts.com

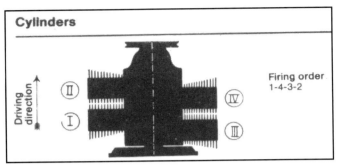

Mark cylinders according to diagram, so that you will know which is which when you are under the car.
www.pelicanparts.com

and endurance with maybe a tad more power versus those who are willing to sacrifice fuel mileage, driveability, and long engine life for instant gratification when they step on the gas. Since the scope of this book is based on a car that can be driven to work and to the occasional autocross or track event, I'll let the big motor crowd fend for themselves. As for the daily drivers, Brian Kumamoto has been driving his 1974 2.0-liter to work for a number of years. I'm going to let him tell you how he took the conservative approach and ended up with a motor that gets him to work every day with no problems, while probably putting out 10 more horses than the stock 2.0-liter. Here's Brian's engine rebuild story.

2.0-Liter Engine Rebuild

By Brian Kumamoto

The 914 engine, when properly maintained, is extremely durable. However, it does have its limits.

When my 914 turned the 200,000 mile mark, its original 2.0 engine was clearly tiring. It still ran well, and very strong, but had increased its appetite for oil and smoked mildly upon hard acceleration. Given that I had just completed a cosmetic restoration of the car, along with a transaxle rebuild, the time seemed right to finish off the car with a complete engine rebuild. My first step was research, and lots of it. Maintaining the fuel injection was a must, but I wanted to gain as much reasonably priced, reliable horsepower as possible. Engine longevity was also a priority. The first engine went 200,000 miles, and I wanted the second engine to at least come close to achieving that feat.

After many months of research, I began assembling parts for the rebuild. I opted to use new European spec pistons and cylinders. European pistons are very closely related to their U.S. cousins, but do not have the "dished" tops of the U.S. pistons. This increases the compression ratio from 7.6 to 8.0, a modest increase worth around five percent more horsepower.

Next came the camshaft. There are a few camshafts available which are reground to supposedly produce more horsepower, even with the stock fuel injection. However, after carefully reviewing as much material as I could find on these camshafts, I decided to stick with a new factory unit. My concerns about the aftermarket grinds were many. First, the D-Jetronic fuel injection system is a "pulse" system, of which piston and valve timing is an integral part. Changing the cam grind could have an effect on the entire system that I could not predict to my satisfaction. Second, all of the claimed increased horsepower (which was not much) appeared to be at the upper end of the rpm range, sometimes right at or

Using a feeler gauge to measure clearance for the exhaust valve on No. 1 cylinder. www.pelicanparts.com

A 13-millimeter wrench will loosen retaining nut for adjustment screw. www.pelicanparts.com

Procedure for tightening retaining nut after valve clearance is adjusted. Screwdriver holds adjusting screw in proper position while nut is tightened. **www.pelican-parts.com**

above redline. On a street driver, this is of limited use. I was not willing to trade a slight horsepower increase at this limited range for the likely loss of horsepower and torque in the midrange (where the vast majority of street driving is done). I bought a new factory camshaft, cam gear, and cam followers.

Aftermarket stainless steel valves are available for the 914, but I opted to buy new OEM valves. The 2.0 exhaust valves are sodium filled, which aids in keeping the valves cool. The stainless steel valves are a lot cheaper, but to me were not worth the risk of a valve overheating, breaking, and getting intimate with one of my brand new pistons at 5,000 rpm. The factory valves lasted 200,000 miles, and that was good enough for me (actually, even at 200,000 miles, the valves still measured within spec and could have been reused, but I felt they had done their job and deserved an "early" retirement).

After carefully marking and removing all of the various connections (watch that transmission ground strap attached to the bottom of the trunk!), I dropped the engine and transmission out of the car. I separated the engine and transmission, and mounted the engine on a rolling engine stand in my garage.

I had originally intended to rebuild the engine myself, farming out the machine work that was beyond my capabilities. However, after looking at the box of fairly expensive new engine parts sitting in the corner, I started to get cold feet. Visions of rods flying through the case because of one slight misstep in assembly haunted me at night.

FAT Performance, in Orange, California, is a well-known builder of Type IV engines, and had helped me in my research of rebuild options. I called and asked how much they would charge to assemble the long block (i.e., the case, pistons, and heads). I was surprised to find out that the labor was less than $400. Additionally, they were more than happy to allow me to come in and follow the project, which was important to me because I intended for this to be a learning experience. Figuring the cost of professional help was cheap insurance, I stripped the engine down to the heads and dropped it off at FAT.

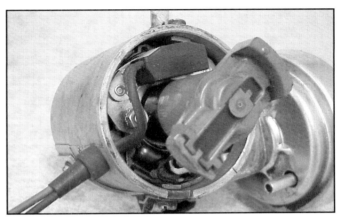

Electronic ignition units use either magnetic or optical sensors and detectors to eliminate the need for adjusting and checking points. Installation is farily easy. **www.pelicanparts.com**

The heart of the engine is the crankshaft. Part of any rebuild should include Magnafluxing the crank to check for cracks. My crank had no cracks, but had a deep groove worn in the flywheel end. This groove was welded up and polished. The crank was then cleaned up, micropolished, and ready to go.

The connecting rods were also checked for cracks (fortunately there were none), and had the small ends rebushed. The rods, pistons, and crank were then carefully balanced to ensure a smooth running engine.

The case was checked for straightness, and align bored to give the crank a nice straight bore to spin in. Prior to bringing the engine in, I had removed all of the factory press-fit oil galley plugs, tapped threads into the oil galleys, and screwed pipe plugs in. This is important, as one of the original galley plugs had once let loose while I was on the road, causing an immediate loss of almost all the oil, and a very soaked clutch.

The heads on the 914 are a bit of a weak spot. While generally in good shape, my heads had cracks around three of the spark plug holes. This is apparently very common. These cracks needed to be welded. Additionally, it is important on a full rebuild that the valve seats be replaced. It is not that uncommon for old valve seats (or new valve seats that were improperly installed) to fall off, causing absolute havoc in the combustion chamber. The new valves were installed, along with new valve guides, adjustment screws, springs, and retainers.

I was presented with a couple of options with the heads, both of which would presumably improve performance. The first was to deck the heads, which essentially reduces the size of the combustion chamber, raising compression. Basically, the compression can be set as high as you dare. I opted to bump the compression ratio from 8 to 1 to 8.5 to 1, a fairly modest increase that I figured would bump horsepower up an additional five percent or so. The second option was to "port" the heads and have the combustion chambers polished. This was supposed to increase flow, and give a bit more power. Because this seemed to not affect reliability, I had the work done. However, I have since learned that polishing the combustion chambers arguably will hurt, rather than help, performance, because air flowing over a smooth surface is actually subject to more surface tension than air flowing over a rougher surface. People probably have different theories on this, but in hindsight I personally would not pay to have the combustion chambers polished again.

I picked the engine up from FAT and brought it home with great excitement. I placed it back on the engine stand and began the task of reassembling the exterior pieces. While the engine was being rebuilt, I had repainted all of the sheet metal. I had also purchased a new alternator, all new sensors and switches, new plugs, wires, rotor, cap, filters, engine mounts, and everything else that could be reasonably replaced. Because I had carefully marked and bagged everything during disassembly, and taken plenty of pictures during the process, everything went back together very nicely. I have enjoyed my rejuvenated 914 for many years now, driving it every day in almost complete reliability.

Epilogue

"Rebuild" means many different things to different people. When having your 914 engine rebuilt, it is important to be involved and know exactly what work is being done, and what kinds of parts are being used. I sometimes see "rebuilt" 914 2.0 engines offered for sale for less than $1,000. Unless the businesses selling these engines are in the business of losing money, it is hard for me to believe they are selling engines that are rebuilt from the crank up using new, factory parts. The cost of the new parts that I used, even at wholesale prices, comes close to or exceeds $1,000. Most likely these engines reuse the old pistons, cylinders, valves, and other parts. While this may be perfectly acceptable, it is important that you at least be aware of what you are (and are not) getting. The same holds true when your engine is being rebuilt by a shop.

Replacing Your Four-Cylinder with a Six-Cylinder

This is a popular but expensive and extensive project. There are a number of companies that will sell you conversion kits to put 911 motors in the engine compartment where a four-banger used to live. Engine options range from the 2.4-liter of the 1972–73 911 era all the way up to 3.2- and even 3.6-liter late-model engines. But if you do it right and upgrade all the necessary components to handle all the extra power, when you are done you will have what is essentially a 911 in 914 clothing. These can be fast, fun, and reliable cars if properly done. I won't get into doing one of these conversions other than to tell you that thorough research will help you best decide what and if you should build one of these cars. Talk to knowledgeable 911 experts about the performance capabilities of engines, transmission, brakes, and suspension components. Talk to people who have built or had cars built for them. Set a realistic budget in time and dollars. If after all that you decide to go ahead with the project, once you have completed the car call me up and let me give it a test drive.

Fuel Injection/ Fuel System

Admittedly, the 914 does have its shortcomings, the brakes and shift mechanism deservedly receiving harsh criticism almost from the beginning, but one area that has unjustifiably suffered at the hands of owners and mechanics is the fuel injection system used on the four-cylinder cars. The 914 was ahead of its time, not only as the first electronically fuel-injected Porsche, but one of the few cars available at all 30 years ago with EFI.

As a result, there were very few mechanics trained to deal with these systems and owners were even less skilled in the proper care and maintenance of such systems. The carburetor was still king, and to anyone caught up in the romance of sports cars and racing, the Weber carb was the king of kings. Remember that this was also the period when enthusiasts saw emissions controls as the death of engine performance. The highly responsive small displacement motors that made entry level sports cars fun were being saddled with auxiliary equipment that eliminated their personalities along with tailpipe emissions. There were even those who viewed this new technology as a step toward eliminating the right of every wrench-toting American to work on his car.

Clogged or leaky injectors need to be replaced with new units. www.pelicanparts.com

The fuel injection suffered by its association with the advent of the smog controls.

The bottom line for the 914's fuel delivery system was that rather than learn to deal with it, owners and mechanics either jury-rigged ways around certain parts of it or tossed it all out and got back to the basics of carburetion.

Living in the enlightened and politically correct period that we do and benefiting from the hindsight that it affords us, almost all 914 enthusiasts realize that Porsche had the right idea when it chose fuel injection over carburetors for the 914, especially for daily driving chores. Stricter emissions laws have also played a role in the trend to reinject, so to speak, originality to the 914 fuel delivery system. For many years, until a recent law excluded cars 25 years and older from emissions testing, carburetted 914s were practically given away in the California used car market because they couldn't be legally registered. And if they somehow were registered, there was the specter of failing the biannual emissions inspection. Replacing the fuel injection, and related emissions equip-

Pressure sensor makes car run lean or rich. www.pelicanparts.com

ment, was the only way to comply with the law. The problem was that over the years discarded smog equipment has become a scarce commodity. It's hard to find the parts necessary to reassemble a complete system.

The change in the California law does take some of the pressure off when it comes to having a complete emissions-friendly setup. Other states are adopting similar laws to California's. Technically, it's still illegal in California to not run the required smog equipment in older cars, but the odds of getting caught have gone way down.

As for running a fuel injection system, as opposed to carburetors, most 914 owners today see a well-maintained, properly adjusted fuel injection system giving better performance over the complete range of daily driving, and with less tinkering than carburetors.

Two kinds of fuel injection were used in the 914. Both were made by Bosch with joint development work by Volkswagen. The 1.7-liter and 2.0-liter engines used the D-Jetronic system, which measured manifold pressure and engine speed to match fuel delivery with engine load. The later 1.8-liter cars used the L-Jetronic system, which used a flap-type sensor that measured incoming air flow, as opposed to manifold pressure. In an odd turn of events during 1976, just as the 914 was being phased out in favor of the 924, Porsche reintroduced a version of the 912, the model that the 914 replaced in 1970. The 1976 912E had the same engine as the 2.0-liter 914, but it used the L-Jetronic fuel injection.

You will also hear the D-Jet referred to as the MPC system, for Manifold Pressure Controlled, and the L-Jet called the AFC, for Air Flow Controlled. Basically, with the exception of measuring manifold pressure versus air flow, both systems operate in a similar fashion. Data collected by engine sensors is relayed to the ECU, or brain box, which processes the data and then transmits electronic signals to the fuel injectors to mete out the proper amount of fuel.

On the D-Jet, a set of contact points located in the base of the distributor determines the opening and closing of the injectors in relation to the crankshaft. For the L-Jet, this information is read by the ECU directly from the distributor and then used to trigger the injectors. Though not exactly the same, the following information is basically the same for both systems. The richness of the mixture is fine-tuned by a temperature sensor located in the right cylinder head near the No. 3 spark plug. It reads engine temperature and relays that information to the ECU for fuel enrichment calculation. Another temperature sensor is located in the air intake to read the temperature of incoming air. A cold-start valve and thermo-time switch spray extra fuel for cold starting when the

Cylinder head temp sensor, temp sensor II, could be the cause of stalling or flat spots at certain rpm levels.
www.pelicanparts.com

With the proper test equipment, a fuel injection expert can take pressure readings at various places in the system to spot any problems in the regulation of either fuel or air supply. This includes testing the injectors for both the quantity of fuel they supply and the spray pattern of the fuel. A reduction in fuel supply by an injector will result in its cylinder suffering fuel starvation in relation to the other three cylinders causing uneven running of the engine and misfiring. Even the smallest difference in spray pattern from one injector versus the others will cause a power loss. Replace any injector that shows evidence of a leak, lack of fuel delivery, or other than perfect spray pattern.

starter is on and the engine is cold. An auxiliary air regulator supplies additional air during the engine warm-up phase.

The 1.7-liter engines used an oil bath air cleaner system that can be updated by fitting the later paper filter units. This is an especially important modification if you plan on doing any competition driving, in which extreme cornering conditions can cause the oil in the filter to slosh into the intake.

An electric fuel pump draws fuel from the front-mounted fuel tank through a series of rubber hoses that lead to the fuel injectors. An adjustable fuel pressure regulator maintains fuel pressure at 28 psi for U.S. cars. The fuel pump was moved to the front of the car in 1975 to cure chronic vapor lock problems in earlier cars. The problem was that the old location of the fuel pump, just in front of the right rear wheel, placed it out of the reach of any cooling airflow and in close proximity to the heat of the exhaust system.

Maintenance and Troubleshooting

Entire books can and have been written on the Bosch fuel injection systems. I don't intend to make you an expert on these systems. I only want to give you an overview of the basic differences between the two systems used on the 914 along with enough information for you to be able to at least understand what may be causing a particular problem. Many running changes were made to these systems over the years. Pressure sensor calibrations are not only distinctive for engine size but, in some cases, model year. Unless you take the time to study and become an expert on your car's fuel injection, it's better to leave any repairs to a trained technician. Tinkering may make a minor problem worse.

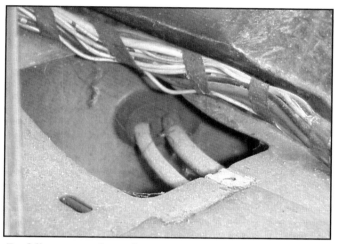

Fuel lines pass through a rubber grommet at the forward part of center tunnel. www.pelicanparts.com

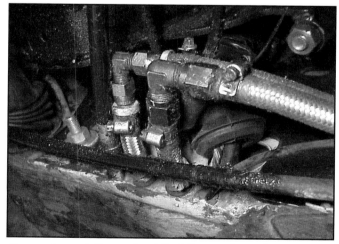

Connectors at the ends of fuel lines, where they exit from the firewall into the engine compartment.
www.pelicanparts.com

Common Problems

Trouble	Cause	Solution
Engine does not start, fuel pump not working	Defective connections to pump or relay Fuse 8A blown	Check connections Replace fuse
Engine does not start, fuel pump is running	No fuel pressure in main line Engine floods with fuel	Check fuel filter and fuel lines for damage Check temperature sensor Check pressure sensor
Engine starts from cold then stalls	Defective trigger contacts in distributor Defective pressure sensor	Clean or replace contacts Replace pressure sensor
Engine misfires and quits	Dirty or defective trigger contacts	Clean or replace trigger contacts
Engine runs poorly, one cylinder not running	Sticking injector	Replace injector
Engine misfires	Loose wiring or ground connections	Check wiring, ground straps, injector wiring
Engine does not produce full power	Defective pressure sensor Clogged injectors	Replace pressure sensor Replace or clean injectors
Excessive fuel consumption	Defective temperature sensor or trigger contact resistance	Test connections, replace parts if necessary

Surging at idle, 1,000 to 2,000 rpm	Leak between auxiliary air regulator
	  and intake distributor
	Leak at throttle valve housing
	Leak in hoses between intake distributor
	  and intake manifold
		Replace hose
		
		Replace gasket
		
		Tighten or replace hoses

Poor idle, hesitation on acceleration	Incorrect timing or idle setting Loose vacuum hoses	Check and adjust Tighten or replace

There are some things you can do to troubleshoot your system. One is to make sure that all hoses and vacuum lines are in good condition and tightly connected. Many of the 914 fuel injection problems can be caused by air leaks. Other causes of problems are broken or loose wiring connections. Just like the hoses, many of these cars have 25-year-old wiring and insulation. Make sure all the contacts are clean, including the extra set of points in the distributor on the D-Jet. The fuel pump relay contacts should also be inspected and cleaned. After 25 years, a new relay may be needed. Make sure the rubber boots on the injectors are in good shape. Double-check the wires of the injectors, especially where they are grounded to the engine case. Make sure the oil filler cap is clean and tight-fitting. A clean air filter is also important.

The above chart depicts common problems with probable causes and solutions. Due to the many variables and interrelated forces at work, there could be other causes and solutions for some of the afore mentioned problems.

Flammable "Fourteens"

Although they don't rival the late Ford Pinto as incendiary devices, 914s do seem to have a slightly higher propensity for fires than other cars. Part of the problem is that, as we have pointed out before, they are around 25 years old and things like rubber or plastic fuel lines tend to decay and leak over the years. Having a battery perched on a tray hovering over the engine and a high pressure (28.5 psi) fuel system adds more volatility to the situation. Some cars were also delivered with faulty fuel lines when new. Porsche issued a safety recall on these cars but who knows how many of these cars were ever brought in to be repaired. It may not be a bad idea to check your car's VIN number with the list that your local dealer should be able to access to see if your car qualifies for this fix.

When replacing the fuel lines in your car, it is important to use the high quality materials. Redoing the plastic lines that run through the car with stainless steel lines is an upgrade that can be carried over to the engine compartment. Make sure that whatever hose you buy can handle the high pressure of the fuel injection. It's a good idea to disconnect the battery for safety's sake when working with fuel lines.

Fuel Tank Removal

You must remove the fuel tank to replace the lines that go from the engine compartment to the fuel tank. Cars made from 1970 through 1974 will require both 7-millimeter and 9-millimeter fuel lines. The smaller lines are the return lines to the tank. The later cars use all 7-millimeter lines.

Some people feel that a good first step is to remove the hood for more maneuvering room and to prevent scratching the hood. Others feel it just slows down the process. Once you've had someone help you take off the hood, it's time to drain the fuel tank. Knowing you were going to tackle this project in advance would let you run down the fuel in the tank until it was nearly empty. Remember to disconnect the battery before draining the fuel tank.

There are also two schools of thought regarding draining the tank. Some people remove the protective plate for the steering rack from the bottom of the car. This allows access for disconnecting the hose that runs from the bottom of the tank to let the gasoline drain into a suitable gasoline container. Once the tank has been drained, remove the overfill canister and disconnect the fuel sender line. Loosen the strap that holds the tank in place. Carefully lift the tank out of the car.

The quick and dirty method is to drive the car until the fuel is at a very low level in the tank. Then you loosen the retaining strap and tilt the tank toward the driver's side of the car so that whatever gas remains won't spill out. After removing the fuel line connections, just lift the tank and pour the remaining gas into a gas can.

Whatever method you choose to remove the tank, now is a good time to inspect the tank inside and out. Clean out any dirt and debris that has gotten inside the tank.

Start removing all the plastic gas lines. Pull up the carpet under the dash. If you have a center console, you will have to remove it to gain access to the center tunnel. Remove the two lines that are attached to a grommet in the wall. Go to the rear of the car and yank these lines out through the engine compartment. It may be necessary to use the access holes in the center tunnel to work the lines through to the rear.

When installing the new lines through the center tunnel, it is a good idea to tape over the ends to avoid getting any dirt inside the hoses. When you go to run the hoses from the hard lines to the tank, make the new lines running to the tank a bit longer than the OEM lines to allow for extra working room the next time you have to remove the tank. Don't make them too long or they may develop kinks. Be sure that no fuel lines or wiring get crimped under or around the sides of the tank when you put the tank back in place. Check for leaks before refilling the tank completely.

Fuel System—914/6

Compared to the four-cylinder cars, the fuel system in the six-cylinder is very simple. The most exotic parts are the two triple-throat Weber carburetors. The setup is very similar to that used in the 911 from 1966 to 1969. A Hardi electric fuel pump is used. The air cleaner uses a paper filter element.

10

Clutch/ Transmission

One of the biggest problems facing engineers who design midengine cars is where and how to locate the transmission and shift linkage. Porsche's solution for the 914 was to reverse its 901 gearbox, the five-speed unit that was used in the 911 until 1972, and mount it backward. The shift linkage design included a series of rods linked together that ran through a tunnel in the chassis and out through the engine compartment all the way to the rear, or tail, of the gearbox. Hence the name tail-shifter.

Anyone who has driven one of the early four-cylinder cars doesn't need to be told that this was not the best arrangement in the world. It was obvious to Porsche's drivetrain engineers who devised a new linkage that first appeared in 1973. Porsche made very few major changes to the 914 in its brief life span, but apparently felt that the shift linkage definitely warranted an upgrade.

What Porsche did was simplify the number of parts used in the linkage and also shorten its path by hooking it up to the side of the gearbox. That's why it's called a side-shifter.

The 901 gearbox is a five-speed that some people call a "dogleg" box, while others also refer to it as having a "racing" shift pattern.

Both these nicknames refer to the shift pattern, which has first gear over to the left and down, while two through five are in the 'H' pattern. Reverse is up from first. During your first day or two in a 914, you may find yourself slogging away from lights in second, but you quickly adapt to this pattern. It's an ideal setup for racing or even spirited street driving because of the straight path between second and third. It's a stout gearbox that saw duty in some of the factory race cars.

Because the 914/6 never survived to see 1973, it never received the linkage upgrade. It used a slightly different version of the early four-cylinder tail-shifter. The legendary 916 had the newer 915 gearbox modified with an endplate to fit in the 914. The gearboxes designed for the 916 are a rarity. Not as rare as the 916 model itself, Porsche having built a few gearboxes before deciding not to go ahead with plans to market the car. You will find many 914 fans referring to them as a 916 gearbox, but the 916 gearbox according to the definitive book of Porsche history, *Excellence Was Expected* by Karl Ludvigsen, was the transaxle originally used in the 908/2 race cars. The 915 was actually a street version adaptation of the racing 916 gearbox.

The later side-shifter is the way to go in any 914. It's still not what you could call slick-shifting or precise by comparison to modern cars like Hondas or the Mazda Miata, but it is serviceable if properly adjusted and maintained. Many early cars have been converted to side-shifters. As we pointed out in the buyer's guide section, if you are contemplating buying a pre-1973 car, the most desirable are those that have had this conversion.

Just because the 914 linkage falls short of modern expectations, don't assume that you should settle for sloppy shifting in any 914, early or later model. These cars are almost all over a quarter of a century old and many have suffered the abuse of people who didn't care or didn't know how to shift or maintain their cars. New bushings can do wonders to improve the feel of 914 shifters. It's also important to remember that Porsches do not like to be hurried or slammed into gear. They respond best to smooth, deliberate movement through the shift pattern from one gear to the next. Try pausing ever so slightly in neutral before selecting the next gear. Your shifting will go a lot better and your synchros will last a lot longer.

Let's take a look at some of the things that can be done to improve the gear selection process in the 914.

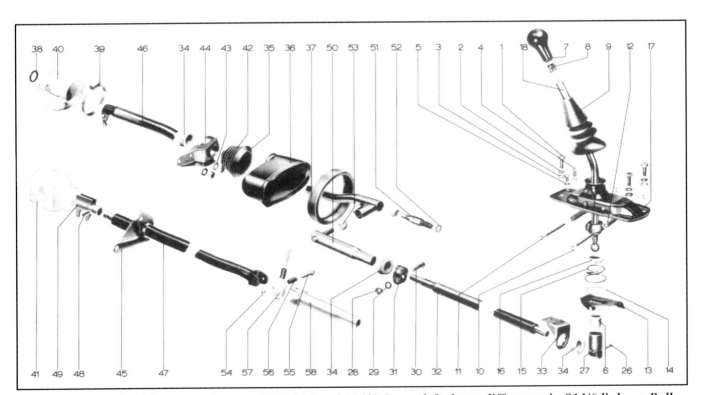

Illustration of tail-shifter, as used on pre-1973 914 and 914/6. Lower left shows differences in 914/6 linkage. Ball socket is No. 6, while two bushings are No. 34. Bushing for 914/6 linkage is No. 56. Porsche AG

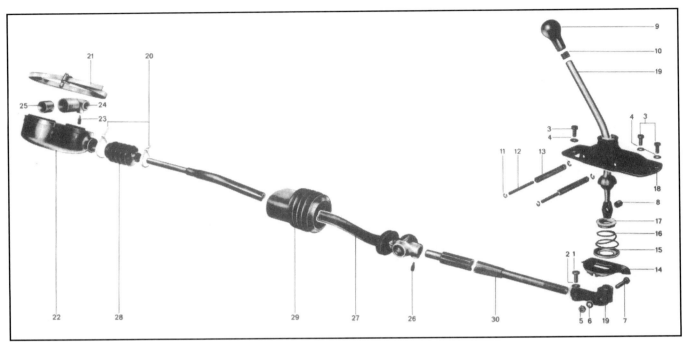

In 1973 the less complicated side-shifter was introduced. Shift rod head is No. 24; ball socket No. 25; and tapered screws are No. 23 and No. 26. Spacer bushing is No. 8; front shift rod is No. 30. Shifter springs are No. 13. **Porsche AG**

Transmission Tune-Up Tips: Don't Settle for Sloppy Seconds, or Thirds, Fourths, and Fifths

Before you start contemplating a rebuild of your 914 transmission, there are a number of inexpensive tune-up procedures you can perform that produce amazing results given the cost and time they require. Rebuilt transmissions are expensive, so it's worth your while to make sure that you really need a new or reconditioned transmission. If you do go transmission shopping, make sure you deal with reputable people and be wary of bargain basement rebuilds. Check out what the parts cost will be if you were to do it yourself and then figure out a reasonable price for labor. Anyone charging less than your estimate must be cutting costs somewhere, probably by not replacing all the parts they should. Averaging out the fact that the necessary new parts needed will vary with the condition of the transmission, presently the wholesale cost of parts to rebuild a 901 transmission would roughly be about $400.

It is possible to nurse a transmission with a worn synchro for a long time before you definitely need to replace it. For a raspy second gear, or any of the higher gears, gently blipping the throttle as you shift should speed up the gears enough to let you ease into gear without grinding.

Before engaging first, it's always a good idea, with any Porsche, to pause a bit after pushing in the clutch. Another trick is to shift into second or third before going into first as a way to take the strain off the first gear synchro.

Straight Talk About Side-Shifters

If you do need a new transmission, the obvious choice would be a side-shifter. This will allow you to move up to the better shifting side-shifter linkage. It is possible to convert the 901 gearbox used in the early cars to a later configuration but it does involve disassembling the gearbox to replace the shift forks and a change of input parts. As long as you're inside, you'll also want to do whatever R and R is necessary on worn parts. In effect, rebuild the gearbox. That's why in most cases it's simpler to just purchase a rebuilt later style gearbox.

Getting the new gearbox is only part of the conversion. Apart from your old shift knob, you will need entirely new linkage. You will also have to change the engine mount bar, since the shift linkage passes through at a different offset. The later cars also have different cooling tin, notably the left side lower deflector plate (022 119 356B), which has an indentation for clearance of the shift rod.

Rear ball cup bushing and shifter rod bushing.
www.pelicanparts.com

Once you have all the parts assembled, it is pretty much a bolt-in operation, albeit an extensive one including the removal of the engine and transmission.

Adding the new engine mount bar points up another solution to loose shifting in the 914. Worn engine mounts can cause the entire engine/transmission assembly to shift under acceleration, throwing off the alignment of the shift linkage, as well as the proper adjustment of the clutch and throttle cables. The later style engine mount bar has the improved silent block rubber bushings for extra cushioning.

When installing the new linkage, make sure that new linkage bushings are added at the same time, making the entire assembly as precise as possible.

The 914/6 can also be converted to a side-shifter. It does not need a new engine mount, but does require modification to the aft shift rod in order to clear the left side heat exchanger.

Tired Shifters Feel Better After Getting Bushed

Having a side-shifter is no guarantee that all your shifting woes will be cured. It's important that all the bushings and couplings between the shift rods and transmission are in optimum condition. One of the first places to attack is the rear ball cup bushing that is located under the large dust boot (No. 22) where the linkage attaches to the gearbox. Refer to the main diagram of the later style linkage for further clarification of this procedure. Loosen and remove the rear tapered screw (No. 23) and the forward tapered screw (No. 26) to separate the rear shift rod (No. 27) from the front rod. This should just pull out. Once you have this bar loose, you can slide the shift rod head (No. 24) off. Remove the old ball cup bushing, and snap on a new one after giving it a light coating of lithium grease. Reassembly is the reverse of disassembly.

Make sure the two tapered screws mentioned in the previous instruction are in good shape and properly secured. Obviously, loose or missing screws will cause shifting problems. The rear shift rod also has a bushing at its end that may require replacement. This may either be replaced by a bronze bushing or a cheaper OEM style plastic bushing. Either one can be changed while you have the rod out for replacement of the rear ball cup bushing.

A bit more complicated to replace is the bushing in the firewall, which keeps the shift rods from wiggling about. To remove this bushing, you must first remove the rear shift rod as previously discussed and then pull out the front shift rod. The latter is best removed by pulling it forward. To do this, you must go inside the car and disconnect the three mounting bolts that hold the shift lever in place. Once the lever is loose, pull it forward, taking the front shift rod with it. This

Shift rod bushing located in firewall. www.pelican-parts.com

Close up of 911 motor mount used in place of 914 transmission mount. This is considered an inexpensive upgrade. www.pelicanparts.com

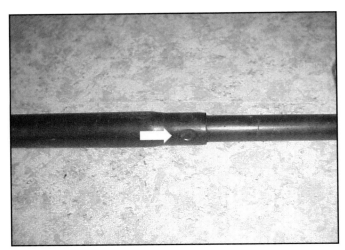

Weld at rear of shift rod on side-shifter linkage.
www.pelicanparts.com

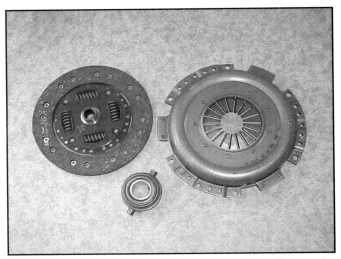

Complete clutch kit includes flywheel, clutch disc, and pressure plate, along with new flywheel bolts and throw-out bearing. Clutch shown is standard 914 unit; the six-spring 911 unit is preferable. www.pelican-parts.com

will save you the problem of readjusting the shift lever linkage after you have finished.

Now you can pry the old bushing out and put a new one in place. The new one will fit a lot tighter than the old one (that's why you're doing this) so it will take a bit to work it in place.

Once you've got the new bushing installed, it's time to reinsert the front shift rod through the firewall. Take off the inspection plate that sits under the center console, between the seats, to get a better grip on the rod to slide it back into the bushing.

Before reassembling everything, you may want to examine the shift lever to make sure it is free from cracks, especially along the seal at its base where it is attached to the ball. Check for missing or loose springs in the shifter assembly. These provide the tension to keep you from nicking reverse as you shift from first to second. Heavier springs are available, if you feel the need for additional protection.

This would also be a good time to make sure that your shift lever is aligned with the shift rod for proper gear selection. The adjustment bolt (No. 1) can be loosened to move the shifter as needed. In neutral, move the shift lever to the right until you hit the stop that would be between fourth and fifth gears. Twist the shift rod to the right (clockwise) to the stop, then tighten the adjustment bolt. You should be able to move easily between all the gears and up from first without hitting reverse. Once you are satisfied, securely tighten down the adjustment bolt and replace the inspection cover plate and anything else that you removed to get to the shifter assembly.

Short shift kits are available that change the ball attached to the base of the shifter in an effort to reduce the length of the throws and improve the feel of the shifting process. They have their advocates and detractors. They will not make up for misalignment or worn bushings. Their detractors say that over time these shifters can cause premature transmission wear. My personal experience is that while I have been happy with short shift kits in 911s, I don't think that they are worth the time and expense to install on a 914. If anything, installing one may be a step backward. Just keep practicing that smooth, steady shifting with a slight pause between

Clutch cable pulley. www.pelicanparts.com

Flywheel is locked with metal bar to allow removal of the flywheel bolts. www.pelicanparts.com

gears and you'll be much better off. As we stated before, the gearbox pattern of having second situated above third negates the need for a shorter route between the two gears you would use most on an autocross or tight road course.

We've already discussed motor mounts as a cause of shifting problems; here are more details on that subject. If you want to check on the condition of your motor and transmission mounts, jack up the car by placing a floor jack under the middle section of the transmission. If the engine/transmission rises without any significant action on the part of the chassis, your mounts have had it. Wayne Dempsey of Pelican Parts suggests using 911 motor mounts as an alternative to the 914 parts. They cost about half as much.

Replacement is a fairly easy process. Jack up the car and place a support under the transmission. Unbolt the transmission mounts, then lower the car slightly to remove and replace the mounts. The engine mounts can be done in similar fashion. Hardcore racers may want to substitute solid transmission mounts to completely remove any flexing of the transmission and its linkage under the stress imposed by track events.

Other Problems and Cures

If your car suddenly develops a will of its own as far as the shift pattern, you may have a broken weld in the shift rod. This will occur near the rear part of the aft shift rod in a later car. On early

cars, the weld will break on the shift rod that is located in the tube that runs through the chassis. Either one can be easily rewelded back together. A more serious problem occurs if the clutch tube breaks loose at the firewall and needs to be rewelded.

Don't forget to replace your transmission fluid at regular intervals. It's a good possibility that some 914s are still running with the fluid Porsche put in at the factory, or whatever portion of it that hasn't leaked out.

Clutch Replacement

Replacing the clutch on your 914 is not especially difficult but it does take, depending on your familiarity with the process and the difficulty of removing certain parts due to rust and long-term neglect, a good bit of time.

Wayne Dempsey of Pelican Parts has compiled a list of the parts necessary to perform the clutch replacement. I have reproduced that list below to give you an idea of the scope and cost of this undertaking. Wayne has also put together another list of contingency items that may be needed to properly complete the job, depending on the condition of these parts in your car. Reviewing this list should give you an idea of whether this is a task that you are willing to tackle yourself, or whether you should hand it off to a professional. If you have never done any of this work before but feel that you would like to take it on, bribing a friend who has had experience working on Porsches or Volkswagens to oversee your work would be well worth the cost of pizza and beer.

Although a picture of a 911 motor, the use of the clutch alignment tool to center the clutch disc is nearly the same for both motors. www.pelicanparts.com

You might be able to do all this in one day, but count on spending a weekend. The poet Robert Burns never got his hands greasy trying to smooth out the shifting of a 914; otherwise, he could have written at least a stanza or two more about the wayward paths that the plans of mice and men and midengine Porsche owners often take.

Ball that holds the throw-out fork may need to be shimmed to get proper half-inch of free play for clutch arm. www.pelicanparts.com

New throw-out bearing and reconditioned fork assembly in place. www.pelicanparts.com

Parts that you will most likely need:

- Pressure plate
- Clutch disc—the early 911 six-spring type is recommended over the virtually identical four-spring 914 type
- Throw-out bearing
- Throw-out fork bushing
- Pilot bearing (for flywheel) and felt
- 2 Throw-out bearing guide clips
- 2 CV joint gaskets
- 2 Muffler gaskets
- New or resurfaced flywheel (good core usually required in trade)
- Flywheel O-ring and metal washer/gasket
- New flywheel bolts
- Transmission fluid

Additional parts that you might need:

- Flywheel seal and mainshaft seal
- New clutch cable
- Throw-out arm retaining fork
- Locking cone screws
- Shift bushings

Following is a list of the tools that you will need in order to complete the job:

- CV bolt removal tool (Quality tool like Snap-On or Mac suggested)
- Large floor jack
- Clutch alignment tool
- A set of metric hex keys (sockets recommended)
- Torque wrench (capable of applying torque between 14.5 and 79.5 lb-ft)
- Flywheel locking tool

Now that you have the parts and tools required for the job, here is a list showing the order that should be followed to assure a complete and proper clutch replacement. Wayne suggests having this list handy while you are doing the work to avoid skipping or performing tasks out of order.

- Clean underside of car (take it to the coin-operated car wash and give the underside a good scrubbing)
- Loosen CV joints
- Elevate car (make sure it is solidly placed on jack stands)
- Remove muffler and muffler bracket (use plenty of WD-40 or Liquid Wrench to soak the bolts, so you don't break any during removal)
- Disconnect battery (VERY IMPORTANT to do before removing starter to avoid electrical shock)
- Disconnect speedometer cable
- Disconnect clutch cable
- Disconnect accelerator cable (914-6 only)
- Remove rear shift linkage
- Disconnect transmission ground strap
- Remove starter cable and backup lamp switch
- Remove starter bolts and starter
- Disconnect and bag CV joints
- Place jack stand under engine case—use a block of wood to maintain the proper height
- Support weight of engine-transmission with floor jack
- Disconnect transmission mounts
- Lower engine-transmission to rest on jack stand
- Unbolt remaining transmission to engine case bolts
- Slide out and lower transmission on floor jack, remove
- Remove one pressure plate bolt
- Attach flywheel lock
- Remove remaining pressure plate bolts
- Remove flywheel lock and pry out pressure plate
- Reattach flywheel lock, remove five flywheel bolts
- Remove flywheel lock, and flywheel
- Check flywheel seal for leakage or damage, replace if necessary
- Check flywheel to see if it is a good core

- Switch pressure plate guide pins from old flywheel to the new one
- Install flywheel O-ring into flywheel
- Install pilot bearing into flywheel
- Place flywheel on car with felt pad and crush washer
- Attach flywheel lock and torque bolts in cross pattern to 79.5 lb-ft
- Remove flywheel lock and place pressure plate disc on flywheel using clutch alignment tool
- Reattach flywheel lock and torque bolts on pressure plate to 14.5 lb-ft
- Remove throw-out arm from transmission
- Replace bushing, and inspect constraint fork
- Replace throw-out bearing and guide clips
- Grease shaft and tip of shaft, reattach throw-out arm
- Check transmission fluid level. Top off if necessary
- Reattach transmission and tighten bolts
- Check throw-out arm for proper clearance (should have half-inch of free play)
- Jack up engine-transmission assembly and reattach mounts
- Bolt on starter
- Reconnect starter electrical cable and back-up switch
- Reattach ground strap
- Reattach CV joints with new gaskets (add joint grease if necessary)
- Reattach clutch cable
- Reattach accelerator cable (914-6 only)
- Reattach speedometer cable
- Reattach shift linkage (replace bushings if needed)
- Reattach muffler and muffler bracket (replace gaskets if old)
- Adjust clutch
- Lower car
- Reattach battery ground
- Drive car, then readjust clutch and check for oil leaks

Wheels and Tires

The 914 sported some pretty sophisticated equipment when it came to market 30 years ago. It had electronic fuel injection, four-wheel disc brakes, a five-speed transmission, and, of course, the midengine layout. It was so far ahead of its time that this same package could debut today and still be considered modern and up-to-date. As long as you don't look down at its wheels and tires. The skinny wheels and tires that were standard equipment under all this sophisticated machinery are comparable to wearing a pair of Chuck Taylor model Converse basketball shoes with an Armani suit.

Not that this was any fault of Porsche, it just shows how much tire technology has advanced over 30 years. Through 1973, the stock wheels on the 914 were a set of Volkswagen painted steel rims measuring 4.5 inches wide and 15 inches tall. Even the base 914/6 rode on silver-painted steel wheels, although they were an inch wider than the four-cylinder wheels. In 1974, the standard steel wheel for the 914 was increased to 5.5 inches by 15 inches. The dated chrome-plated hubcaps were also deleted that year, as the standard wheel took on a hipper "mag wheel look," trimmed with black plastic covers for each lug bolt and a small center cap.

Mahle alloy wheels were an option on the 914/6. Said to be the lightest alloy wheels Porsche ever had, they are referred to as "gas-burners," not because of fuel mileage but for resemblance to the top of a kitchen stove. www.pelicanparts.com

Tires were either the standard 155x15 radials or the extra cost 165x15 radials.

An optional 5.5-inch steel wheel with a deeper offset was offered for the four-cylinder cars from 1970 to 1973. An alloy wheel manufactured by Pedrini that also measured 5.5x15

was yet another option on the four-cylinder cars from 1970 to 1973. The Fuchs (pronounced "fewks" in case your mom is listening) "2.0-liter" forged alloy made its debut in 1973 as part of the Appearance Group option package available for 2.0-liter cars. This wheel has four slightly raised spokes and bears a slight family resemblance to the famous five-spoke Fuchs alloy that has become synonymous with the early 911. The 2.0-liter Fuchs alloy used the same lug bolts and center caps as the Pedrini wheels.

The Mahle alloy wheel also shared those same lug bolts and center caps. It was first used on 1973 2.0-liter cars without the Appearance Group option. Its claim to fame was being fitted on the 1974 Limited Edition cars, painted to match the stripes and rocker trim. Painted silver, it was optional equipment for all other four-cylinder cars from 1974 to 1976. An important safety point concerning 914 wheels is that all the alloy wheels used lug bolts that were longer than the lug bolts that came with the steel wheels. If your 914 has any of these alloys make sure the longer lug bolts (40-millimeter versus 25-millimeter) are used to secure them.

As for the 914/6, it could be ordered with optional 5.5x14 inch 911-style Fuchs forged alloys, as fitted to the 911E of the time. A cast magnesium Mahle wheel was also available for those who preferred the larger 15-inch-high

Pedrini alloys were optional for 914 owners who wanted sporty looks to match their active lifestyles. **Porsche AG**

The 914/6 came with 14-inch Fuchs alloys. **Porsche AG**

One other change worth noting occurred in 1973. All the 914 wheels were changed to a hub-centric design. A raised center ring, on which the wheel could be centered before the lug bolts were screwed in, was cast in the hubs. Prior to this change, mounting the wheels followed the archaic VW method of relying on the lug bolts to center the wheel. Why Porsche would use a system that required balancing the tire on your toe, while fiddling about trying to get a lug bolt started, instead of using the standard and safer combination of studded wheels and lug nuts is a mystery. It's an example of those strange quirks of German engineering genius that will equip a state-of-the-art sports car with all the wonderful goodies we listed at the beginning of the chapter, and then borrow an idea from Barney Rubble's dinosaur cart to hang on the wheels.

Speaking of Volkswagens, a number of aftermarket wheels were offered for the 914 over the years, many of them also applicable to the VW Bug (the original). True Porsche wheels will have Porsche part numbers stamped inside. The most popular aftermarket wheels, in terms of sales but not necessarily in the eyes of hardcore 914 aficionados, are the Riviera five-spoke wheel and the reproduction of the Fuchs 2.0-liter wheel. Either type works fine for street cars (the fit of the Riviera limits its use to narrow 165 tires) but anyone who plans on subjecting their 914 to the rigors of the track should rely on the stronger forged factory alloys or aftermarket race wheels of comparable quality. Cast wheels are subject to

wheel. The M471 option package used 6-inch-wide 15 inch Fuchs 911 alloys with wheel spacers and longer lugs. The 916 used 7-inch Fuchs alloys, while the 914/6 GT used either the 7- or 8-inch variants of the Fuchs wheel. The front and rear fender flares of the later two 914 derivations were what allowed the use of the larger wheels.

Hubcaps were still available on the 914 through 1973. **Porsche AG**

developing stress cracks over the years, so they should be carefully inspected before hitting the track. Alloys can also be damaged around the bolt hole faces by the overzealous use of air wrenches at tire stores and brake shops that subscribe to the "parts is parts" theory of auto repair. And last but not least, when your life and limbs are on the line, beware of poor quality aftermarket wheels of unknown origin that were probably made in factories that now turn out toy stuffed animals.

When dealing with aftermarket wheels or factory wheels from other models, the key to proper fit within the stock wheelwells is what is known as backspacing. Some people call this the wheel's offset but that is not technically correct. Offset is the dimension from the outside lip of the wheel rim to the mounting surface. Backspacing is measured from the rear of the wheel. It's the distance from the rear lip of the wheel rim to the surface of the mounting face. A good way to measure backspacing is by laying a wheel (without a tire on it) face down. Place a straightedge across the diameter of the back rim, then measure the distance from the straightedge down to the mounting surface, the flat part of the wheel that snugs up against the hub when the lug bolts are tightened. For the 914 four-cylinder factory wheels, this measurement is 120 millimeters, about 4 5/8 inches. On the 914/6 and early 911 wheels it should be 125 millimeters, or 4 7/8 inches.

When using a 5.5-inch wheel that conforms to the factory backspacing, it should be possible to comfortably fit a 195/60x15 tire inside the stock wheelwells of a 914. This should give adequate clearance in the rear and little, if any, rubbing on the front inner fenders under very tight turning situations like parallel parking. Many people have reported no problems on going up to 205/60x15 tires. Remember that changes in tire height will alter speedometer accuracy. A 195/65x15 tire will let you move up in size while maintaining the integrity of your speedometer readout.

Not all 914s and not all tires measure up exactly the same. Obviously spring rates, shock settings, ride height, load weight, and wheel dimensions are also variables to be considered when fitting tires. Even though tires are classified by size, a 205-millimeter-wide tire from one manufacturer may be a bit wider or narrower than similar sized tires from other companies. Your best bet is to try before you buy. It also pays to ask other 914 owners what their experience has been.

One method of checking clearance is to have someone press down on the rear bumper or trunk while you try to fit your finger between the inside of the fender lip and the tire sidewall. If you can do that, you're OK. Some people go so far as to say that sufficient clearance is there as long as you can get something even thinner than your fingertip in this space. An important but maybe not so obvious part of this test is that you have your helper push down on the suspension before you stick your finger in the space, otherwise your swollen fingers lose their value as precision measuring devices. If you don't want to let your fingers do the measuring, another method of checking is to drive the car over a bumpy surface at moderate speeds while listening for rubbing sounds. When you stop, inspect the sidewalls for any scuff marks. Be sure to look on the inner side as well as the outside of the tire. You can also look up into the fender wells for shiny spots where the tires may have come in contact.

If things look like they just about fit but you feel that a little extra room would take the worry out of being close, you

2.0-liter Fuchs alloys debuted in 1973 and became the classic 914 four-cylinder wheel, sparking cheaper repro models. **Porsche AG**

To guarantee authenticity, look for a Porsche part number or the name of a wheel maker, like Mahle, cast in reverse side of wheel.

can always roll in the lip or slightly flare out the rear fenders. This is an old Porsche owner trick that often involves the use of a baseball bat. The idea is to use a stout, round object (baseball bat) to gently stretch out the sheet metal, giving it a slight flare. The key to this procedure is going slowly and applying only enough force to gradually create the additional space you need. Going at it like Mark McGwire could crease the rear panel or crack the paint.

There are a couple of ways to roll the rear fenders. One way is to remove the rear wheel and tire. The car should be on a lift or otherwise securely supported. Look up inside the wheelwell and you will see a ridge that runs along the top of it. Place the knob end of the bat inside the fender well up against the outer edge of this ridge so that the bat becomes wedged between the ridge and the fender lip. Gripping the barrel of the bat, roll it along the fender lip in a front to rear direction at the same time you are exerting upward pressure. How much pressure to apply is a trial and error process but it's better to err on the gentle side to avoid expensive fender damage. Work carefully, and you should have no problems.

Another way to do this without removing the wheel and tire is to find a bat or similar object that can be wedged in between the tire and wheel and just roll it back and forth. Wrapping the bat in a cloth would be a good idea to prevent scratches or nicks to the paint. This is also a good way to flatten the fender lip without trying to put a bulge in the fender panel. That's good for almost an extra half-inch of clearance. The more meticulous body shapers will snip out the inner part of the lip and then flatten the remainder so that there will be no sharp edges to cut the tire. This would require priming and painting any metal that gets exposed in the process. Starting in 1973, I have heard of cars that came from the factory with this surgery already done.

Adding GT-style fender flares is the more obvious way to get additional clearance for bigger wheels and tires. The steel flares are very expensive to buy and install. The fiberglass flares are much cheaper but beware, as quality and fit do vary among brands. Again, this is something that is worth discussing with someone who has been there, done that to save yourself time, money, and wavy fenders. After flares are

Riviera wheels are a popular aftermarket wheel for 914s.

The 914 six-cylinder conversion sports 911 five-bolt wheels and subtle flares to give them room to work.

Simple way to convert to five-bolt wheels is by drilling new bolt pattern in front rotor/hub. www.pelicanparts.com

This is what you want, the larger calipers and vented rotors from a 911SC. www.pelicanparts.com

Rear hub and rotor drilled for five-bolt wheels.
www.pelicanparts.com

The quick and dirty way is to use wheel adapters that bolt to the stock four-bolt hub and have five bolt studs for mounting the five-bolt wheels. The safety of this method is questionable. Don't even think about racing if you do this.

The next method is to have your stock hubs redrilled to a five-bolt pattern. Studs will have to be threaded through the hubs to mount the 911 wheels. On the 1970–71 cars, the rear hubs came from the factory with mounting bosses where the five-bolt pattern could be drilled out. Later hubs do not have this thicker space between the four-bolt hole mounting pads. Even though there is less metal surrounding the new holes, drilling the later hubs is still considered to be acceptable as far as reliability is concerned. Using 914/6 rear brake rotors is a cheaper alternative than having the rear four-cylinder rotors redrilled to a five-bolt pattern. This still allows the

Rear brake rotor and hub from 914/6. www.pelican-parts.com

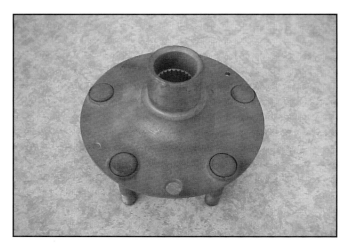

Two views of the early 911 hub used on the 914/6.
www.pelicanparts.com

added, longer (70-millimeter) lug bolts and wheel spacers are then used to move the wheels out the proper distance. The wheel spacers come in 1/4-inch widths and may be stacked to achieve the needed distance. Two inches is about the maximum width that can be safely obtained using wheel spacers. The other option is, of course, to pass on the adapters and just stuff bigger wheels and tires in the additional space.

Five-Bolt Conversion

Converting your four-bolt wheel pattern to the five-bolt pattern used on the 914/6 and 911 opens up a whole new world of possibilities as far as wheel and tire options. There are a few ways to do this but, as usual, the preferred and safest method takes a bit more work than the others.

The 914/6 stub axle. www.pelicanparts.com

Rear brake caliper and rotor from 914/6. www.pelican-parts.com

use of the stock 914 four-cylinder rear calipers and the emergency brake.

The best method of adding five-bolt wheels is to convert the suspension to that of the 911 or 914/6. Up front, this can be accomplished by adding 911 front struts, which include the spindle/hub assembly and the vented rotors and 911 calipers. Or you can add the entire 911 front suspension, including the torsion bars, steering rack, and sway bar. Up to 1989, 911 parts will fit. This means you can upgrade to more recent equipment like larger brakes and torsion bars. The later suspensions also have a lighter, aluminum steering rack mount. If you choose to go down the 911 conversion path, a 19-millimeter brake cylinder must be added if you haven't already done so. In the rear, you will want to convert to a 914/6 setup as using 911 rear calipers will eliminate the emergency brake. Not such a big problem for track cars, but

definitely not a good idea if you drive your 914 on the street. There are hydraulic emergency brake systems available, but it's easier to use the stock handbrake and 914/6 rotors and the four-cylinder calipers. Using 914/6 calipers is an option, but the parts are scarce.

To handle the rear conversion to 914/6 specs while retaining your old calipers, you will also need a pair of 1969–1971 911 hubs, 914/6 stub axles, and the 914/6 brake discs. You will also need to replace the rear wheel bearings when you switch over. The early 911 hubs and both models of the 914 use identical rear wheel bearings. The 914/6 stub axles fit the splines of the 911 rear hub and also bolt up to the

914/6 CV joint. www.pelicanparts.com

Early Fuchs alloy with proper backspacing for 914/6 or five-bolt conversions. www.pelicanparts.com

four-cylinder CV joints. For the record, the 914/6 uses different CV joints than the four-cylinder cars.

The options described above are not the only alternatives to those seeking improved braking performance. Other more exotic and expensive methods are available. Studying the ads in Porsche-related magazines and talking to serious Porsche racers can provide more information for those interested.

Tire Talk

You probably already know more about tires beyond the fact that they are round, black, and smell funny, but let's go over a few basic bits of information. Back in the days when the 914 came into the world, tire technology, as we have said, was nowhere near as sophisticated as it is today. You didn't see all the writing on the sidewall that you see today. The 914 had 155x15 tires and that was all they said. This meant that the tread width was roughly 155 millimeters from sidewall to sidewall and that the tire fit wheels 15 inches in diameter. There was no need to list any additional information about things like the aspect ratio, that is, the proportional relationship of the height of the sidewall to the width of the tire as measured across the tread from sidewall to sidewall. That's because all the tires back then had the same aspect ratio. In other words, the aspect ratio was understood to be 82 because the sidewall height of all tires was 82 percent of the tread section's width.

This changed when lower profile tires came on the scene. Their aspect ratio was only 70 percent of the width so it became necessary to label them as such. You may recall that 911s of the early 1970s carried tires listed as 185/70x15. That meant that the height of the sidewall was 70 percent of the 185-millimeter width of the tread. The 15, of course, referred to the 15-inch diameter wheels that it was made to fit.

Today you will also see letters like "P" or "LT" on tires. This differentiates between passenger car (P) and light truck (LT) tires, the main difference between the two being increased load capacity in the truck tires.

Other letters on the sidewall of tires these days refer to the tire's construction and its speed rating. Thus, 205/60HR15 designates a tire that is 205 millimeters wide from sidewall to sidewall, with a sidewall that measures 60 percent of that width (/60) has a speed rating (H) of 130 miles per hour, radial construction (R), that fits a 15-inch wheel. We don't need to go into how speed ratings are determined, but a good rule of thumb is to buy tires rated for the number that exceeds your car's top speed. The original 914 tires were "S" rated, which meant 112 miles per hour. Some other speed ratings that relate to Porsches are "U"=124 miles per hour, "V"=149 miles per hour, and "Z"= over 149 miles per hour.

One other number appears on new tires that is important when doing Porsche tire buying. This is the UTQGS (Universal Tire Quality Grading System) number, which is used to rate a tire's treadwear. To keep it simple, the lower the number, the faster the tire will wear out. Of course, there are other factors involved, and the one we're most interested in is the tradeoff that usually exists between a tire built for long wear versus one built for handling. With few exceptions, a hard tire wears longer and a soft tire handles better. The grades run from 60 to 620. Street-approved (DOT) race tires usually have a wear rating below 90. If you want a great handling street tire, the wear rating will usually be between 100 and 150, maybe 200. As they say, your mileage may vary. In other words, ask around to see what works on other 914s.

Once you settle on those new treads, it's important that your wheels are properly balanced, inflation pressures kept within specs, and proper alignment maintained. Avoid heavy wheel locks that may throw your wheels off balance and create mysterious vibrations at freeway speeds. Try to have the wheels balanced on the car to avoid this kind of problem.

Taking Your 914 to the Race Track

The 914 may have started life as an entry level Porsche sports car, but these days it lives on as an extremely popular entry level Porsche race car. Entry level in that it is fairly cheap to purchase, yet in virtually stock form, out-handles cars costing much more. That includes the 911. And it's a car that responds well to tuning so that as the driver's interest and skill level increases, he or she won't outgrow the capabilities of the car. A wealth of parts and technical knowledge has built up over the years to further enhance the 914's competitive nature. It also helps that the Porsche Club of America and the Porsche Owner's Club have aggressive club racing programs that rank at the top among any owner's marques in this country. These programs support a strong calendar of events in almost every geographic zone of the country, backed up by excellent driver training programs. The popularity of Porsche club racing and the enthusiasm generated by its participants have also established a strong aftermarket of companies providing Porsche racing-specific goods and services. All this activity generates a big market for used parts and recycled race cars, so building a car on a budget is possible, as is the potential for recouping part of your investment should the unthinkable happen

123

License plate on this 914 sums up the reason many current owners purchase 914s.

The tight and twisty confines of the autocross course are a perfect playground for the agile 914.

and you lose interest in racing. With all this activity, no wonder the 914 retains its popularity as the people's Porsche. It's the cheapest ticket to get into the show.

Autocross

The best way to acquaint yourself with the acceleration, shifting, braking, and handling of your 914 without endangering yourself or others on the open road is by taking part in a slalom or autocross competition. It's also a great way to build-up your racing skills before taking to the big tracks. By definition, an autocross is a low-speed event that tests a driver's skill at successfully maneuvering around a tight, twisty course in the quickest time possible. It's a race against the clock, so there is no fear of fender banging with a competitor. Low speed means that although speeds as high as 70 miles per hour may be reached briefly, most turns will be negotiated in second and occasionally first gear. Some courses could be as long as a mile in length, but most are half that distance, possibly even less. Usually held in wide-open areas like parking lots, the course is marked by a series of orange cones. A driver is penalized for hitting cones

(called cone crushing) or driving off course. The key is to be smooth. That smoothness applies to braking, shifting, accelerating, and making quick directional changes. The same things happen on an autocross course that happen on a bigger race track. At an autocross they happen at lower speeds, which makes autocrossing a great way to build your skills before tackling the high speeds of a race track. The quick reactions and knowledge of vehicle dynamics that you learn autocrossing also make you a better street driver. Anyone who competes can provide you with stories of how they were able to avoid a potential highway disaster by instinctively reacting the way they would on the track.

You can find out when and where the next autocross will be held in your area by contacting the local PCA or POC chapter for a calendar of such events. The SCCA (Sports Car Club of America) or other local car clubs may also hold autocrosses in your locale. The advantage of running an event put on by a Porsche club is that the people you meet will be able to give you specific tips and instructions relating to driving a 914 or other Porsches. By seeing what they have done to their cars, you will have real world knowledge of what works best in modifying your car. Some of these people have been driving 914s as long as 914s have been around.

It's a good idea to let some of these experienced 914 pilots drive your car in order to give you pointers on how you can make improvements to it. More importantly, you can observe their driving styles and techniques. Whether you are driving or just riding along, having an experienced racer in the car will make you a better Porsche driver. The instructors are all volunteers and most take a relaxed, low key approach. They were all novices themselves at one time and know what it's like the first few times you stare through your windshield at a parking lot filled with a maze of orange cones and try to figure out which way to go.

Getting started autocrossing is pretty simple. All it takes is a driver, a car, and a few pieces of safety equipment. That safety equipment includes a set of working seatbelts like the ones you hopefully use everyday when you go to work. You will also need a helmet. Loaner helmets may be available when you get to an event, but it's best to bring one along just in case. It's also a good idea to check beforehand as to the type of helmets that are allowed. Some clubs let you wear a motorcycle helmet

(these have stickers saying they are M rated) while others will only allow SA rated helmets. The M and SA ratings are based on tests performed by the Snell Foundation, a research organization devoted to helmet safety. The SA helmets are specific to automobile racing and the major difference between them and the motorcycle helmets are the fire resistant linings and materials used in their construction. The Snell test procedures are periodically updated and helmets carry a stamp as to the latest Snell specifications to which they conform. Current helmets carry a 1995 sticker. Some organizations may let you run with a helmet bearing a 1990 sticker. Check with the rules that apply to the events in your area. Motorcycle helmets are generally much cheaper than SA rated helmets. Just remember that before you go helmet shopping, if your future plans include any wheel-to-wheel club or vintage racing, you will need an approved SA rated helmet.

Other items that you will want to include in your autocross essentials whether you are a novice or a pro are comfortable driving shoes that let you easily maneuver your feet around the pedals. Good low-buck alternatives to racing booties or Italian driving moccasins are wrestling shoes that

Dodging cones teaches a driver to react quickly.

Lessons learned on the autocross course are a good foundation for driving on big tracks.

you can pick up at the larger discount sports equipment warehouses. You should be able to pick up a pair for 35 bucks or less. You won't want to walk around in them all day but they give you great feel for working the pedals and at a quick glance they can pass for fancy Formula One footwear.

Driving gloves are another good idea. You have to work the wheel very quickly in autocrossing and gloves can give you added grip and protection from nicks, cuts, and blisters. Long sleeve cotton shirts and pants may also be required while on course. Even if they aren't required for driving, they can come in handy to protect you from the sun and wind. Along those same lines, don't forget a hat and sunscreen.

Water is almost as essential as gasoline for race drivers. Staying properly hydrated helps you fight fatigue. Fatigue is a driver's worst enemy. Driving is strenuous work and a long day in the sun can take its toll by slowing down your ability to react quickly. Drink plenty of water. A decent fitness program will also improve your life at and away from the race track. While we're on the subject of drinking, common sense and insurance requirements ban alcoholic beverages while events are going on.

Other things to bring to the track are a tool kit, duct tape, an air tank for adding air to your tires, a tire gauge, white liquid shoe polish, a stopwatch, pen and notebook, an extra fan belt, rags, and oil. The shoe polish comes in handy for writing your car's number on the windows. If you bring along race tires then you'll need a jack and the tools necessary to change tires. A torque wrench with a socket that fits your wheel lug bolts or nuts is handy for making sure the wheel bolts are properly tightened. If you value the appearance of your lug bolts, a special "soft socket" with a plastic inner lining to protect their finish is a worthwhile investment.

Driver's Education and Other Weighty Advice

So far we've been discussing a lot of generic stuff that applies whether you drive a 914 or not. We'll get to more specific car prep in a minute, but there are a couple more important things to discuss before we do that. The key component of any race car, 914 or otherwise, is the driver. Before you start adding or modifying equipment on your car, the biggest gains in performance

Having the proper combination of torsion bars, springs, shocks, and anti-sway bars lets you track through the corners smoothly and with little body lean.

will come as you improve your skills as a driver. Listen and learn from the instructors and the other experienced drivers.

Listen to what your car is telling you, too. Understanding vehicle dynamics will make you a faster and safer driver, on and off the track. As a car accelerates, brakes, or goes either to the left or the right, it experiences changes in how its weight is balanced. Step on the gas and the car's weight shifts to the rear. Braking has the opposite reaction. Going around a corner forces the car's weight to shift to the outside or away from the direction that you are turning. The changes while going up or down hill should be obvious.

Bearing the burden of this shift in weight are the car's tires. They are, and should be, the car's only contact with the ground. The place where the tires meet the ground is called the contact patch. Tire size, construction, and inflation pressure all determine the size of any given tire's contact patch. The bigger the contact patch, the better a tire should be able to grip the road.

Equipment	Increases oversteer	Decreases understeer	Decreases oversteer	Increases understeer
Front sway bar	Smaller diameter	Lengthen setting	Larger diameter	Shorten setting
Rear sway bar (optional)	Larger diameter	Shorten setting	Smaller diameter	Lengthen setting
Front torsion bars		Lighter		Heavier
Rear spring rate		Heavier		Lighter
Front shocks	Softer setting		Harder setting	
Rear shocks	Harder setting		Softer setting	
Front camber	Increase negative	Less negative		
Rear camber	Less negative		More negative	
Front tire pressure	Higher			Lower
Rear tire pressure	Lower			Higher

When the tires are standing still or moving at a steady speed in a straight line, all four tires roughly bear an equal amount of the load. Step on the gas and the back tires will be bearing more of the load while the front tires have less weight pressing on them and therefore less traction. Under very heavy acceleration, not only will the front tires have less traction but the rears may not be able to handle all that weight and power causing them to lose their grip. Try braking downhill and a similar shift occurs, only toward the front tires. Now for a disastrous worst case scenario: Let's say you're heading downhill toward a left-hand bend and you realize that you are going way too fast. You jam on the brakes and the next thing you see is the rear end of your car trying to pass you on the right and then you are off making donuts in the dirt. What happened? You forced all the weight of the car onto the front tires because you were heading downhill and then braking hard. A bad move, but maybe one both front tires could handle. Things really got out of hand, however, when you turned left, putting all that weight on the right front tire. With little or no weight to hold them down, the rear tires lost contact, and then were swung to the right by the force of you turning left.

You can read more details of vehicle dynamics in both of the high performance driving books that I have listed in the appendix. Bob Bondurant has spent over 30 years teaching people how to drive fast and smart. His book is the next best thing to attending his driving school. I have had the chance to sample a number of driving schools and Bondurant is No. 1 in my opinion. The other book I have included is by long-time Porsche racer Vic Elford. Elford thoroughly covers the topic of high performance driving with Porsches specifically in mind. He doesn't have much to say about the 914, but the book is still highly recommended. Elford, like a lot of professional drivers who honed their driving skills in the days when four-wheel drifts and sliding the tail out were considered the fast line around corners, prefers a car with the tail-happy attitude of the 911. These drivers have developed a feel for exactly how far to let it all hang out and are comfortable with that feeling. Midengine cars like the 914 take a more neutral attitude through turns and feel more stable to most drivers. They do have high cornering limits, but people like Elford don't like the fact that a midengine doesn't give as much warning once it has reached its limit of adhesion. Like they say

A good view of what oversteer looks like when you are following someone.

This is what oversteer looks like when someone is coming at you.

in Porsche circles, the 914 may be a hard car to spin, but once you do get it spinning it will spin for a long time. That's why I have said it is very important to listen to your car to find out when it is reaching its limit. It is also why I recommend starting with the slower speeds generated in autocrossing to explore those limits.

Getting Things to Go Your Way

We need to discuss understeer and oversteer. Understeer is the feeling you get when approaching a turn that the car does not want to turn in the direction that you want it to go. It prefers to "plow" straight ahead instead of turning. And the more you turn the wheel, the more it refuses to turn in. Oversteer is when the rear of the car wants to swap ends with the front as you turn into a corner. The rear end feels "light" and out of control.

Cynics will say that understeer means the front end will hit the tree first while oversteer means the back end will hit first. I feel a better description is that oversteer is when the passenger soils his pants, while understeer is when the driver needs to change underwear.

How you set up your car depends on how comfortable you are with either understeer or oversteer. The ideal would be a neutral handling setup. There are a number of things you can do to your car to cure or at least compensate for a handling problem causing it to understeer or oversteer. Remember that there are changes that can be made at either end of the car to reach the ideal setup. The following chart lists some of the options available to you. Talking to other drivers with similar cars about their setups is advisable before making big changes to your car. You should also determine a satisfactory base setup that matches your driving style and comfort level before tinkering with a lot of different variables. Establish torsion bar and spring rates, sway bar size, and shock settings that make the car handle the way you want. After that you can experiment with tire pressures and sway bar settings.

Tires: The Black Art

Once you decide that autocrossing is something you would like to do on a regular basis, the best thing you can do to improve your times and the car's handling is to get a set of sticky racing tires. You will also need an extra set of wheels on

A good example of how weight shifts to the outside when a car is negotiating a turn.

which to mount these tires. You can save money by picking up a set of used wheels from a fellow racer who has decided to move up to wider wheels and bigger tires. You can even get by with a used set of tires. The life span and usability of racing tires depends a great deal on heat cycles. Race tires work best when they get hot and sticky. A heat cycle is when a tire goes from the ambient temperature to its operating heat range and then cools down again. The number of heat cycles a tire can stand varies with each make and compound of tire. Usually the tire manufacturer's technical rep or a knowledgeable sales person can give you this information. Of course, this assumes that the tires were properly heated up or cooled down during each heat cycle. Again, the manufacturer can tell you how the tires should be broken in. Your fellow racers can also tell you what works best. When inspecting used tires look for irregularities and flat spots or scuff marks. Tires that feel more like petrified wood than rubber will probably handle as they feel.

Read the rule book to see whether you must run street legal treaded tires or if you can run slicks. Usually slicks are only run by the highly modified cars. Putting them on a car that is basically stock may move you into a class where you will be hopelessly out of contention. This advice also applies

to certain engine and chassis modifications. Read the rule book and ask questions before installing anything that will move you into a higher class.

Special DOT (Department of Transportation)-approved race tires are usually the way to go. These tires usually have a shaved or shallow tread pattern that makes them legal for street use. With most of them, you can put them on at home the day before and then drive back and forth to your autocross. They aren't cheap, about $500 to $600 a set, and they wear very quickly in street use, so most people only use them for competition. Why waste them on street driving when you can get all your money's worth out of them at the track? Hoosier, Yokohama, Kumho, and B.F. Goodrich are the more popular brands. Different brands work better with different suspension settings or air pressures. Some tires trade maximum handling for maximum wear. Going with such tires instead of marginally slower but better wearing tires depends on how fast you want to go and how often you want to replace tires. Once again, ask around before making your choice.

Adjusting tire pressure is probably the easiest way to fine-tune your handling at the track. Buy a good tire gauge with a valve that lets you bleed off excess air. Modern tires usually don't require the high pressures that racers were advised to run 10 to 15 years ago. Don't make big changes in adding or deleting air. Work in increments of a half to one pound at a time. Remember to be consistent as to when you read the air pressure. A hot tire will register a higher air pressure than it does once it has cooled down. Bleeding off excess air based on hot tire readings may leave them underinflated when they cool down.

One other valuable lesson I learned is not to use Armor All or similar products on your race tires. Hard cornering may have you running a bit on the sidewalls, which can get very slippery when they are all shined up.

A Budget Based Suspension Build-up

Now let's get to some specific improvements you can make to your 914 even if you are watching your pennies. Even if money is no object, the following is a good logical progression to follow before you get to the expensive tricky stuff.

Check out the results of any PCA autocross and you'll see that 914s often run rings around the more powerful 911 and the high tech 944/968. That's because the 914's midengine layout has what's known as a low polar moment of inertia. Having most of its weight in the middle of the car causes it to react rapidly to steering input. In other words, it can change direction very quickly. A 914's handling, for the most part, is neutral, although oversteer can be provoked if you're into tail-wagging around the cones. Just remember that the darker side of a low polar moment of inertia is that once you start to spin you end up doing a pretty good imitation of a top.

Besides good handling, another virtue of the 914 is that it is relatively cheap to buy and modify. Getting the most bang for your buck can be accomplished by carefully shopping at swap meets and wrecking yards. It also pays to talk to people who know 914s and can tell you how to spend your money wisely even if you're buying new parts. Bill Bartee (see sidebar) was one of those people, so I have included some of the tips he shared with me on the fundamentals of 914 suspension modifications.

Another advantage of the 914 is that you don't need a big rig to haul it to the track. Note interesting front aerodynamic treatment.

It's important to read the rule book before you modify your car. Adding the wrong piece of equipment may move you up into a class in which your competition looks like this.

Jason Burkett runs Paragon Products, a mail order firm that specializes in selling Porsche parts and accessories at discount prices. Having raced a 914 for a number of years, he can not only dispense parts at a savings to budget-conscious racers, he also has practical hands-on experience to share.

Racing on a budget is a good test of shopping skills as well as driving skills. Just remember that you don't want to sacrifice quality or safety to save a few bucks.

Before we get started spending your money, let's cover some basic ground rules. The first rule is that before you start modifying any car, make sure it's basically sound and safe to drive. You may go faster on the freeway than at an autocross, but those tight turns and directional changes put a tremendous strain on the chassis, suspension, and brakes. Safety and reliability are priorities. Speaking of rules, both Bartee and Burkett stress the importance of reading the rule book before modifying your car. Don't waste your money on that trick suspension modification that will move you up into a class where you are no longer competitive. Finally, Bartee pointed out that the best thing you can do to go

faster is to spend time, instead of money, developing your skills as a driver.

"You can have the best suspension in the world, but it doesn't know what to do without the proper driver input," is how he put it.

OK, lets get down to the basics. Here's how to modify your Porsche in roughly $500 installments. These changes should give you the best return on your investment.

Let's start with stopping. I've already made a few enemies among the 914 purists by criticizing its braking in chapter 7, but when you're on the track it's every man for himself anyway, so good brakes are a necessity. For less than a hundred bucks and an hour of time you can make a vast improvement to your 914's stopping ability. A set of new carbon Kevlar brake pads for your front brakes will do wonders in decreasing your stopping distance and increasing pedal modulation. You'll pick up valuable time by being able to brake deeper into a corner. You'll probably have to put up with a bit of brake dust on your wheels and some squeal when you stop. But at least you will stop a lot quicker and with more confidence.

Despite its modest beginnings, the 914 doesn't need to back down to 911s on the race track.

Stainless steel brake lines, a larger 19-millimeter brake cylinder, and some high temperature brake fluid are also worthy improvements to your car.

The other weak point of the 914 is the shift linkage. New bushings and solid transmission mounts will keep things from twisting around and make shifting more precise.

Green lights are usually good things, but if you see one on the dash of your 914 it means bad things are happening with your oil supply. Hard cornering and tight turns force oil away from the stock pick-up tube. A Weltmeister Oil Trap has an extended pick-up tube and a reservoir for additional oil. It allows you to add about a half quart more oil, which should aid in cooling and in keeping things lubricated in the turns. It easily attaches to the bottom of your engine's sump in place of the oil strainer cover.

Since you don't have a lot of horsepower to waste in a 914, especially with a 1.7-liter engine, it's a good idea to try to get the most out of what you have. High quality plug wires and a solid state electronic ignition will go a long way to keep

every one of the small herd of ponies pulling its share of the load. The Pertronix Ignitor is a magnetic pickup ignition system that fits inside your distributor and eliminates the points. Eliminating the points means no point bounce at high rpm. It also means less maintenance, since you don't have to replace or set points at tune-up time.

What's the best way to spend $500 on improving a 914's handling? Everyone is pretty much in agreement that it is a good set of shocks. Bartee and Burkett both like Konis because of their adjustability. Buy the sport shocks and avoid the temptation to run them at too hard of a setting. Bartee told me a trick he learned years ago from the people at Automotion regarding installation. Up front, two thin rubber snubbers should be removed from the shock, while, in the rear, about two-thirds of the snubbers should be removed.

Next up is an adjustable front sway bar. Burkett and Bartee both agree that a 19-millimeter bar is a good choice for street and track use. See chapter 6 for installation techniques, especially if your car did not come equipped with an anti-sway bar from the factory. You will need to purchase the necessary mounting kit to mount the new bar. At the rear, you'll need a set of 140-pound springs and adjustable spring perches. The stiffer springs should lower the car about an inch. Burkett feels that while 185-pound springs are the hot setup for a track car, an autocross car may develop too much wheelspin in the tighter turns of an autocross. The heavier springs will also destroy whatever meager ride comfort the 914 delivers in street driving. The spring perch kit will allow infinite ride height adjustment for proper corner weighting to achieve the optimum handling setup.

Moving on to the next step in the process, we get to the front torsion bars. Tubular torsion bars reduce unsprung weight, react quicker to suspension inputs, and offer better ride quality than their solid counterparts. They only cost about $30 more than their solid counterparts, so your decision here is a no brainer, according to Burkett. He likes the 21-millimeter bars for street/autocross use. Bartee preferred larger 22- or 23-millimeter bars. He said that the smoother the surface you run on, the heavier the bar you can use. In either case, the stock torsion bars are slightly larger than 17

millimeters, so even the 21 millimeter bars should produce a notable change in your 914's attitude.

For years, many people, Bartee included, did not run rear sway bars on 914s. Bartee experimented with both the stock 15-millimeter and the optional 16-millimeter rear bars, and found they allowed him a way to further refine his car's handling. The only time he ran with them disconnected was at very tight autocross courses. Many people feel that a limited slip differential is essential to avoid excessive wheelslip when using a rear bar. See chapter 6 for tips on installing a rear anti-sway bar.

Weltmeister polygraphite suspension bushings can take out the sloppy feel of the stock rubber parts. They do ride harder and transmit more road noise. If you replace the rear bushings, be sure to routinely check the tightness of the trailing arm mounting bolts.

A turbo tie rod kit provides more precise and quicker steering feel. If your stock tie rod ends are in good shape, this is something that can wait until they need replacing. Steering rack spacers are a must if you have lowered your car. They restore proper steering geometry and eliminate bump steer.

Club racing allows you the chance to "go faster," in case you didn't get the message.

The 914 responds well to race tuning. A good car for beginning racers, it can still be satisfying to an experienced driver.

Bump steer is excessive feedback through the steering wheel when driving over rough or uneven roads.

Speaking of ride height, a good rule of thumb is to set the front about a 1/2-inch lower than the rear. Use the adjustment ratchets on the torsion bars that should be visible when you look under the car just aft of the front wheel. Each 1/4 turn of this adjusting screw makes about a 1/4-inch adjustment in ride height. The acceptable rear setting for ride height should be 1 3/4 inches between the fender lip and the wheel rim.

As for alignment settings, the more negative camber up front the better. Try for 1.5 degrees of negative camber in front, if you can get it. Some cars will only give you 1 degree. Jason Burkett likes a little toe out up front for easier turn in. This counteracts understeer but can cause the car to wander down the straight at high speed. It's not something that's recommended for a car that sees a lot of street use. The rear setting should be 2 degrees of negative camber. These settings are also affected by what brand of tires you run. In the past some of the stickier street tires preferred a lot of negative camber while others did not.

Check with tire manufacturers and other racers for your tire's specific needs.

Finally, the twists and turns of autocrossing can put a tremendous strain on the chassis of a 914 with a very stiff suspension. Welding in a chassis strengthening kit can help relieve some of that stress. Trailing arms can also be bent hitting curbs or going off course. "Boxing" the trailing arms with additional bracing can prevent this. Care must be taken when welding on these kits, because if not properly done it can actually bend the trailing arm out of shape.

Driver also take their share of abuse under hard cornering. Five-point safety harnesses keep a driver securely in place, which not only avoids the morning-after aches and pains, but lets him or her use the steering wheel solely as a driving tool and not a handle. On the 914, a harness bar attaches easily, using the upper seatbelt mounting bolts. Depending on your club's rules, it can be used to mount the shoulder straps of a racing harness. It provides the proper height for these belts to keep them from compressing your spine in case of an accident. Bolting in a roll cage may be a

Some 914s start to look like 911s as they move up to the higher classes of club racing.

bit much for an autocross car, but it certainly is strongly suggested for anyone who runs time trials or hot laps on a real race track. The cage also does a great job of providing additional stiffness to the 914 chassis so it has performance benefits in addition to the more important safety aspects.

A number of aftermarket racing seats can be fitted to a 914, but they usually must be bolted to the floor to provide enough headroom for most drivers when wearing a helmet. This fixed mounting also rules out adjustability. This could be a problem when two drivers of different height share a car. Lars Frohm is a guy who is at home racing anything from Mini Coopers to Corvettes. He also has a surprisingly fast 914 that is a rolling lesson in low-budget, do-it-yourself tweaks. It's fun to see him blow off cars with fancier and more expensive equipment. Here's how he tackled the seating arrangements in the 914 he shares with his wife, Bev. Lars also shares some advice on the mental and physical attitude adjustments you make when you start going faster.

914 Seating Modifications

By Lars Frohm

This may sound like an odd subject to discuss in conjunction with mechanical modifications to make the car handle better

and go faster. The old conventional wisdom guides us in our efforts to make more horsepower, how to make the car handle better, and how to make it stop better, but it fails to address the issue of the driver's ability to handle and extract the most from all the newfound performance. For a driver who may have had lots of experience with high performance, and perhaps, competition driving, any modification to the car will require an adjustment in how to operate the car for maximum benefit. As an example of what happens when you fail to make these mental adjustments, I can draw from a multitude of personal experiences and screwups.

Picture your favorite on/off ramp or a certain turn at a race track. You have perfected your approach to the turn. You have your braking points memorized and you know exactly when to begin to turn in toward the apex. You have done this so many times that, if checked with a stopwatch, your times through this section would be amazingly identical. Now, what if this is your first time through this section with your newfound horsepower behind you? You probably haven't noticed, but because of the extra power, you carried a little more speed on your approach to the turn. All of a sudden, the feeling that all is not well arrives with accompanying butterflies in the stomach and you start thinking that this is not

Mahle alloys are the unfair advantage for 914 racers, because of their light weight and high strength.

going to work out! With your finely honed driving skills, and a fair amount of luck, you will hopefully not spin or hurt anything, except maybe a slight bruising of the ego.

What happened? With an increase in approach speed, you have to make adjustments to your braking. If the brakes haven't been modified from the time before, you simply need to get on the brakes earlier to scrub off enough speed to safely execute the turn. If the braking performance has been increased to match the higher speed, perhaps the same braking point can be used as before. If there has been a significant improvement in braking, you may even be able to delay your braking more than before. With improvements in the suspension, steering, and perhaps, also with better tires, you could have carried that extra speed through the turn. When you change one thing, everything else is affected by the change. An improvement in one area, like more power, should, whenever possible, be matched with an improvement somewhere else, like better brakes, in order to extract the most of the changes done to the car.

Another important factor related to changes that increase acceleration, braking, and lateral forces is the effect on the driver. Acceleration pushes you back into the seat and it just feels great! Hard braking causes your body to lurch forward and you end up having to use your arms and legs to stay in the seat. The stock seatbelt does not do a lot to keep you firmly and safely in the seat as it very likely will not feel enough forces to lock up the retracting mechanism, so you end up doing some of the work. Lateral forces during cornering tend to make you lean into the turn to prevent yourself from flying out of the seat.

There is a simple fact with the stock seats in the 914: They have no lateral support whatsoever! In order to facilitate getting in and out of the car, there are no side bolsters on the seats. Perhaps they designed them this way for styling, but one way or the other, they do not help you stay where you belong during performance driving. You end up having to use your arms and hands on the steering wheel to remain upright when you should be using them to steer the car. You also use your legs to brace yourself against the door or against the center console, if your car is equipped with one. Without the center console, your right leg has nothing to hold it in place and only

Club racing can get very serious. A parts house for a sponsor helps.

the heel against the center tunnel prevents it from ending up in the passenger side footwell. Your legs and feet need to work the pedals and your hands and arms should focus on steering the car. Trying to perform double duties with your arms and legs has a negative effect on your concentration.

A high performance driver needs to be seated comfortably and his body should be supported as much as possible. The ultimate solution is a properly designed seat. It should be comfortable, but snug. It should have high sides to keep your legs in place and also prevent any sideways motion of your upper body at the same time allowing your arms to move freely. There are many good seats available on the market but there is a problem as far as the 914 is concerned. Most aftermarket seats are not directly made to fit the 914. Of course, anything can be made to fit, but it may be more of a compromise than you are willing to allow. Because of the upholstered part of the firewall, the fore/aft movement of an aftermarket seat becomes very restricted. Konig and Scheel offer special seats for 914s, but they can be hard to find and expensive. If you plan to use your 914 for organized competition, be sure to check the rules regarding which aftermarket seats you can mount and how you can mount them.

If you cannot find an aftermarket seat to suit your car, your budget, or your club's rules, there is still a way to modify the stock seat to make drastic improvements in how it can support you. It takes a little work and it will not be very pretty, but it is cheap! You will need a high-back seat cover, some fabric, foam rubber, contact cement and, if you are really crafty, a sewing machine. We are going to build a slip-on racing seat! Even if some clubs may have rules against installing a racing seat, I have never seen a rule that prevents you from having a seat cover on your stock seat.

The 914 has a removable seat cushion. Lift it up from the rear, detach the sensor wires (on the later models), and carefully slide the assembly toward the rear to disengage the clip that holds the front of the seat in place. You have now created a partial racing seat. If applicable, push the sensor wires through the hole and let them lie on the floor. Take a piece of foam rubber, approximately 1 inch thick, and cut to fit the area at the bottom of the seat. You can use the bottom of the seat cushion as a template, but cut the foam a little oversize so that it snugs up under the sides of the seat. Cut another strip of 1-inch foam, approximately 3 or 4 inches wide. This strip will be attached at the front edge of the seat, under the full-size piece, and it will serve to boost the front of the

Tires play an important role in handling. Bigger is better.

A helmet, sticky tires, and 914 GT body kit with lightweight racing wheels by Revolution in a four-bolt pattern all add up to fun at the track. Bruce Sutherland and son Robert built the 2.4-liter four-cylinder car as Robert's first car. Bruce Sutherland

"Boxed" rear trailing arms keep them from bending under strains of racing.

Harness bar is easily installed, by using bolts for the stock upper seatbelt mounting position.

cushion up a little bit so that your legs won't rub on the hard molded edge of the seat bottom. We want to eliminate any irritations, since our purpose for this project is to concentrate our focus on driving.

Experiment by positioning and cutting foam rubber to suit your physique. When you are satisfied, glue the pieces together. Position the new cushion in the seat and put a towel or something similar over it to simulate the thickness of the seat cover. Cut pieces of foam to shapes you think will be comfortable and attach temporarily with duct tape or other suitable means to the side bolsters of the seat frame. Make them bigger than you think is appropriate, as there will be some trimming and shaping taking place for final fit. These pieces should span a distance from at least your waist to just below the armpits. Extend them all the way down to the hip area and all the way out on both sides of the seat area, if your body shape allows this and if you have foam large enough to do this. If possible, cut the foam in one piece as it will add a small amount of structural support. Cut and shape and keep fitting until you have something that looks like a real bucket. Take the high-back seat cover and open the seams at the sides where the seat bottom cover attaches to the side pieces. Carefully slide the seat cover over the foam that is still temporarily attached to the seat. When in place, make patterns of the areas that need to have material spliced in and sew the whole thing together.

Test the fit as many times as you need to until you are satisfied with it. Remove most of the tape and leave just enough to hold the foam in place. Slide the seat cover over the seat and attach to the foam by hand sewing in a few places, just to hold the foam in place. Carefully remove the whole assembly, taking extra care not to disturb the location

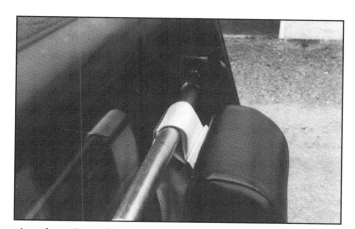

Another view of harness bar installation.

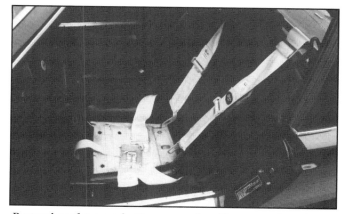

Removing the seat bottom may be all you need to do to get more support from the stock seat. It also lowers you in the car for added helmet clearance.

Oil trap adds a half-quart more oil capacity for additional cooling and lubrication under hard cornering.

of the foam against the seat cover. Glue the foam onto the back of the seat cover, including the seat cushion. After gluing, sew through the seat cover and foam to add a little extra assurance that the pieces will stay in place. Reinstall on the seat and you now have a racing seat whenever you want one and without having altered the original interior.

You will be surprised how much this will help you focus on your driving instead of wasting energy on bracing yourself. Guaranteed better lap times at the lowest possible dollar investment! What could be better than that?

Wheel-to-Wheel Racing

The precision driving and car control required in autocrossing can be exciting and challenging, but to any person who yearns to race on the big tracks there is nothing like wheel-to-wheel competition against other cars. Once you have had the thrill of stalking another driver through the turns and then

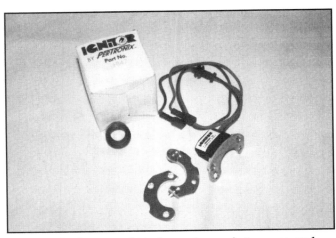

Ignitor eliminates points for easier maintenance and better ignition performance.

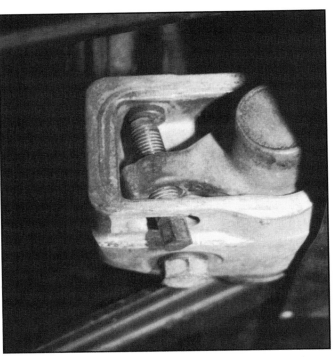

Close-up of the torsion bar adjusting screw, for setting front ride height. There is one on each side.

pulled off a passing maneuver exactly to plan, it's hard to go racing against a stopwatch.

With a 914, you have a number of options when it comes to racing. Both the PCA and POC have what they call club racing. Club racing defines itself as a little more low-key than the all-out combat of SCCA racing. The object is to make racing fun and safe without tearing up a lot of equipment. Aggressive driving and ill-conceived passing maneuvers will get you barred from racing for a number of events.

There are a variety of classes in both clubs to let you race anything from a basically stock car to an all-out racer. Safety harnesses and a fire extinguisher (always a good idea in any 914) are mandatory minimum requirements in the lower classes while full roll cages and fire suppressant systems become required as you move up. Contact either PCA or POC for more details and a rule book before you start building a car.

The 914 is also eligible for some vintage racing organizations. It depends on what the organization has decided is the cut-off year to qualify as a vintage racer. Contact the vintage group in your area for its rules. Vintage racing tends to be more low-key than the Porsche events. You get to race against and hang out with a bunch of unique and interesting cars and people. Instead of just racing against Porsches, you may be dicing with Alfas and BMWs and other types of cars.

SCCA club racing also lets you race against other marques. Because of the need to seek parity over a diverse group of cars in each class, the SCCA rules will vary a great deal from Porsche club rules. Drivers have a tendency to bang fenders and bend sheet metal more than in the other types of racing so it could get expensive. You'll miss out on the camaraderie that goes along with the all-Porsche events but you'll also be entertained by a diverse group of cars and drivers. SCCA rules may be a little harder to figure out, since you are building a car to meet generic standards instead of ones with specific Porsche models in mind. Your best bet is to attend a few SCCA Regional or National events and see if you prefer this style of racing.

A Club Racer

By Mitchell Sam Rossi

Over the years many 914s have been transformed from sprightly little midengine sports cars to dedicated racers. Yet few can boast a nearly 20-year evolution like the 1970 914 of the late Bill Bartee. A long-time member of the California-

Bill Bartee was a guy who knew as much about racing 914s as anyone. And he was always willing to share that knowledge. He also had a great love of the 914. Fortunately he got to build his ultimate 914 race car before cancer shortened his life.

Mitch Rossi gives us a look at how Bill started out, like many 914 owners who first buy it as an affordable sports car that can do double duty as a daily driver and the occasional weekend racer. Then Bill let his knowledge and enthusiasm run wild. I was planning on having Bill share some of his 914 racing knowledge with the readers of this book. Unfortunately that was not to be. The information he provided me a while back on setting up a 914 for autocrossing has been included in this chapter. I hope Mitch's story will provide more of Bill's inspiration and knowledge in building a competitive 914. PCP

Bill Bartee's car started out as a daily driver 1.7-liter he acquired in 1979. Mitch Rossi

Bartee's driving prowess evolved along with his car's modifications. He was chief driving instructor for the Porsche Owner's Club. Mitch Rossi

Car was completed in time for Bartee to race it a few times before succumbing to illness. Mitch Rossi

The 3.2-liter with Motec engine management pumps out 338 horsepower to push the car up to 160 miles per hour. Mitch Rossi

based Porsche Owners Club, Bartee originally purchased the somewhat haggard VW-Porsche in 1979 for his wife. Although he intended to run the car at local events, what the weekender became was a high tech front-runner that not only earned but demanded respect at every West Coast track on which Bartee turned a wheel.

Starting its competition career in the club's A stock class, which included 356s, 912s, and 924s, the 914 quickly revealed the inherent qualities of its midengine design by propelling Bartee to class champion. For Bartee himself, his driving skills and long dedication to the POC garnered him the position of chief driving instructor.

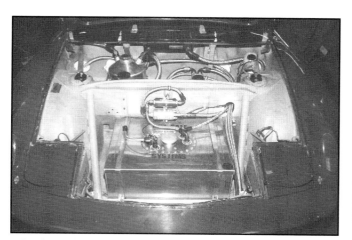

The fuel cell dominates the front trunk. Mitch Rossi

The rear trunk houses the battery and electronics for engine control. Mitch Rossi

Safety and comfort are stressed in this cockpit, framed in roll cage. Furnishings include Sparco seats, MOMO wheel, fire system, and lap timer. Mitch Rossi

Twelve-inch cross-drilled rotors stop things out back. Mitch Rossi

Eisenlohr Racing Products suspension replaces the stock front 914 components. Mitch Rossi

RSR coil-over struts, Eibach springs, and Bilstein shocks keep things moving smoothly up front. Big red calipers and 13-inch discs handle stopping chores. Mitch Rossi

Over the years, the car's original 1.7-liter VW-based engine was tweaked and stretched until it became a highly tuned 2.0-liter motor, which relegated Bartee and his ride to one of the upper four-cylinder competition classes. But as most racers know, car development is similar to natural evolution. Once set in motion, it is difficult to stop.

In 1995, Bartee decided he had pumped as many steroids into the motor as it could handle. It was time to slip a full six-pack into the midship bay. A lot of 914-4s undergo such conversions, but being competitive in the class Bartee was targeting meant more than simply shoe-horning a big displacement six into where its smaller cousin once rode. This was especially true as the chief instructor had his sights set on a powerplant that would launch the 914 to over 160 miles per hour.

Bartee tucked behind his seat a 3.2-liter long-stroke motor generating 338 horsepower at 5,700 rpm, a torque of 343 lb-ft at 4,800 rpm, and a screaming redline of 8,200 rpm. Inside, Mahle cylinders surround 11:1 Cosworth pistons under ported and polished twin-plug heads. Titanium retainers and Aasco valve springs keep the valve train reliable. To ensure that the car would see years of racing, the motor was assembled with aircraft quality Raceware fasteners, while the case was strengthened by inserting shuffle pins at each main bearing joint.

In keeping with the car's balance, a Peterson 12-quart engine oil tank was mounted in the forward trunk. Filled with Kendall lubricant, the system is kept to temperature by a large Setrab front cooler and cleansed by a System One filtering unit.

If the motor is the heart of this 914, then its cerebral cortex is the Motec M4 Pro engine management system. A small gold anodized box mounted in the rear trunk houses the Motorola 32-bit 33 MHz microprocessor. Using a network of on-board sensors to monitor a wide range of chosen parameters, the Motec is in constant control of the electronic twin-plug ignition and fuel injection systems and thus keeps the engine performance at its optimum level.

With each sensor transmitting its data 2,400 times a second, the Motec can adjust the ignition timing for each cylinder between compression cycles. And that's at over 8,000 rpm.

The Motec also monitors the crank and cam position, air temperature at the intake manifold, and the ambient air pressure. The microprocessor's control of the injector pulse helps generate maximum horsepower throughout the throttle range. The key to having a Motec type management system aboard is its ability to fine-tune the engine on the fly and thus achieve the car's full potential. This is the realm of Formula One technology inside a club racer.

To transfer this kind of power through the car's flywheel to its rear tires, Bartee decided to keep the early style five-speed transmission. To assure reliability with a component that was only designed to handle a maximum of 200 horsepower, a few modifications were needed. After closing the gear ratios to minimize the rpm drop between shifts, Bartee upgraded the 901 gearbox with an interior spray bar to shower oil onto each gear set and onto the ring and pinion. Equipped with its own Setrab cooler, Bartee's gearbox uses twice as much oil as the factory unit. To aid in feeding this racer under hard cornering, a high volume 911 turbo fuel pump was installed with 1/2-inch diameter solid lines running between the engine and the Fuel Safe cell in the nose.

A roadracer must always balance its engine power with enough braking might to hold it back. To this end, Bartee opted for the big "reds," the massive four-piston calipers from a late-model 993 Turbo. This wasn't a mere swap. The larger front clampers from two donor cars were used at each

corner of the 914. With the brake bias adjusted from the cockpit, a hefty 25-millimeter master-cylinder put the squeeze on 13-inch ventilated, cross-drilled rotors up front and 12-inch disks in the rear.

Early in its career, Bartee's 914 hit the track with 165/70s on 15-inch steel rims. Now, the car presses the tarmac with Godzilla-sized 315/35ZR17 B.F. Goodrich Comp T/A R1 tires at the rear and 275/40ZR17 T/As in the front, each wrapped around light-weight Kinesis three-piece wheels with gunmetal gray centers.

Inside the rear fender wells, reinforced trailing arms swing on solid monoball hinges and rest upon coil-overs and Koni shocks. At the front end of the 914, the factory A-arms have been replaced with an Eisenlohr Racing Products suspension system. The new components use polished spherical bearings in place of the car's archaic rubber bushings, adding precision to the 914's vertical wheel travel. Although the completely adjustable system raises the car's original pick-up points, it retains the correct geometry. The front end package is completed with factory RSR coil-over struts with threaded bodies, stiff Eibach springs, Bilstein dampeners, and an adjustable Charlie anti-sway bar.

After all the time and effort invested into the 914, flaring the fenders with a baseball bat and hacksaw was unthinkable. The German steel was stripped off and the car was reskinned with removable rear quarter-panels and a one-piece nose and fender combination. The rear deck is an off-the-shelf piece, while the forward lid was custom designed, incorporating louvers to disperse the airflow through the oil cooler. The car's expressionistic paint scheme was envisioned by Bartee himself.

Inside, a full roll cage cocoons the 914's cockpit. It is surprisingly well appointed with RS-like door panels, black Sparco seats, and a red detachable Momo steering wheel. Aside from the usual array of gauges and a Hot Lap track timer, the dash panel to the right of the instrument pod is equipped with two large red T-handled pull switches; one for the battery cut-off and one for the emergency SPA fire system. As weight is always a factor with track cars, Lexan windows replaced the factory glass.

Bartee never had an opportunity to campaign his car for a full season, but during his dashes to the checkered flag, it was clear it was near the top of the POC's highly contested V0 class. The level of performance reached by this club racer should not be surprising when one remembers that the factory's ultimate competitor, the GT-1 98, saddles the engine amidship just like the potent 914 brought to life by Bill Bartee.

Maintaining Your Car's Appearance

As a relatively cheap, highly maneuverable sports car that readily converts into a race car, the 914's greatest appeal is as a driver's car. As a result, very few end up living the life of a pampered garage queen. They are too much fun to drive or race to keep covered up in the barn.

That's why when you attend Porsche Club events, you expect to see the 914s out on the track as opposed to posing on the lawn. If you're like most 914 owners, you'll spend more time modifying and tuning your car than washing and waxing it.

This doesn't mean that the proper care and maintenance of your 914's appearance should be neglected. If you have invested a lot of time and money in your car, you want to be able to proudly show off your investment. More importantly, remember that rust is the 914's biggest enemy. Taking the time to properly keep up your car's appearance also employs methods that can protect your investment from being eaten away by the rust bug.

One of the other attributes of the 914 that we mentioned early on was that it's a low-cost way to gain admittance to the Porsche Club of America. That, in turn, leads to an opportunity to take part in many fine driving and social events. You'll also enter the highly competitive and fanatically spotless realm of people who show their cars at concours events. While some of these people resort to tactics like keeping their tires in plastic bags until the car is rolled into place for judging, there is a "wash 'n' shine" category that allows the less compulsive cleaners to compete against people who actually drive their cars more than once a year.

All joking aside, some of the more fastidious Porsches are driven frequently by their owners. The hardest part is getting your car super clean in every nook and cranny the first time, after that it's just maintaining that cleanliness and

touching up the dirty spots. Who knows, once you get your 914 in shape, even if you autocross it, you may want to see how many trophies your car can win standing still.

Most of you probably won't succumb to the urge to concours your cars. I never have, but I felt a chapter about properly cleaning and protecting your car's appearance is important to anyone who is proud of their car. I decided to go to the experts at Meguiar's for most of the advice you'll see here. I also wanted to present a few tricks of the trade from the concours crowd. I asked Beverly Frohm, who, along with her husband, Lars, has won a number of PCA concours awards, to share a few detailing secrets. Lars and Bev have won their trophies with a pristine 1970 911E Targa, a car that they aren't afraid to drive on tours and rallies, by the way. The reason I felt they could relate to the readers of this book is because they also have a modified 914 with which

Bev Frohm is barely visible as she looks for the last speck of dirt in concours-winning 911 Targa. Lars Frohm prefers racing the family 914, but does his cleaning chores as well.

they do very well when it comes to more serious driving events like autocrosses and time trials.

Take Five—The Five-Step Plan to a Pristine Porsche 914

Meguiar's has been in business since 1901, so it has a pretty good handle on how to care for your car's appearance, whether it is painted with Henry's basic black or one of the current clear coat finishes. I spoke with Mike Pennington, director of training, to get an overview on what it takes to give your 914 an appearance makeover that will have it looking like new again and how to keep it looking that way. Mike's job is to instruct both amateurs and pros on everything from the proper way to wash a car to specifically how and when to use one of the many products Meguiar's has developed over its 98 years in business.

Mike says that whether you are maintaining a daily driver or preparing a concours queen, there are five basic steps to taking care of your car's appearance. These are steps that you can do regardless of what company's products you choose. Meguiar's does offer a comprehensive line of products that are designed for specific applications like treating clear coat painted surfaces, leather cleaners, cleaning or polishing clear plastic, vinyl treatment, wheel cleaners, and more. Some of these products may be designed for professional detailers while others are geared to the person looking for a quick and easy way to keep the car shiny.

While we're taking a generic approach to presenting this five-step program, Meguiar's does offer a free analysis personalized to your specific needs to anyone who fills out a survey similar to the one you see in Figure 13-1. It includes variables like where you live, the color and condition of your car's paint, and how much time and effort you are willing to

If you got it, flaunt it. 914/6GT is a good show car when it's not busy at the track.

devote to maintain your car's appearance. Look in the appendix for Meguiar's phone number or website if you are interested in this free service.

Step One—Wash and Dry

Frequent washing, ideally once a week, is the key to keeping your car's finish free of what Meguiar's calls "loose contaminants" that can build-up over time and bond themselves to the paint. Some of these contaminants may also scratch the paint's surface. Washing removes them before they can do much harm.

Washing and drying the car is also the first step in evaluating the surface and determining the condition of your car's paint. Once the car is dry, run your hand over the paint. You should be able to easily feel any scratches, contaminants, or oxidation. You want the surface to be shiny and smooth like glass. Visually inspect it from various angles and in different types of light to spot any scratches or contaminants.

If your car fails the touch test or the visual inspection then you must move on to the next step, cleaning the surface. Before we get to that step, here are some pointers on how to properly wash your car.

- Do it yourself to control the conditions and materials used. Avoid using any kind of detergent, including dish washing liquid, or household cleaners. They can strip away the wax. Choose a commercial car wash solution formulated to be gentle to your car's paint and avoid water spotting.
- Avoid washing your car in direct sunlight or when the surface is hot. This can cause water spots on the paint. Try to find a cool, shady spot or wash your car early in the morning or later in the day when the sun is not as strong.
- Hose down the entire car to loosen any dirt and debris to avoid scratching the paint. This also cools down the surface of the car.
- Wash from the top down to avoid dirty rinse water going over clean parts.
- Do one section at a time.
- Keep your mitt or sponge well lubricated with soapy water to minimize scratches.
- Rinse the car off by letting the water gently flow over the surface in a sheeting effect rather than a high-pressure spray. This cuts down on water beads that can dry as spots. It also lets more water flow off the car's surface, cutting down on drying time.
- Use a chamois or 100 percent cotton terry towel to dry the car as quickly and completely as possible.

Step Two—Cleaning the Surface

If your car's paint is shiny and smooth as glass after you have done the touch test, you can skip this step and move on to the next one. If not, you need to clean it before you can polish it.

When cleaning your car's surface of contaminants like tree sap, tar, and bugs, or scratches, swirls, and oxidation, Mike Pennington's Golden Rule is to stay away from rubbing compounds and harsh abrasives. Pennington prefers a chemical paint cleaner that contains very mild abrasives. Using a cleaner is much better because it allows you to take the paint down little by little as opposed to a harsh abrasive that may take too much off or scour the surface. If your 914 still has its original paint job, or an older repaint, you have a surface that is a bit easier to work with and not as susceptible to scratching as the newer clear coat finishes.

The majority of metallic paint jobs will be clear coated, but if yours is not, be very careful when working on it with cleaners. Rubbing too hard may alter the color of the car. Never use a buffing machine on a metallic car that does not have clear coat.

Deep scratches that go through the clear coat cannot be corrected without repainting.

Step Three—Polishing

Polishing is what gives your car that glossy shine. If you have a white or lighter color car, this is a step you could skip. For people with black or dark colored cars this step is a must, especially if you want that deep, "wet look" shine. Polishing restores the natural oils in your car's paint. Polish one section at a time and don't allow the polish to dry. Make sure you use enough to condition the paint but don't apply too much at once. Allow the polish to penetrate into the surface. When buffing, either by hand or machine, use light pressure and overlapping strokes.

Step Four—Protection

Pennington says a daily driver definitely needs a coat of protection. It's your choice as far as a carnauba wax or one of the newer polymers, resins, or synthetic products. Carnauba is the hardest natural wax known to man and became a buzzword for high quality wax a few years ago. Pennington says that the newer tech polymer-based products actually provide better protection.

Whatever you use, make sure you let the product dry before removing it. Multiple thin coats are better than one thick coat. For horizontal surfaces that are more exposed to the elements, Meguiar's suggests two thin coats for extra protection.

Use clean 100 percent cotton terry towels to remove the wax. Change them frequently to avoid wax build-up.

Step Five—Maintenance

"Frequent car care is easy car care" is the Meguiar's slogan. Wash the car once a week and constantly evaluate the surface for contaminants. Every three to four months, especially for a daily driver, something needs to be done as far as cleaning, polishing, and waxing. If your car passes the touch test, then you may only need to polish it and add a protective coat of wax. It's possible that only a section of the car has been subjected to some sort of contaminant. Clean that section only, then polish and wax the entire car.

Spray detailers can be used to keep your car clean between washes or for spot cleaning contaminants before they bond to the finish. Avoid using these products in the hot sun to prevent streaking. Apply them as a mist over a broad surface as opposed to a direct spray. Work one section at a time and remove with a 100 percent cotton terry cloth.

Pennington also had maintenance tips for the rubber, vinyl, and metal trim parts of the 914. He cautions against using any abrasives or metal polish on the windshield trim. Ditto that for the aluminum trim around the vinyl cladding on the sides of the targa bar for cars so equipped. You run the risk of having some spots shinier than others if you rub harder in some sections than others.

As for the targa top itself, Pennington couldn't recommend a specific Meguiar's product. The uneven surface precludes waxing it since some waxes dry white (most Meguiar's waxes dry clear), making it difficult to remove all the wax residue. When black shoe polish was mentioned, he called it "the wrong means to an end, but it works." The problem being that you must keep redoing it.

Vinyl and rubber can be treated in the same way. Do a good scrub with a cleaner formulated for vinyl and rubber, then apply a vinyl dressing, being careful not to get it on the paint. Leather, of course, requires its own formulation of cleaners and conditioners.

For cleaning wheels, the recommended procedure is soap and water, or a nonacidic wheel cleaner, and a soft scrub

Some people just prefer knowing that they have the cleanest 914 around.

Don Bierce is proud of his 914 six-cylinder conversion, so he keeps it extra clean.

brush or special mitt. Alloys that have turned milky white need to be refinished or polished.

Perfectly smooth, nonporous plastic pieces can be polished and waxed like the painted metal. If the plastic has any pores or a textured surface, then treat it with vinyl care products.

Meguiar's has yet to find a suitable glass cleaner, and doesn't offer one in its catalog. Pennington uses the same home remedies as everyone else—from newspapers to towels. A 50/50 mix of white vinegar and water does an acceptable job. He also prefers to use a wet towel followed by a dry one. One bit of advice he does offer for concours fanatics is to wipe the outside of the glass in one direction, say horizontally, and the inside vertically. That way if you do see streaks, you at least know which side they are on.

As for removing any wax that has strayed onto those rubber bumpers, use a toothbrush and vinyl cleaner along with elbow grease to scrub it out. You need to break it down to remove it. It's a good idea to cover up the paint in the area

that you are working, as the vinyl cleaner can leave streaks or other adverse effects on the paint.

Where you live, how much driving you do, and how much protection your car gets from the elements are all factors that affect the life of your car's paint job. These factors should be considered in the routine maintenance of your car's appearance. A good baseline is weekly washing and evaluating of your car's surfaces plus regular polishing and waxing at least three times a year. Remember, the more you do it, the easier it is to do.

Polishing Up Your Act—Concours Tips

Having a thoroughly clean car is a good idea even if you don't care to massage the crevices of your 914 with Q-tips and toothbrushes. I'll tell you what Bev Frohm has to say on those two items in a second. The practical side of cleaning out all the grit and crud from under and around your car is that when you do need to work on it, your job will certainly be cleaner and easier. It also makes it easier to spot leaks. And, although it might

Bierce also races the immaculate black 914.

FREE OFFER APPLICATION

This form must be **COMPLETELY FILLED OUT** if you want to receive your free sample of Endurance Tire Gel and the free personalized Car Care RX. *The information you submit will be kept confidential and your name and address will never be sold, rented or exchanged. The information is needed to provide you with a computerized Car Care RX that meets your needs and to help us serve you better.*

☐ Male   ☐ Mr.   ☐ Ms.   ☐ Dr.
☐ Female   ☐ Mrs.   ☐ Miss   ☐ Rev.

First Name _____ M.I. _____

Last Name _____

Address _____ Apt. # _____

City _____ State/Province _____

Zip/Postal Code _____ Country _____

Car Make (Oldsmobile, Toyota, etc.) _____

Car Model (Cutlass, Camry, etc.) _____

Year: _____

New Car?   ☐ New car (6 months old or newer)

Odometer: _____

Approximate miles driven per month:
☐ 0-500   ☐ 501-1000
☐ 1001-2000   ☐ 2001-2500
☐ Over 2500

Your car's current paint condition (check one):
☐ New/Like New   ☐ Average
☐ Neglected

Your car's color (check one):
☐ Light Color   ☐ Medium Color
☐ Dark Color   ☐ Two-Tone

Your car's finish (check one):
☐ Standard   ☐ Clear Coat
☐ Don't Know

Is your car's current paint (check one):
☐ Original   ☐ Repainted
    If repainted:
        ☐ Within Last 6 Months
        ☐ Over 6 Months
        ☐ Entirely Repainted
        ☐ Partly Repainted

Time car is parked indoors (check one):
☐ Never   ☐ 1-6 Hours/Day
☐ 7-12 Hours   ☐ 13-18 Hours
☐ 19-24 Hours

I use a car cover when my car is outdoors (check one):
☐ Often   ☐ Sometimes
☐ Almost Never   ☐ Never

Which statement BEST describes your car care finish goal (check one):
☐ I want my car to look its absolute best all the time
☐ I want my car to look good most of the time
☐ I only want it looking good for special occasions
☐ I want to protect the finish, shine isn't that important

Which statement BEST describes your car care time goal (check one):
☐ I enjoy spending whatever time it takes to make my car look its best
☐ I'm willing to spend 4 hours (or more) per month on my car's appearance
☐ I'm willing to spend 2-4 hours per month on my car's appearance
☐ I'm willing to spend 1-2 hours per month on my car's appearance
☐ I would like to spend less than 1 hour per month on my car's appearance

Are you currently a Mirror Glaze (beige bottle) user?
☐ Yes   ☐ No
☐ Don't know

Do you frequently park:
☐ Near an airport   ☐ Near a factory
☐ Near trees   ☐ Near the beach

Method used to polish/wax your car (check one):
☐ Hand   ☐ Rotary Buffer
                     ☐ Orbital Buffer

Method used to wash your car:
By Hand:
☐ Usually   ☐ Seldom   ☐ Never
Auto Car Wash:
☐ Usually   ☐ Seldom   ☐ Never

How often was your car waxed in the past?:
☐ 1-2 times per month   ☐ 4-5 times a year
☐ 2 times a year   ☐ Once a year
☐ Rarely

How often do you usually apply a protectant or dressing to your tires?
☐ Weekly   ☐ Twice a month
☐ Once a month   ☐ 8-11 times a year
☐ 4-7 times a year   ☐ 1-3 times a year
☐ Never

Select your three most difficult surface care problems:
☐ Tree Sap Mist   ☐ Light Scratches
☐ Bugs   ☐ Spider Webs
☐ Road Tar   ☐ Stains
☐ Fresh overspray   ☐ Chemical Fallout
☐ Old overspray   ☐ Flaking/Chipping
☐ Bird Droppings (baked on) ☐ Oxidation
☐ Bird Droppings (fresh)   ☐ Rust
☐ Swirls   ☐ Road Salt
☐ Tire Browning

I usually shop for my car care products at (check one):
☐ Auto Parts Store   ☐ Hardware Store
☐ Paint & Body Dealer   ☐ Grocery/Drug Store
☐ Discount /Dept. Store ☐ Independent Auto Parts

If you weren't able to fill this form out at the event, you can still get free offers if you phone in this information within the next 30 days. Call 1-800-347-5700 Monday-Friday from 6am-6pm Pacific, or Saturday from 7am-3pm.

Meguiar's offers free car care consultation, based on your specific needs and willingness to work on your car. **Meguiar's**

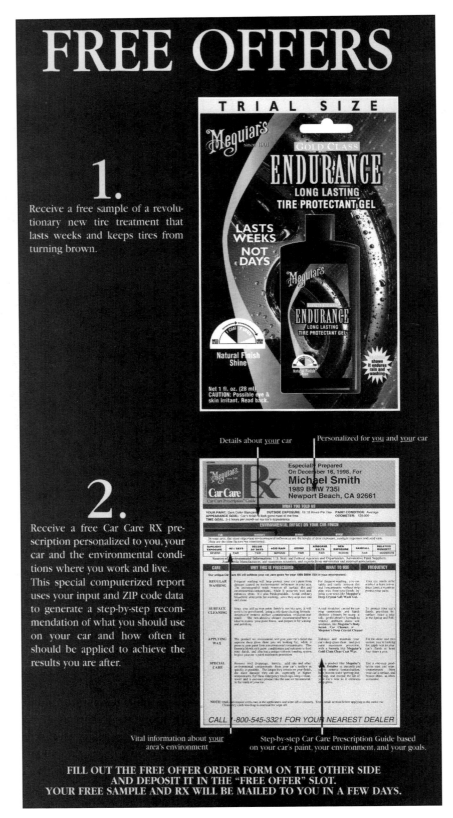

Printout from Meguiar's gives specific instructions for washing, waxing, and maintaining your car's finish and appearance. Meguiar's

Jeff Brubaker restored and modified this 3.2-liter six-cylinder for the track and concours. Jeff Brubaker

be a minor detail, those hardcore racers who drill out the pedals and do whatever they can to shed excess weight but ignore their car's cleanliness might be missing out on saving more weight. They could be carrying around an extra pound or two in terms of dirt and tire debris stuck to the wheelwells and undercarriage.

It pays to head on down to the local spray and wash with a handful of quarters and rags plus a set of jack stands to scrub out the underside of your 914. This is also a good idea for anyone who lives in the rustbelt where salt and/or cinders are sprayed on the roads when it snows.

Pull the car into a bay, jack it up, remove the wheels and place the car securely on the jack stands. Drop your quarters in the slot, then select the wheel scrubbing setting to clean out the wheelwells. If your car wash lacks that option, just go at it with the high-pressure wash setting. As long as you're careful and don't get anything on the exterior paint, you can spray a household cleaner like Simple

Green or 409 into the wheelwells to loosen up some of the harder grit. Just make sure you hose everything off thoroughly. This is a dirty job, but after you do it once, you should only have to touch it up every so often. Make sure you clean out the rocker panels and up under the front and rear valances.

That's my few quarters' worth of cleanliness tips. Here's what Bev Frohm has to pass on from her duels with dirt on the concours battlefield.

Car Washing Basics

Plain water is the liquid of choice when the car hasn't been driven much since its last bath and is basically just dusty from sitting in the garage. If it carries souvenirs from a rally or tour, car wash is added to the water to get things clean. Bev cautions against detergent for the same reasons as the people at Meguiar's. For drying the car, she prefers 100 percent cotton terry towels, switching to a dry one when the one she is using becomes damp. She'll keep the damp towels handy for wiping out any potential water spots before they dry and bond with the paint.

Another note on the towels. When you wash them, don't use any fabric softener. The fabric softener retards the absorbency of the towel and can leave streaks when you use the towels.

Another good point to remember is to drive your car a bit before putting it in the garage after washing. This cuts down on the chance of any water resting in places where it can cause rust. A quick drive will blow this out and also let you dry off the brake rotors so they don't get rusty as well.

Toothbrush Tactics

The toothbrush is the essential tool of the dedicated concours participant. Bev has a number of ways to use hers as part of her automotive hygiene program long after they have done their part in her dental hygiene program.

She uses the ones that have become well-worn and frayed to remove freshly applied wax from the rubber weather stripping. The bristles are tough enough to dislodge the wax residue but soft enough to avoid damage to the paint or rubber. She avoids using her fingers or a towel to wipe away the wax dislodged by the toothbrush. Instead, she uses a can of compressed air, the kind you use to clean computer keyboards, to blow away the wax particles.

A different technique, and toothbrush, is used on dried wax that has been sitting for a few months. A newer toothbrush, with stiffer bristles that have not yet become frayed along the edges, is used to break through the dried crust of the wax and then gently remove the rest. This is tedious work. You must rub gently and without excessive pressure or you will scratch the paint. It's a long, slow process but one of the little details that makes a major improvement when you study the final result.

Rear view of Brubaker's car reveals details of rear wing and ominous looking tailpipes. **Jeff Brubaker**

A stiffer brush is used to remove the dirt that works its way in between the paint and the rubber near the bumpers. Don't use too stiff a brush or you may scratch the paint. Just gently work the dirt off the surface. Do not wet the brush. This could cause bits of dirt to meld with the wet bristles to turn your cleaning tool into sandpaper. Just go slow and gently lift off the dirt. Being fastidious can be tedious.

Save your stiffest toothbrushes for cleaning in the engine compartment. They are a good way to apply cleaners and solvents to smaller parts that you want to spiff up.

Cleaning and Conditioning Rubber Trim

Keeping your rubber trim from showing the effects of the hot sun and ozone in the air is a constant battle, whether you show your car or just want to keep it looking new. There are a number of products that people use but some of them can create as many problems as they solve.

Petroleum jelly—Vaseline—seems like a good idea but it actually will dry out the rubber over the course of time. It's also messy and looks a little too slick when applied.

Armor All has both its devotees and its detractors. It should be buffed off after applying for a natural sheen. Otherwise it leaves a slick, oily residue. It also requires frequent applications as it tends to dry out quickly. I have found that Clear Guard looks a bit more natural and lasts longer than Armor All. Meguiar's has products that clean and condition rubber and vinyl trim. For tires, they have recently introduced a protectant that comes in gel form to avoid the problem of overspray or drips on wheels and painted surfaces.

An insider's tip that Bev passes on should do wonders for 914 owners with big rubber bumpers, and maybe targa tops. Furniture spray wax, like Pledge, is a secret weapon of many concours competitors.

And what would a concours discussion be without bringing up the topic of Q-tips. Bev uses them to apply rubber conditioner to the rubber trim and weather stripping. She uses them as applicators and as buffing tools. Only don't use the wooden style, as they may gouge or tear your rubber.

Exotica

Andy Leaney of Renegade Hybrids tells a story about a guy driving one of his V-8 powered 914 conversions who was goaded into a stoplight grand prix by the driver of a hot rod Mustang. The 914 driver started slowly to save his gearbox and then demonstrated just enough second gear power to make his point to the Mustang driver before shutting down. Unfortunately, the local police had earlier decided that this Mustang was a ticket waiting to happen, and were waiting to pounce on him as soon as he made his move. Both drivers got cited for racing, the Porsche driver opting to go to court to plead his case for a lesser conviction. When his day in court arrived, the Porsche driver was shuffled from crowded courtroom to crowded courtroom until he ended up in front of a harried judge who was eager to dispense some quick justice at the end of a long day.

The Porsche driver told the judge he was unfairly accused of racing. The judge asked what kind of car he had. When told it was a 914, the judge said, "Oh, I had one of those, it could barely get out of its own way. There's no way you could race anybody with one of those. Case dismissed."

I know it's a true story because I've withheld the name of the 914 driver to protect the guilty. I like it because it illustrates the lack of respect 914s get from the general public who see performance based on 0 to 60 times rather than the ability to slice around autocross cones. Throughout this book, I've taken a fairly conservative approach to modifying your car. Here's where we bust loose. If you're a 1.7-liter driver who's tired of getting sand kicked in your face by those bullies in the Honda Civics, maybe it's time to do the Charles Atlas bit and add some muscle to your 914. All you guys building, and rebuilding, those "big bang" 2.4 motors might also want to listen up. You could end up saying, "Wow! I could have had a V-8."

Andy Leaney first got started putting V-8s in Porsches back in 1983, when a friend got him involved in his company, Renegade Hybrids. Like the Remington shaver guy, Andy enjoyed it so much he eventually bought the company. He currently has a personal fleet of Chevy-powered Porsches that includes a 911, 928, 944 turbo V-8, and a 924. Although he's built a number of V-8 914s over the years, he doesn't own a completed one at this time. He was in the middle of building one for himself when I last paid him a visit.

The car pictured here is actually the first V-8 conversion of a 914 ever done. It's a 1970 914 that Rod Simpson converted and had for about a year until he sold it to its current owner. This gentleman drove it for many years before bringing it to Renegade Hybrids some years ago for upgrading. During the course of its life, it has gone through a number of changes including three different brake systems. It was also wrecked once, the front end totaled. After the accident, because of all the work and money that had gone into the original chassis, the decision was made to rebuild the car rather than strip it and start over with a new body.

Presently it has an aluminum 350-cubic inch Chevy V-8 featuring a Donovan block and Brodix heads. Andy says it puts out 376 horsepower. This is in a car that weighed 2,290 pounds when it still had the heavier stock 911 SC brakes. Those were later changed to 930 brakes, which stayed in the car for about 500 miles before it was in the previously mentioned accident. Rebuilding the car has been a slow process, as the owner has pursued other interests over the years. Porsche brake systems have moved at a faster pace, so along the way Cooltech rotors and Big Red calipers have been installed.

Look closely, and you'll see that it has a 916 transaxle and a 21-millimeter Weltmeister adjustable front sway bar. The rare factory racing tranny turns a factory limited-slip differen-

Renegade Hybrids is updating the first 914 ever converted to a V-8.

C-2 wheels only hint at changes inside the white 1970 914.

tial set at 80 percent and a tall 3.1 ring and pinion, as opposed to the stock 3.88 unit. This lets the motor wind out an additional 9 miles per hour in first and 36 miles per hour in fifth. Front suspension is a mix of 911 parts from the SC and 1980's Carrera eras. The spindles have been moved up the struts 1 inch for proper steering geometry to compensate for lowering the ride height. Out back, 200-pound springs, boxed control arms, and chassis stiffeners handle the added weight in the engine compartment and the additional accelerative forces. The 17-inch wheels were lifted from a Porsche 911 C2. They carry Yokohama 008P tires that measure 205/50x17 in front and 225/45x17 in the rear.

Cooling is done by a pair of thermostatically controlled fans drawing air through a front trunk–mounted radiator. The radiator is 14 inches high and about 29 inches wide with two rows of aluminum cooling fins that make it about 3 inches thick. Huge rectangular air holes are cut in the front fender wells to expel the hot air. Because they are forward of the front suspension mounting points, the structural integrity of the car is not affected. Leaney reports that the modified cars run cool, with temperatures only getting to the 200 degree mark on extremely hot days. The fans are switched on automatically by a fan switch pirated from a VW Rabbit.

Adding structural integrity, and occupant protection, a roll hoop is welded into the car to eliminate any chassis flex. It attaches at the top to the seatbelt anchors and then extends through the boxed frame section under the car, where it protrudes about an inch. Here it is tied into tubes that run along the longitudinals on either side of the car. These tubes go from the attachment point of the rear suspension all the way to the attachment point for the front suspension. It's a neat and tidy way to add rigidity to the inherent flexibility of the 914 chassis.

We weren't able to do any timed acceleration runs because the car was just coming back together after sitting idle for a few years and had yet to be removed from its non-operating status with the DMV. A couple of quick blasts through the back roads in the orange groves near Andy's shop were enough to convince me, once my head stopped spinning and my heart started beating again, that it will definitely run, and stop, with the big dog exotics. Forget bacon frying, coffee brewing, or lighting the day's first cigarette. I have found the ultimate wake up call. Man, I love the smell of clutch smoke in the morning.

This particular car would be very expensive to duplicate, but Andy says that the average do-it-yourself 914 owner could build a basic conversion in 60 to 80 hours using his kit and a chassis that has already had the stock engine removed. The cost would be around $9,000 plus the chassis and the suspension upgrades. Add about $7,000 for Andy to do it. The latter is the way to go if you're in a hurry. After gathering all the necessary parts, Leaney did one conversion in 23 hours.

With slight flare to rear quarters and discrete dual exhaust outlet, car has the appearance of a sleeper until the V-8 wakes up.

Because he's converted so many cars over the years, Andy is able to make running changes to his kits if needed to make sure that all components fit as advertised. "Everything lines up," he says. "The bolts go in the holes like they should; otherwise we go to our machine shop and change it."

Leaney says the best "bang for the buck" would involve a 300-horsepower V-8, a Chevy 283-, 327-, or 350-cubic inch motor. He says the stock 914 transmission is good for that much horsepower if you use a special clutch. Renegade Hybrids has a custom-made unit, 9 1/8 inches in diameter, that is the biggest that will fit in the bellhousing. Another piece in the basic conversion kit is the adapter plate that mates the engine to the transaxle. It's an aluminum aircraft alloy casting. Transmission and engine mounts are also included, along with all the radiator pieces.

The hoses that run to the radiator are Gates green stripe truck-rated heater hoses. Andy says it's the easiest way to plumb the radiators, and the hoses are super strong. When the white car was in the accident that totaled its front end, it ran over a curb that blew out the tires and bent the wheels and suspension. The hoses only had a few scrape marks.

To avoid the need to modify the firewall of the 914, Renegade Hybrids custom manufactures a water pump that mounts to the left side of the engine and runs off a belt to the modified harmonic balancer. The alternator mounts in a similar fashion on the right side of the engine. These modifications shorten the space needed for the engine by about 5 inches. This is also part of the basic kit.

Other parts of the kit include a tachometer recalibrated for eight cylinders and a pair of VDO Cockpit gauges for reading water temperature and oil pressure. Stock Porsche fuel lines, clutch, speedometer, and accelerator cables are used.

For suspension, Andy says the only mandatory change is to 200-pound springs. Just for the record, a cast-iron engine adds about 220 pounds to the middle of the car while the radiator filled with water tips the scales at about 40 pounds. To deal with this added weight, Leaney recommends the 911 front suspension, along with a 21-millimeter front sway bar. For wheels, his choice is a set of wheels and tires that could be picked up at a reasonable price as "take-offs" when someone switches their 911 to custom wheels. He says that 16-inch wheels, sixes in front and sevens in the rear, work very well. A very subtle flare will be needed in the rear fenders to clear the bigger wheels.

Renegade Hybrids also supplies a complete exhaust system with its basic conversion kit. This consists of the headers,

Surprisingly, the V-8 doesn't look crammed into the engine compartment.

mufflers, tailpipe, hangers, gaskets, and miscellaneous pieces. The parts are all designed to work together as a unit by Renegade Hybrids.

If you can afford it, worthwhile options to the basic kit would be bigger torsion bars in front and boxed control arms and chassis stiffeners for the rear.

If you love the way Porsches look, handle, and stop but prefer the sound and easy maintenance of a good old American V-8, one of these cars could be your ultimate thrill ride. A V-8 powered 914 may not get everyone's approval, but it will get their attention. And once you step on the gas, it will also get their respect.

A Totally Tubular 914 GT-1 of a Kind

Barely belt high to a stock 914 and standing 37 inches from the top of the air scoop to the pavement, Ron Mistak's ground-hugging racer demonstrates how far imagination and ingenuity can stretch the viability of Porsche's first attempt at a midengine sports car. Despite what it looks like, it's not exactly a 914 GT-1. This car is actually 2.5 inches lower than a GT-1! But it's as close as anyone could ever hope to imagine for the VW-Porsche love child born in 1969. Much closer than long-time POC/PCA club racer Mistak intended when he set out to upgrade his aging 914 race car.

Not that the former appearance of Mistak's car would have been mistaken for a run-of-the-mill 914. With its 935-style slope-nose and 962-sized rear wing, the little red rocket already resembled a couple of famous racing Porsches even before he started this project.

"The car was falling apart from years and years of use and the aerodynamics were like moving a brick through the air," says Mistak, who purchased the purpose-built race car in

Detail shows off right side headers and plumbing for the radiator overflow tank.

Rear trunk contains electronic engine controls.

Main components for the engine swap are aircraft quality engine mount cross bar (top) and engine/ transmission mounting plate.

1983 from Alan Johnson Racing. Almost right out of the box, Mistak was setting the amateur Porsche racing world on its ear by showing people what a properly set up 914 could do. "I raced the car in the 1984 Parade (autocross) and had the top time of the day." He repeated that feat in Dallas at the 1986 Porsche Parade. In 1992, Mistak and his 914 were the overall winners of the first ever PCA Club Race, held at Second Creek Raceway near Denver.

"My original plan was to lay the windshield down and chop the top," he recalls of the December 1996 visit to Bobby Hart's California Motorsports shop in Riverside. "We just got a little carried away," he adds with a big grin when he nods toward the tube frame chassis that eventually sprouted from and through what Mistak calls the "tub" of his 914.

"There was a 911 roof laying around and we put it on just to see what it would look like," Mistak says of the creative spark that eventually fanned the flames of the major transformation. The similarity to the Porsche GT-1's silhouette was noted and things grew from there.

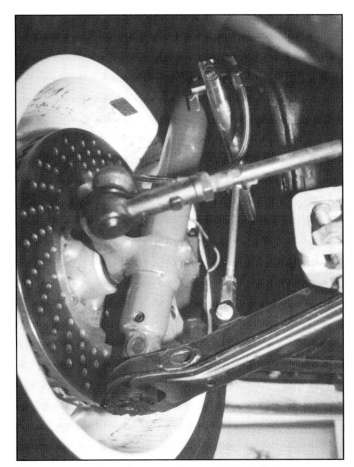

Front suspension close-up shows off Cool Tech cross-drilled rotors, turbo tie rods, and lowered spindles.

Front trunk doesn't even hold air anymore, thanks to huge cutouts that aid flow through the radiator (right).

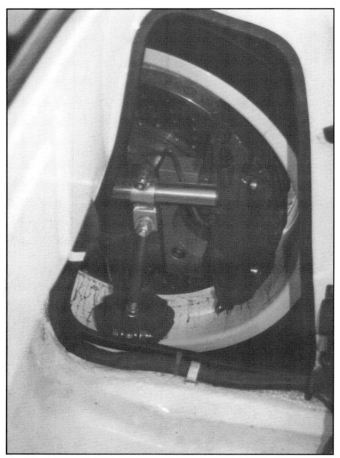

Looking through hole in trunk reveals big red calipers, and the end of adjustable front sway bar.

Welding up "boxed" bracing for rear trailing arms helps them cope with torque generated by the Chevy V-8.

Rare 916 transaxle is bolted in place similar to stock 914 unit.

Thermostatically controlled electric fans draw air through heavy-duty radiator in the front trunk to keep things cool.

Another view from underneath shows radiator lines going off toward front-mounted radiator.

View from underneath shows how nicely the V-8 matches up to the 916 transaxle. Note the headers and how the alternator is mounted off to the side, so that the firewall doesn't need any modifications to accommodate the length of the V-8.

It was soon determined that a Pro Stock drag racer hood scoop might be a good way to emulate the Porsche factory racer's distinctive roof-mounted air duct. While Mistak carved away on the fitment of this scoop, fellow 914 club racer Randy Beck, whose dad Chuck is famous for creating the Beck 550 Spyder, was busy using his inherited fiberglass skills to lay up the rest of the body panels.

To create the large rear wing, Mistak measured the wing on a 1/43rd scale model of the GT-1 he had and multiplied the results to achieve full-size dimensions. The FIA GT race at Laguna Seca in October 1997 also provided an opportunity to study a 1:1 scale model up close.

Anyone who has seen a seminude 914 will immediately recognize the floor pan and side rails, door frames, and front fenderwalls on Mistak's car. The roll cage that ties together the wealth of triangulated tubing that forms the remainder of the chassis is firmly attached to the original 914 pieces in accordance with PCA racing rules.

Mistak points to the door opening and says, "These are the original door striker plates from the 914 in their original place." All the measurements used to lay out the car were indexed to the location of these striker plates.

The main cage is 1.5-inch DOM tubing with a .120 wall thickness. The frame that extends from the cage is fashioned of Chrome Moly 1.5-inch tubing of varying thickness, from .095 down to .049 depending on PCA rules and stress loads.

The eclectic nature of projects conducted at Hart's immaculate shop contributed to a 914 that bridges the culture gap of different types of racing. His experienced team of craftsmen is adept at building or restoring anything from hot rods to off-road vehicles to racing cars of all types. A 1947

Kurtis midget racer belonging to Porsche racer and parts purveyor Dennis Aase was sunning its bare metal flanks outside the shop when I first stopped by to see the 914 coming together. Hart, who spent six years specializing in rebuilding transmissions at Aase's Porsche wrecking yard, is restoring the midget racer and its 100-cubic inch Offenhauser engine for his ex-boss. Such diverse activity played a big role in the creativity and open-minded thinking that went into the 914 project. Having Dennis Aase's wealth of knowledge and experience in the preparation of racing Porsches as a ready reference library was also an enormous advantage.

The goal was to make the car stronger and lighter with the weight carried as low as possible. In addition to the dragster air scoop, components from all forms of racing, including off-roading and circle track, were utilized if they were the best suited for the intended purposes. Examples of this include the Peterson NASCAR oil tank that not only offered flexibility as far as locating it in the chassis, but is lightweight, inexpensive, and easily disassembled for cleaning. A Tilton pedal assembly (hanging pedals, as opposed to floor-mount) comes complete with a clutch master cylinder and front and rear brake master cylinders to adjust brake bias.

About two weeks into the project, the decision was made to go with 993 suspension components. The only change to the stock Porsche suspension parts was the substitution of mono–ball bearings for the rubber bushings. Bilstein sport shocks are used front and rear, with 993 RSR struts up front.

All alone and at speed, Mistak's 914 is a GT1 look-alike.

The plan was to locate the suspension at its stock ride height position and avoid any major adjustments affecting camber angles or bump steer settings. The stock geometry of the suspension was not to be disturbed.

Hart and Mistak first determined where they needed to locate the suspension in relation to the rest of the car to avoid radical changes to its stock geometry. This came after many hours of head-scratching, visualization, and just staring off into space while sifting through all the information they had gathered from observing other cars and talking to people like Dennis Aase. Then, placing the tub and 993 parts on an arrow-straight platform to serve as a jig, to ensure that everything would come together properly aligned, they began running tubes from the roll cage to the attachment bungs that had been welded on the suspension pieces. That's how they built up the chassis. In effect, what they did was to lower the car around the suspension.

Both Mistak and Hart credit Dennis Aase's generosity in giving up his time and ideas to make this car come together as quickly as it did. They were able to do a track test in nine months' time with a car that was pretty close to being "dialed in" right out of the box. They openly attribute this to the help they received from a number of sources. Aase was a major contributor, along with Mark Anderson and Alex Cross, both of Swift Engineering.

Swift is a company with a long history of building successful race cars including the current Newman-Haas Indy Cars. Anderson provided valuable assistance in the structural analysis of the chassis tubing, along with some insights into airflow and race cars.

"Swift held our hand along the way so we weren't guessing," Hart relates. "They would check formulas for triangulation and let us know if we were doing good or needed to change a little here or a little there."

While the car is not lighter than its predecessor, as Mistak had hoped, the new chassis configuration did allow for relocating components to achieve better weight distribution and balance. One obvious change is moving the driver to the center of the car. The constraints of using the original tub plus engine placement for proper cooling didn't allow putting Mistak any farther back in the car, so his racing seat, which came out of a 935, was tilted as far back as possible. This served to aid the balance of weight distribution and to ensure that his helmet cleared the inside of the low profile roofline. Once the center tunnel was cut out of the tub, a new floor fabricated, and the ideal driving position determined, Mistak still had to put in more static seat time. His role was that of an ergonomic "dummy" while Hart went through the trial and error process of fabricating a new steering system and shift linkage based on the center seat driving configuration.

Rear view shows off triangulation of tube frame and rear suspension from 993.

Adapting the 993 steering rack and knuckles required all other components, apart from universal joints, to be custom made. Hart estimates a good 25 hours of his time was spent coming close to a workable setup. Having built similar systems for other racing and off-road cars was a big time-saver.

The shift linkage also drew heavily from Hart's past experience. The desire for precise and positive shifting ruled out a cable-actuated system. The shift tower, shift lever, and the three bars that make up the linkage to the transmission are all made of Chrome Moly. Heim joints and a stiffening sleeve over one of the bars ensure smooth operation without unwanted flexing.

Once the suspension was mounted and the primary components of driver and engine situated, accessories like the battery and oil tank were shifted from place to place within the car, using scales to monitor weight balance from side-to-side and front-to-rear. The fuel tank was designed to carry the weight of the fuel as low as possible in the chassis. Hart's craftsmanship and his understanding of all the diverse factors affecting a race car's construction quality are evident

in his work on fabricating the fuel tank. Not only is it shaped to clear a major structural piece of the chassis, but it also conforms to the air duct for the oil cooler, while still providing enough capacity to feed a thirsty RSR engine during a three-hour enduro.

Old meets new. Close up of 993 rear suspension mounted over 901 transaxle.

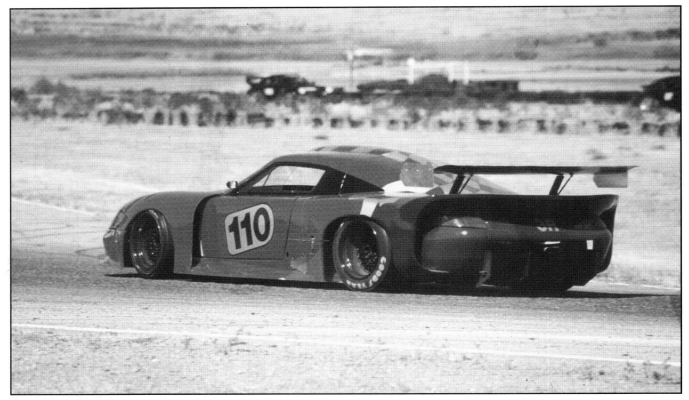

Car debuted in new form at PCA club race at Second Creek Raceway in Colorado, site of the first PCA club race a few years ago. Overall winner at that first race was Mistak, in an old version of the same car.

Once completed, the fuel tank was sent to Fuel-Safe for a custom safety bladder to be fitted. Three fuel pumps complete the package, two for delivery to the surge tanks and a rear-mounted third pump that delivers fuel to the engine.

Because no one had been running a midengine car with 993 suspension, special front and rear sway bars were ordered from Wrightwood Racing Products.

Choosing drivetrain components was an easy matter. Deciding to stick with proven equipment wherever possible for reasons of cost and durability, the 901 transmission and 2.8 RSR motor were carried over from Ron's original car.

"I wanted a faster car but didn't need to reinvent the wheel," claims Mistak.

Hart, who also spent time working for Aase's racing team, was confident that the 901, now mounted upside down, would continue to stand up to the 300 horsepower motor. The extra weight penalty that would have been incurred by using a newer Porsche transmission was also a factor in sticking with the 901. The 901 weighs 75 pounds, as opposed to the 915's 125 pounds and the more than twice as hefty, 175-pound G50 unit of later 911s.

"Ron is easy on the tranny," he says. "He's never ruined one, he just wears them out." Hart's confidence was also boosted by the positive shifting provided by the new linkage and the 80 hours of work that he devoted to getting the new system to

Can you spot the original OEM 914 parts still lurking under the state-of-the-art skin?

Rear wing generates a bit more downforce than the trunk-lip units used on the first 914 race cars in 1970.

work. That said, Mistak reports that as soon as PCA approves a rule change, the car will switch to a sequential shifter.

The transmission was inverted to get the motor as low in the car as possible to reduce the car's center of gravity. Bellhousing mounting holes were relocated and the unit completely disassembled to put in spray bars and pinion squirters to improve lubrication. A Tilton electric pump was also fitted to pull out the gear oil, put it through a cooler and then pressurize it back into the gearbox. The mainshaft was modified (welded and re-splined) to accept second and third gears in the first gear position and third gear in the second gear position, to allow Mistak a wide range of options for matching his engine's power band to various race track layouts.

According to Greg Brown of Precision Motorwerks in Orange, California, who last freshened the engine in Mistak's racer about five years ago, the most unique feature about the motor is that it's an original factory 2.8-liter RSR that was acquired years ago from Porsche's Motorsports department. With twin plugs and high-butterfly injection, it is factory rated at 300 horsepower.

A number of K&N air filters were measured to fit the induction opening from the roof-mounted air intake and, oddly enough, the application that dropped right in was the filter for a Porsche 928. The most significant change in mounting the engine to the new chassis involved the slight reconfiguration of the headers where, because the motor now sits lower to the ground, one of the pipes on each side had to be raised slightly to avoid dragging along the ground. The header tubes run into a drainpipe-sized collector (another NASCAR item) that exits in the opening above the rear diffuser. The reason for having this opening, created by mounting the rear portion of the undertray two inches lower than the body, just as on Porsche's GT-1, is to provide an escape route for hot air. Mistak, looking much like any other Cheshire cat with a supertrick 914, hints that his Indy car contacts also provided another reason to choose this location for the exhaust, but prefers to let anyone who is interested work out the solution on their backyard wind tunnel.

Brakes continue the theme of using stock 993 parts as much as possible. "They are stock 993. Not big red calipers, not RSR calipers," Mistak says. Carbon-Kevlar racing pads do replace the standard units. After watching him drive smoothly past competitors deep into the tight corners of Second Creek Raceway, when the car made its debut at a 1998 PCA club race, I could see why Mistak has good reason to chuckle when he deems his car's braking system to be "adequate."

Wheels and tires remain the same as fitted to the old car. The front BBS alloys measure 16 x11.5 inches, while the rears are 16x14 inches. They carry Goodyear Eagle Radial Special slicks sized at 23.5/10.5 x16 up front and 25.5/14x16 in the rear. The wheelbase came out to be slightly longer than a stock 914, primarily because of engine cooling and driver placement requirements.

Mistak says his new central seating position and shift linkage make him feel as if he were driving a Formula Ford. He also reports that turn-in response when entering a corner is much like an open-wheeled racer. Also similar to formula cars, especially Formula 1 and CART, is the Pi data acquisition system that has been mounted in the car. He can use it as a digital dash to monitor the standard oper-

ating functions like rpm and various temperatures and pressures while on track. When he pulls into his pit he can then download to a laptop computer additional information including lap segment times, throttle position, and corner entry speeds. In this way, he can separate driver input from car setup to improve the performance capabilities of both.

Mistak prefers not to quote lap times or speeds for the car, but the telemetry tells him that the thousands of hours of work were well spent. Improvements in lap times from the old car can be measured in whole seconds, rather than fractions, which is significant, considering that the engine and tires have been carried over unchanged.

After starting in 12th position for the car's coming-out party at Second Creek Raceway, fuel delivery problems forced Mistak to drop out about halfway into the race, just as he was ready to overtake the leader. As this is written, the car has spent less than a couple of hours on a race track. Final spring rates and suspension settings are still being worked out, but one thing is apparent. Because of the low center of gravity, weight distribution, and suspension placement in relation to

Rear undertray air diffuser was inspired by Indy cars.

Center seat cockpit involved a lot of work in converting the steering and shifting controls.

Car shows how serious even club racing can get.

the chassis, the car can run at spring rates that are significantly lower than similar racers. This is something that Mistak is very pleased about, since he is not a driver who favors a very stiff suspension setup.

He also feels that building a car similar to his can be done for less money than converting a stock late-model 911 to a race car. In fact, Mistak is prepared to go into business building one of these "baby" GT-1s for anyone who is interested.

Porsche may have given up on the 914 many years ago, but thanks to the evolutionary work of devoted owners and racers, the 914 may be back in production again. Only this time around no one should have any complaints about its looks or its performance.

Mistak's red rocket is dwarfed by standard-sized 914.

Appendix A

Owner's Clubs and Racing Organizations

914 Owners Association
100 South Sunrise Way, Suite 116
Palm Springs, CA 92662
e-mail: autobahn914@hotmail.com

Porsche 914 Club
4300 Sand Mound Blvd.
Oakley, CA 94561
phone: (925) 684-2199
FAX: (925) 684-9566
www.dgi.net/914/

Porsche Club of America
PCA National Office
P.O. Box 30100
Alexandria, VA 22310
phone: (703) 922-9300
www.pca.org

Porsche Owners Club
Membership Information
P.O. Box 9000-277
Seal Beach, CA 90740
phone: (310) 784-5653
www.porscheclub.com

SCCA
Sports Car Club of America
phone: (800) 972-6662
www.scca.org

Appendix B

Suggested Reading

Books and Manuals
Porsche 914/4 and 914/6 Handbook l,
Lash International
Formerly the *Clymer Manual*. Basic
technical procedures and tune-up specs.

*Haynes Porsche 914 Automotive Repair
Manual*, Haynes Publications, Inc.
Typical Haynes manual. Good
supplement to Factory Service Manuals.

Porsche 911 Performance Book,
MBI Publishing Company
Author Bruce Anderson is guru of 911
technical knowledge. Covers modifying
all years of 911 engines. Overall
technical review and racing/
performance tips on suspensions,
brakes, gearbox, and tires.

*How to Rebuild Your Volkswagen Air-
Cooled Engine* by Tom Wilson
The engine bible for 914 owners.

How to Hot Rod Volkswagen Engines by
Bill Fisher
The title says it all.

*How to Understand, Service & Modify
Bosch Fuel Injection and Engine
Management* by Charles O. Probst, SAE
Everything you wanted to know and
more about Bosch fuel injection.

*How to Tune & Modify Bosch Fuel
Injection* by Ben Watson
Covers a wide range of applications,
but a little less intimidating than
Probst's book.

*Bob Bondurant on High Performance
Driving* by Bob Bondurant and John
Blakemore
The Master speaks. Read it, learn it,
know it, and you'll be a better driver
on the track and highway.

*Porsche High-Performance Driving
Handbook* by Vic Elford
This famous Porsche racer shares
driving knowledge and interesting
racing anecdotes. Handy if you ever
trade a 914 for a 917.

Porsche, Excellence was Expected by
Karl Ludvigsen
THE history of Porsche. Getting a little
dated but contains good coverage of
914s including photos of racing,
concept, and special models.

Up-Fixin der Porsche, Porsche Club of
America
Reprints of technical advice appearing
in the club's magazine *Panorama* over
the years.

Magazines and Periodicals
european car
McMullen Argus Publishing Inc.
774 South Placentia Avenue
Placentia, CA 92870-6846
phone: (714) 572-2255
Frequent technical and how-to articles
on older Porsches. Decent amount of
Porsche parts and accessories
advertising.

excellence
42 Digital Drive, Number 5
Novato, CA 94949
phone: (415) 383-0580
All Porsche, all the time. Decent
classifieds and abundance of
advertisers for parts and other goodies.

Grassroots Motorsports
425 Parque Drive
Ormond Beach, FL 32174
phone: (904) 673-4148
Loves 914s and early 911s. Real racers
with many how-to and technical stories.

PML
Porsche Market Letter
P.O. Box 6010
Oceanside, CA 92058
phone: (888) 928-9111
Monthly collection of nationwide
listing of cars for sale. Editorial
highlights 914 and vintage racing a
couple of issues a year.

Websites Worth a Visit
In addition to those listed under
organizations or suppliers here are a
few places to click on for Porsche
stuff.

www.914fan.net

www.porsche-net.com

www.porschefans.com

www.porsche.com
Official site of Porsche Cars North
America

Appendix C

Parts and Accessories

Aase Bros.
701 Cypress Street
Anaheim, CA 92805
phone: (800) 444-7444
FAX: (714) 956-2635
www.aasebros.com

AIR
9830-2 San Fernando Road
Pacoima, CA 91331
phone: (818) 890-5878
FAX: (818) 504-9348
Fiberglass body parts and aero kits

Automobile Atlanta
505E South Marietta Parkway
Marietta, GA 30060
phone: (770) 427-2844
www.autoatlanta.com

Automotion
193P Commercial Street
Sunnyvale, CA 94086
phone: (800) 777-8881
FAX: (408) 736-9013
www.automotion.com

Best Deal, Inc.
8171 Monroe Avenue
Stanton, CA 90680
phone: (714) 995-0081
FAX: (714) 995-5918

FAT Performance
1558 North Case
Dept. EXCL
Orange, CA 92667
phone: (714) 637-2889
FAX: (714) 637-7352

GPR
German Parts & Restoration
202 Tank Farm Road, Bldg. #5
San Luis Obispo, CA 93401
phone: (877) 321-5432
FAX: (805) 549-8994

Kerry Hunter Enterprise
phone: (805) 623-1581
Headers

Original Fit Interior
P.O. Box 269
298 Harmony Drive
Roseburg, OR 97470
phone: (541) 679-4460
Discount carpet and interior

Otto's
707 South Hampton Drive
Venice, CA 90291
phone: (888) 901-OTTO
www.ottosparts.com

Paragon Products
5602 Old Brownsville Road, F-3
Corpus Christi, TX 78417
phone: (800) 200-9366
FAX: (512) 289-5682 FAX
www.paragon-products.com

Patrick Motorsports
Phoenix, AZ
phone: (602) 244-0911
FAX: (602) 244-0900
www.patrickmotorsports.com

Pelican Parts
111 Eucalyptus Drive
El Segundo, CA 90245
phone: (888) 280-7799
FAX: (310) 640-2632
www.pelicanparts.com
Be sure to visit this site; it contains a
wealth of 914 technical and
miscellaneous information

Performance Products
16129 Leadwell Street
Box # B-4
Van Nuys, CA 91406-3488
phone: (800) 789-1891
FAX: (818) 787-2396
www.performanceproducts.com

Renegade Hybrids
610 Amigos Drive, #B
Redlands, CA 92373
phone: (909) 307-2150
www.RenegadeHybrids.com
V-8 conversions

Troutman
P.O. Box 737
Temecula, CA 92593
phone: (800) 356-9307
FAX: (909) 699-5290

Tweeks
1125 L.
Brookside Avenue
Indianapolis, IN 46202
phone: (800) 428-2200
FAX: (317) 974-5757

George Vellios Co.
4145 West 163rd Street
Lawndale, CA 90260
phone: (310) 542-0806
FAX: (310) 370-6382
914/6 conversion kits

Zims
1804 Reliance Parkway
Bedford, TX 76021
phone: (800) 356-2964
FAX: (817) 545-2002

Index